GOLD

B2 First

NEW EDITION

CONTENTS

Exam information

The *Cambridge English: First* examination is made up of four papers, each testing a different area of ability in English. The Reading and Use of English paper is worth 40 percent of the marks (80 marks), and each of the other papers is worth 20 percent (40 marks each). There are five grades. A, B and C are pass grades; D and E are fail grades.

Reading and Use of English (1 hour 15 minutes)

Paper 1 has seven parts. Parts 1–4 contain grammar and vocabulary tasks within texts or as discrete items. Parts 5–7 contain texts and accompanying reading comprehension tasks. You write your answers on an answer sheet during the test.

Part 1 **Multiple-choice cloze**	*Focus*	Vocabulary/Lexico-grammatical
	Task	You read a text with eight gaps. You choose the best word or phrase to fit in each gap from a set of four options (A, B, C or D).
Part 2 **Open cloze**	*Focus*	Grammar/Lexico-grammatical
	Task	You read a text with eight gaps. You have to think of the most appropriate word to fill each gap. You must use one word only. No options are provided.
Part 3 **Word formation**	*Focus*	Vocabulary/Lexico-grammatical
	Task	You read a text with eight gaps. You are given the stems of the missing words in capitals at the ends of the lines with gaps. You have to change the form of each word to fit the context.
Part 4 **Key word transformation**	*Focus*	Grammar and vocabulary
	Task	There are six items. You are given a sentence and a 'key word'. You have to complete a second, gapped sentence using the key word. The second sentence has a different grammatical structure but must have a similar meaning to the original.
Part 5 **Multiple-choice questions**	*Focus*	Detail, opinion, attitude, text organisation features (e.g. exemplification, reference), tone, purpose, main idea, implication
	Task	There are six four-option multiple-choice questions. You have to choose the correct option (A, B, C or D) based on the information in the text.
Part 6 **Gapped text**	*Focus*	Understanding text structure, cohesion, coherence, global meaning
	Task	You read a text from which six sentences have been removed and placed in jumbled order after the text. There is one extra sentence that you do not need to use. You must decide from where in the text the sentences have been removed.
Part 7 **Multiple matching**	*Focus*	Specific information, detail, opinion and attitude
	Task	You read ten questions or statements about a text which has been divided into sections, or several short texts. You have to decide which section or text contains the information relating to each question or statement.

Writing (1 hour 20 minutes)

The Writing paper is divided into two parts, and you have to complete one task from each part. Each answer carries equal marks, so you should not spend longer on one than another.

Part 1	*Focus*	Outlining and discussing issues on a particular topic
	Task	Part 1 is compulsory, and there is no choice of questions. You have to write an essay based on a title and notes. You have to write 140–190 words.
Part 2	*Focus*	Writing a task for a particular purpose based on a specific topic, context and target reader.
	Task	Part 2 has three tasks to choose from which may include: • a letter or email • an article • a report • a review. You have to write 140–190 words for Part 2.

Listening (approximately 40 minutes)

There are four parts in the Listening paper, with a total of thirty questions. You write your answers on the question paper and then you have five minutes at the end of the exam to transfer them to an answer sheet. In each part you will hear the text(s) twice. The texts may be monologues or conversations between interacting speakers. There will be a variety of accents.

Part 1 Extracts with multiple-choice questions	Focus	Each extract will have a different focus, which could be: main point, detail, speaker purpose, feeling, attitude and opinion, function and agreement between speakers.
	Task	You hear eight short, unrelated extracts of about thirty seconds each. They may be monologues or conversations. You have to answer one three-option multiple-choice question (A, B or C) for each extract.
Part 2 Sentence completion	Focus	Specific information, detail, stated opinion
	Task	You hear a monologue lasting about three minutes. You complete ten sentences with information heard on the recording.
Part 3 Multiple matching	Focus	Gist, detail, function, attitude, purpose, opinion
	Task	You hear a series of five monologues, lasting about thirty seconds each. The speakers in each extract are different, but the situations or topics are all related to each other. You have to match each speaker to one of eight statements or questions (A–H). There are three extra options that you do not need to use.
Part 4 Multiple-choice questions	Focus	Opinion, attitude, gist, main idea
	Task	You hear an interview or conversation which lasts about three minutes. There are seven questions. You have to choose the correct option (A, B or C).

Speaking (approximately 14 minutes)

You take the Speaking test with a partner. There are two examiners. One is the 'interlocutor', who speaks to you, and the other is the 'assessor', who just listens. There are four different parts in the test.

Part 1 Interview (2 minutes)	Focus	General interactional and social language
	Task	The interlocutor asks each of you questions about yourself, such as where you come from or what you do in your free time.
Part 2 Individual long turn (4 minutes)	Focus	Organising your ideas, comparing, describing, expressing opinions
	Task	The interlocutor gives you a pair of photographs to compare, answer a question about and give a personal reaction to. You speak by yourself for about a minute while your partner listens. Then the interlocutor asks your partner a question related to the topic. A shorter answer is expected. You then change roles.
Part 3 Collaborative task (4 minutes)	Focus	Interacting with your partner, exchanging ideas, expressing and justifying opinions, agreeing and/or disagreeing, suggesting, speculating, evaluating, reaching a decision through negotiation
	Task	You are given a task to discuss together for 1–2 minutes, based on a written instruction and prompts. You then have a minute to try and reach a decision together. There is no right or wrong answer to the task and you don't have to agree with each other. It is the interaction between you that is important.
Part 4 Discussion (4 minutes)	Focus	Expressing and justifying opinions, agreeing and disagreeing
	Task	The interlocutor asks you both general questions related to the topic of Part 3, and gives you the chance to give your opinions on other aspects of the same topic.

For more information see the **Writing reference** (page 165), the **General marking guidelines** (page 180) and the **Exam focus** (page 186).

Bands and fans

Vocabulary
free-time activities

1 Work in pairs and discuss what activities you enjoy, either alone or with friends and family, e.g. sport, cultural events, classes, visiting new places.

2 Look at the activities in the box and give examples of verbs often used with them, e.g. *do, go, have, listen, make, play, watch*. Add a preposition if necessary.

Example: *have friends round; spend time with my friends*

clubbing   computer games   exercise   friends   gigs   guitar   museums   music
pizza   social media   sport   TV   shopping   yoga

3 Complete the sentences with details about what you do in your spare time.

Example: *I quite enjoy learning Spanish. Playing sports doesn't appeal to me at all.*

1   I quite enjoy ....
2   .... doesn't appeal to me at all.
3   I absolutely love ....
4   I can't stand ....
5   I'm very keen on ....

4 Work in pairs. Compare your sentences and report back to the class.

Example: *We both enjoy shopping; Neither of us likes going to the gym; Franco likes … but I prefer …*

Listening and speaking
asking and answering questions

5 ▶ 01 Read and listen to the questions about free time. Underline the words which are stressed. Are these mainly grammar words or content words such as nouns and adjectives?

1   How do you usually relax when you have some free time?
2   What do you do when you stay in? Where do you go when you go out?
3   Do you like being in a large group or would you rather be with a few close friends?

6 ▶ 02 **Listen to the students' answers and complete the sentences.**

1 I usually find .... quite relaxing but it depends on ....

2 I tend to .... on weekdays though I sometimes ....

3 .... is good fun.

4 .... helps me to switch off.

5 I'm really into ....

6 I go out .... now and again.

7 **Work in pairs. Ask and answer the questions in Activity 5.**

▶ **GRAMMAR** REFERENCE p.140

Interview (Part 1)
listening to and answering questions

▶ **EXAM** FOCUS p.189

8 **In Part 1 of the Speaking test, you have two minutes to answer some questions in which you give personal information and opinions. Match questions 1–6 to typical topics A–F.**

1 How important is music to you?

2 Tell us about your closest friend.

3 What do you like about the place where you were brought up?

4 What subject did you enjoy most at school?

5 What do you think you'll be doing in five years' time?

6 Where do you think you'll go on holiday this year?

A your personal relationships

B your home town

C your job or studies

D your free-time activities

E your travel plans

F your future plans

9 **Write two more questions for each topic A–F. Use question words such as** *what (kind), when, how (many), who, why, where.*

10 ▶ 03 **Listen to Julia and Stefan and answer the questions.**

1 Which of the questions in Activity 8 were they each asked?

2 What did Stefan say when he didn't understand the question?

3 What could Julia have said when she didn't know the word for *marks*?

11 **How well did they both answer the questions? Use a number between 1 (lowest) and 5 (highest) to give your opinion on the areas assessed in the Speaking test.**

• range of grammar and vocabulary

• developing an answer without too much hesitation

• pronunciation

12 **Choose one question from each topic in Activities 8 and 9 and ask your partner.**

LANGUAGE TIP

Adverbs of frequency (*usually, never, hardly ever,* etc.) come before a main verb and after auxiliary verbs such as *be.*

I hardly ever go shopping. I'm always busy.

Longer adverbials (*from time to time, every day, now and again,* etc.) can come at the beginning or end of a sentence.

I go running every evening. Now and again I play squash.

EXAM TIP

Answer in full, giving reasons. Avoid one-word answers and don't move away from the question to talk about something else.

1 Look at the photos and discuss the questions.

1 Name as many different kinds of music genres as you can. Which are the most popular in your country?

2 What is the attraction of going to music festivals like the one in the photograph? What negative aspects might there be?

3 Have you ever been to a music festival like the one in the photograph? If so, which bands or musicians did you see? If not, would you like to go?

2 You are going to read a newspaper article about an American music festival, Coachella. Read the article quickly for gist and choose the phrase 1–7 which best summarises each paragraph A–G. The first one is done for you.

1 appealing to the target market D

2 getting bigger and better

3 choosing between two attractions

4 the original inspiration for Coachella

5 a fashionable destination

6 a money-making success

7 overcoming problematic beginnings

How a music festival turned into a money-making monster

A When the American 90s rock band Pearl Jam put on a concert in the dried-up, baking-hot Coachella Valley in California, *it* was an attempt to prove that *they* could break away from the monopoly of the concert giant TicketMaster, *who*, they believed, was using *its* considerable power to <u>exploit</u> music fans by continually increasing prices. *Their* concert was well attended and <u>inspired</u> the idea for a future, more <u>ambitious</u> event. Naturally, nobody could have predicted quite how important Coachella would eventually become.

B Six years later, in 1999, the same venue hosted its first weekend-long music festival. Although initially making a loss, this was blamed on the unbearably high temperatures and the lack of available campsite facilities. ☐ 1 ☐ E ☐ What's more, it took only a few more years until its quality line-ups, from small bands to headliners, were attracting worldwide attention.

C If one band is responsible for <u>confirming</u> Coachella's arrival on the world stage, it is Daft Punk's <u>iconic</u> appearance there in 2006. ☐ 2 ☐ As a direct result of the festival's success, promoters expanded it to a three-day event, and in 2009, Coachella presented its most mainstream line-up, including Paul McCartney, the Killers and The Cure. The following year Jay-Z became the first rap headliner and by 2012 such was the popularity of Coachella that it had developed into two weekends of three-day shows.

D In an effort to attract America's <u>impoverished</u> younger generation to an expensive annual visit to the desert, the promoters made two clever decisions. One smart move was to get a much-missed band or singer such as Rage Against the Machine to reform every year. Most notable was a holographic representation of the late rapper 2Pac in 2012. ☐ 3 ☐ In a stroke of genius, they decided to <u>cater for</u> the section of the audience who adored the music that used to be labelled electronic and who <u>flocked</u> to dance in big tents to their favourite DJs.

E By keeping its cool musical reputation, the festival would go from strength to strength. In 2016, half a million fans bought their tickets in under 20 minutes and each year around 100,000 attendees a day now <u>splash out</u> around $375 on admission. Of course, the costs don't stop there. ☐ 4 ☐ It is now the most <u>profitable</u> festival in the world.

F Just two hours from Los Angeles, Coachella swiftly became the place to see and be seen. ☐ 5 ☐ The presence of models and other celebrities soon began to attract style bloggers, drawn by the fashion rather than the music. Which, in turn, has made Coachella <u>irresistible</u> to fashion houses, beauty companies and other lifestyle labels.

G Although for several years luxury brands have been hosting free concerts and pool parties for invited guests and photographing Instagram stars modelling designer clothes, this has until recently been outside festival hours. ☐ 6 ☐ As a result, they are now effectively separate events, to the point that 'No-chella' as it has become known, is, in the opinion of some, in danger of <u>overshadowing</u> the 'real' festival.

Coachella has certainly come a long way from the original anti-establishment Pearl Jam gig.

3 Read the first two paragraphs again and answer the questions.

1 In the first paragraph, what do the referencing words in italics link to?

2 Read option E in Activity 6. What does *these issues* refer back to in the second paragraph? What other links can you find in the sentence following gap 1?

4 Read the text before and after gaps 2–6 and guess what information might be missing.

5 Underline the referencing words around the gaps and in the options and work out what ideas or synonyms they refer to.

EXAM TIP

Look for words in the options which link to the ideas and language before and after each gap in the text.

Gapped text (Part 6)

▶ **EXAM** FOCUS p.187

6 Six sentences have been removed from the article. Choose from sentences A–G the one which fits each gap. There is one extra sentence which you do not need to use.

A The appeal of its location – palm trees, guaranteed sunshine, warm temperatures – is not difficult to understand.

B When refreshments, merchandise, transport and accommodation are <u>taken into account</u>, the expense of attending rises dramatically.

C Fear of missing out on another such memorable performance caused huge demand for tickets the following year.

D Lately, however, increasingly extravagant marketing by the fashion industry means that attendees are now preferring to stay away from the music concert itself.

E Fortunately, *these issues* were soon <u>resolved</u>.

F On this occasion, medical professionals treated numerous audience members for heatstroke.

G Their other idea was even more brilliant.

7 Compare your answers and give reasons for your choices based on Activity 4. Then re-read the text with your answers in the gaps to check it makes sense.

8 Write down five reasons why you would or wouldn't like to go to Coachella. Think about the music, location, cost, facilities, etc. Then discuss your answers in groups.

Vocabulary
deducing words in context

9 Look at the underlined words and phrases in the article and options and try to work out the meaning from the context or from the word itself. Then match each one to a definition of the verbs 1–9 and the adjectives 10–14.

Example: *splash out is 1 (… $375 … costs don't stop there …)*

1 spend a lot of money

2 show something is definitely true

3 find a solution (to a problem)

4 go in large numbers

5 try to get as much as possible (sometimes unfairly)

6 consider facts when making a decision

7 make something seem less important

8 provide people with what they want

9 give the idea for

10 good but difficult

11 someone or something famous and important

12 impossible to refuse

13 makes a lot of money

14 very poor

10 Work in pairs. Compare your answers, then work out the meaning of five more new words from the article.

Present time

▶ **GRAMMAR** REFERENCE p.140

simple and continuous forms

1 Look at the pairs of sentences and say why the speaker has used the present simple or present continuous in each case.

Example: *1A means possess (stative), whereas 1B means taking, happening now (dynamic).*

1 A I <u>have</u> a ticket to see Rihanna.
  B I'<u>m having</u> a shower.
2 A That singer <u>appears</u> to be doing well.
  B Do you know who'<u>s appearing</u> at Coachella this year?
3 A He'<u>s being</u> really kind.
  B He'<u>s</u> really kind.
4 A It <u>depends</u> on how much money I've got.
  B I'<u>m depending</u> on her to organise everything.
5 A This soup <u>tastes</u> good.
  B Joe'<u>s tasting</u> the soup.
6 A My computer'<u>s always crashing</u> these days, for some reason.
  B He always helps me with my computer when it <u>crashes</u>.

2 Read the text quickly for gist. What kind of people are buying vinyl these days?

3 Complete the text with the present simple or present continuous form of the verbs in brackets.

VINYL REVIVAL

These days vinyl **(1)**............. (*enjoy*) a remarkable comeback in many countries all over the world. In fact, it is so popular in some places nowadays that even mainstream supermarkets **(2)** .... (*begin*) to stock it and it **(3)** .... (*appear*) that the reason for buying vinyl is not just older people being nostalgic. There is also a generation of younger music fans who **(4)** .... (*like*) the original look and sound of vinyl. Furthermore, vinyl often **(5)** .... (*come*) with artistic covers and sleeve notes that people **(6)** .... (*want*) to collect and show off to their friends. Apparently, men **(7)** .... (*be*) still the most serious collectors of vinyl but things **(8)** .... (*change*). Increasingly, people **(9)** .... (*bring*) their parents' old records down from dusty lofts and **(10)** .... (*make*) a design feature of their record players and vinyl collections in their living rooms.

present habit: *be used to/get used to*

▶ **GRAMMAR** REFERENCE p.141

4 What do you think you would have to get accustomed to if you went to a music festival for the first time?

5 Read the extracts from Sarah's messages about her experiences of camping at a music festival. Decide whether statements 1–3 are true (T) or false (F).

> I don't sleep very well because I'm not used to lying on the hard ground with so little space to move around.

> I'm getting used to paying a fortune every time I want something to eat.

> Are you getting used to the peace and quiet now that Dan and I aren't around?

1 Sarah often goes camping and sleeps in uncomfortable places.
2 Sarah doesn't find it any easier to pay so much for her food.
3 Sarah wants to know whether her parents are accustomed to being on their own yet.

6 Which form of the verb follows *used to* in the present: *-ing* or *to* infinitive?

7 Imagine that you have just started work for the first time after leaving college. Write sentences about two things that

1 you do on a regular basis.
2 you are doing now (but not necessarily at this exact moment).
3 you are getting used to doing.
4 you are not yet used to doing.

8 Work in pairs and compare your sentences. Do you have anything in common?

Multiple-choice cloze (Part I)

▶ **EXAM** FOCUS p.186

1 Quickly read the text about a musician and say what is unusual about Josh Freese's relationship with his fans. Don't worry about the gaps yet.

2 Look at the example (0). Why are options A, B and D wrong? Think about which two verbs are used with places rather than people, and which one does not fit grammatically.

3 Read the text around gap 1 and answer the questions.

1 Which word do you think might fit here?
2 Look at the options. Which of the verbs A–D can be followed by *of*?
3 Choose the phrase which means *be familiar with*.

EXAM TIP

Decide what kind of word might fit each gap before looking at the options. Then check around each gap to make sure that the option you choose fits with the other words.

4 For questions 2–8, decide which answer (A, B, C or D) best fits each gap.

DRUMMING UP BUSINESS

Josh Freese is a very successful drummer **(0)** *C, based* in Los Angeles. You probably won't have **(1)** .... of him but he's played with some very successful bands. When Freese **(2)** .... his first solo album, called *Since 1972*, he decided to set up a system where fans could buy something unique. By **(3)** .... with fans directly, he hoped to sell more of his music.

The idea was that if you paid $50 for his music, you would also get a personal five-minute 'thank you' phone call. Sales of the album quickly took **(4)** .... But there were other possible choices which gave fans the opportunity to meet Freese in **(5)** .... The option to have lunch with Freese for $250 **(6)** .... out in about a week. Fans could also **(7)** .... a private drum lesson from Freese for $2,500. There were other offers ranging from $10,000 to $75,000.

Not all of these were taken **(8)** .... by fans, but a teenager from Florida actually purchased the $20,000 option and spent a week on tour with Freese.

0	A situated	B located	C based	D lived
1	A recognised	B noticed	C heard	D known
2	A released	B sent	C presented	D brought
3	A joining	B discussing	C contacting	D communicating
4	A after	B out	C off	D in
5	A person	B reality	C life	D face
6	A stayed	B gave	C sold	D let
7	A achieve	B receive	C collect	D gain
8	A over	B back	C away	D up

5 Work in pairs. Compare your answers and say why you chose them.

6 Discuss the questions.

1 Do you think this is a good way for artists to promote their music?
2 Would any of these offers attract you?

Vocabulary

phrasal verbs with *take*

7 Complete the sentences with the correct form of the phrasal verbs in the box. One phrasal verb is used twice with different meanings.

take after   take back
take off   take over   take up

1 His career .... as soon as he won the prize and now he's really successful.
2 He .... his father, who's also really musical.
3 I gave up the piano and .... the saxophone instead.
4 He finally .... my invitation to join the band.
5 Tom .... as the band's manager when Sam left.
6 I made him .... what he said about my taste in music.

LANGUAGE TIP

If the phrasal verb has an object, the particle can sometimes come either before or after the object. This is shown by the symbol <-> in the dictionary.
I have taken up the saxophone.
I have taken the saxophone up.
However, if there is a pronoun, the particle must come after the object.
I have taken it up.
NOT *I have taken up it.*

Multiple matching (Part 3)

▶ **EXAM** FOCUS p.189

1 Tick the statements which are true for you. Then work in pairs and compare.

A   I like following my favourite musicians on social media.

B   I often buy albums online.

C   I spend a lot of time watching music videos.

D   I like music that most other people haven't heard of.

E   I have quite a varied taste in music.

F   I enjoy sharing music with my friends.

G   I always listen to music when I'm in a bad mood.

H   I often disagree with my friends about music.

2 ▶ 04   You will hear five people talking about listening to music. Listen to Speaker 1. Which things does he mention?

his favourite bands   his taste in music   social media

LANGUAGE TIP

Notice that sometimes *will* is used to talk about present habits.

My friends and I will spend hours playing different tracks …

3 Look at the extracts from Speaker 1 (1–4). Which one matches one of the statements A–H in Activity 1? Underline the words which say the same thing in a different way.

1   Now I'm just into the same stuff as everyone else – hip hop mainly.

2   Some people I know always want to be different so they'll only listen to new bands that haven't become popular yet.

3   My friends and I will spend hours playing different tracks to each other and making up new playlists. It's fun.

4   I don't really bother with following my favourite bands on Instagram or anything like that.

4 ▶ 05   Now listen to Speakers 2–5. Match statements from the list A–H in Activity 1 with what each speaker says. Use the letters only once. There are three extra letters which you do not need to use.

Speaker 2 [   ]
Speaker 3 [   ]
Speaker 4 [   ]
Speaker 5 [   ]

5 Work in pairs and compare your answers. Which paraphrases did you hear? Listen again to check.

EXAM TIP

Listen for words and phrases that are synonyms or paraphrases of the key words in the statements.

6 Work in pairs and discuss the questions.

1   Compare the kinds of music you like listening to, and how and when you listen to it.

2   What kind of music do you dislike, and in what situations do you prefer not to have to listen to it?

Habit in the past
used to/would

▶ **GRAMMAR** REFERENCE p.141

1 **Look at the extracts from the recording and answer the questions.**

I <u>used to watch</u> a lot of videos on YouTube.

I <u>used to be</u> obsessed with music videos.

When I was growing up, my mum <u>would</u> often <u>play</u> 70s disco music and dance around the kitchen.

1 Does she still watch videos on YouTube?
2 Is she still obsessed with music videos?
3 Did her mother listen to 70s music?
4 Which underlined verb describes a past state?
5 Which underlined verbs describe a past habit?
6 Which of the underlined verbs can you use to describe both past states and habits?

LANGUAGE TIP

Be careful not to confuse *used to do* (describing past habit and states) with *be/get used to doing* (be accustomed to doing something in the present or the past).

Used to + bare infinitive describes past habits and states.

I used to hate classical music. (= but now I like it)

Did you use to like disco music? (= at a time in the past)

I was/got used to being alone as a child. (= It's something that happened a lot and I don't mind it.)

---

2 **Choose the correct option in italics to complete the sentences. Sometimes both options are possible. Explain your choices.**

1 My parents *would always/always used to* listen to classical music in the car.
2 Every year they *would/used to* go to a jazz festival which took place near our home.
3 I remember my dad *would/used to* have a huge collection of vinyl when we were young.
4 My mum *would/used to* know all the words to every song by Madonna.

3 **Work in pairs.**

1 Talk about the kind of music your family would listen to when you were younger.
2 What kind of music did you use to like and didn't you use to like?
3 What did you get used to? Is there something you never got used to?

4 **Complete the text with the present simple, present continuous, *used to* or *would* form of the verbs in brackets. Sometimes more than one answer is possible.**

Tom Carter is now a farmer, but his life was once very different.

Until a few years ago, I **(1)** .... (*be*) the lead vocalist in a band. In the old days, record companies **(2)** .... (*give*) musicians a cash advance to make albums and videos and then after the album was released, we **(3)** .... (*go*) on tour. When we got back, we **(4)** .... (*start*) work on a new album. We **(5)** .... (*have*) a lot of fun, even though we **(6)** .... (*also/have to*) be away from our families for months at a time.

It's all completely different these days. It's often necessary for musicians **(7)** .... (*raise*) money themselves to release their own records, which can be very difficult. Because of the crowded media market they **(8)** .... (*compete*) even harder with other bands. In the age of social media, fans also play a bigger role. They **(9)** .... (*want*) new albums all the time and also **(10)** .... (*expect*) to hear from the musicians directly on Twitter.

I know musicians of my age **(11)** .... (*find*) it all very difficult to get used to.

5 **Work in pairs and discuss the questions.**

1 How has accessing music changed over the years?
2 Do you follow any musicians on social media? Which ones?
3 In what ways has your taste in music changed over the last ten years?

Informal email (Part 2)
using informal language

▶ **WRITING** REFERENCE p.168

1 **Work in pairs and discuss the questions.**

1 How easy is it to see live music where you live?

2 Would you travel abroad to go to a music festival or concert?

3 What advice would you give to someone who is visiting your country about where to see live music?

2 **Read the exam task and answer the questions.**

1 Who do you have to write to?

2 Why are you writing?

3 What kind of style do you have to write in?

> You've received an email from your English friend Josh. Read this part of the email and write your email to Josh.
>
> > I'm really looking forward to visiting you this summer.
> >
> > If possible, I'd really like to see some live music. Can you tell me what kind of music is popular with you and your friends? How easy is it to get tickets for concerts?
> >
> > Thanks
> >
> > Josh
>
> Write your email in **140–190** words in an appropriate style.

3 **Look at the model answer and choose the most suitable word or phrase in italics for an informal email.**

Hi Josh

Yes, can't wait to see you, too! It's good you want to see some live music while you're here because in my town **(1)** *there's a music festival every summer/an annual music festival takes place* so **(2)** *you will have the opportunity/you'll be able* to see lots of local bands play. Unfortunately, none of them is very famous but there's a fantastic atmosphere there and I always **(3)** *find it very enjoyable/enjoy going a lot*. Also, the tickets are very reasonable and you can spend the whole day there. Of course, like all my friends, I **(4)** *am mainly interested in/have a preference for* rock bands but you can find reggae and traditional music there too – **(5)** *you won't be disappointed because there's something for everyone/it offers something for everyone, which means no one will be disappointed*.

There aren't any large music venues near where I live, so it's not that easy for me to go to big concerts very often. **(6)** *But/However*, one of my favourite bands, Soundtracks, is playing in the nearest city on 22 August, so **(7)** *if you like, I could/if you're interested, I'd be willing to* get tickets for us to go to that.

(8) *Let me know what you think./Please reply as soon as possible.*

Alice

4 **Which of the expressions 1–4 could you use to end the email to Josh?**

1 Hope to hear from you soon.

2 I look forward to hearing from you.

3 Can't wait to see you in the summer.

4 Don't hesitate to get in touch if you have any more questions.

5 **Read the exam task and tick the information (1–6) you could include in your email to Max.**

> You have received an email from a student called Max. Read this part of the email and write your email to Max.
>
> > I'm moving to your town soon to go to college. Can you tell me what kinds of things there are to do in the evening for students and what you like doing best?
> >
> > Thanks
> >
> > Max
>
> Write your email in **140–190** words in an appropriate style.

1 recommend some places to go

2 offer to take Max out one evening

3 tell him about the most expensive restaurants in your town

4 complain about the lack of entertainment venues

5 describe a typical evening out in detail

6 describe your favourite kind of evening out and why you like it

6 **Write I (informal) or F (formal) next to the phrases 1–6 and add any other ways of recommending or suggesting.**

1 I would advise you to …

2 The best place to eat is …

3 You really must go to …

4 If you feel like dancing, there's a good club in …

5 You should definitely try …

6 I'd highly recommend visiting …

7 **Write your email, using some of the language from Activities 3 and 6. Then check your work, using the writing checklist on page 165.**

EXAM TIP

Don't mix informal and formal styles in your email. Learn some different ways of starting and ending your informal emails.

1 Complete the second sentence so that it has a similar meaning to the first sentence, using the word given. Use between two and five words, including the word given.

Example:

I was given responsibility for booking gigs for our band.

OVER

Last month I took over booking gigs for our band.

1 I enjoyed learning to play the guitar and I'd like to take it up again one day.

   USED

   I .... learning to play the guitar and I'd like to take it up again one day.

2 We always went to the jazz festival every July.

   WOULD

   We .... to the jazz festival every July.

3 I perform in front of people all the time, so I don't mind doing it.

   USED

   I .... in front of people, so I don't mind doing it.

4 Her career was an instant success as soon as she appeared in a TV advert.

   TOOK

   Her career .... as soon as she appeared in a TV advert.

5 Unfortunately, I'm not like my grandfather, who could play the piano really well.

   AFTER

   Unfortunately, I .... my grandfather, who could play the piano really well.

6 When we started going out, I disliked my boyfriend's taste in music but it's becoming less of a problem.

   USE

   I .... my boyfriend's taste in music but it's becoming less of a problem.

2 Complete the sentences with the present simple or present continuous form of the verbs in brackets.

1 I .... (*not like*) classical music.

2 I don't understand what you .... (*say*). Can you say it again, please?

3 My teacher .... (*not think*) it's a good idea to learn an instrument when you're too young.

4 She's never at home. She .... (*always do*) something in the evening.

5 Traditional music .... (*get*) more and more popular.

6 You .... (*play*) really well today.

3 Choose the correct option (A, B, C or D) to complete the sentences.

1 My brother's always .... computer games instead of doing his homework.

   A playing   **B** doing   **C** play   **D** do

2 Do you enjoy .... time with your friends?

   A doing   **B** spending   **C** do   **D** spend

3 I'm determined to learn the .... this year.

   A water skiing   **B** yoga   **C** guitar   **D** Spanish

4 When I lived on my own, I .... much more exercise.

   A went   **B** practised   **C** did   **D** made

4 Complete the text with the words in the box.

ambitious confirm exploit person profitable
put raise release

BANDS AND FANS

In the old days, young people used to join a fan club, and receiving signed photographs from their heroes was probably enough to keep them happy. These days, however, the balance of power has shifted. In order to **(1)** .... money for new projects, musicians are now turning to their fans to crowd-fund them so that they can afford to **(2)** .... new music. For artists who want to stay in the public eye, it is no longer enough to simply **(3)** .... on a concert or appear at a festival: if they want their work to be **(4)** .... , they must also encourage their fans to **(5)** .... their popularity by 'liking' videos repeatedly on social media.

However, if they are not to **(6)** .... them, musicians are required to give their fans something in return and autographs, or even selfies, are no longer enough. Fans are now more **(7)** .... , and 'meet and greet' sessions, where they can meet their heroes in **(8)** .... , are becoming increasingly more common.

2 Relative values

1 **Discuss the questions.**

1 How do you think your friends would describe your personality?

2 What personality characteristics do you share with other members of your family?

2 **Do the personality quiz.**

PERSONALITY QUIZ

How likely are you to ...	Very likely	Quite likely	Neither likely nor unlikely	Quite unlikely	Very unlikely
1 spend most evenings on social media?					
2 get talking to people on a train or plane?					
3 always think you are right?					
4 make decisions quickly?					
5 organise a party?					
6 discuss a problem openly with friends or family?					

3 **Turn to page 138 to get your results. Then complete sentences 1–6 so they are true for you.**

1 I'm very likely to ...

2 I tend to ...

3 I'm good at ... *-ing*.

4 I find it difficult to ...

5 There's no way I'd ...

6 There's a slight chance I might ...

4 **Work in pairs. Compare your sentences and discuss the questions.**

1 How much do you have in common?

2 What did you learn from your results?

3 Do you think this is an accurate test of personality?

Vocabulary
formation of adjectives

5 Copy and complete the table with the adjective forms of the nouns in the box.

care caution comfort drama emotion generosity harm help hope love
meaning pessimist prediction reliability sympathy use

-able	-ous	-ic	-al	-ful
sociable	adventurous	realistic	practical	thoughtful

6 ▶ 06 Mark the stress on each adjective, then listen and check. Practise saying the words. Which adjectives have the stress on different syllables from the noun form?

7 Which of the nouns in Activity 5 can be used with *-less* to form an adjective with a negative meaning? How does the meaning change?

Example: *hopeless*

Word formation (Part 3)

▶ **EXAM** FOCUS p.186

8 Read the text quickly without worrying about the gaps. What problem with describing people's personalities is mentioned?

How well do you know yourself?

When trying to understand our own or other people's
(0) *behaviour* , we tend to over-simplify things. We use one or two adjectives to sum each other up. We think of one friend as having a generally **(1)** .... and positive outlook, while another friend is considered **(2)** .... and negative. Of course, in **(3)** ...., none of us is so easily defined. The truth is that we are all made up of inconsistent and contradictory **(4)** ....; we can be serious and reliable with our colleagues at work but in our personal relationships at home we are more **(5)** .... and emotional. With some friends we can be very cautious, while we are **(6)** .... thrill-seekers with other friends.

So can people be neatly divided into personality types? Or do we alter our personality according to the **(7)** .... in our changing moods and situations? Maybe we can never really get to know ourselves and the idea of a fixed personality is completely unrealistic and **(8)** ....

BEHAVE

HOPE
PESSIMIST
REAL
CHARACTER

PREDICT

ADVENTURE

DIFFERENT

MEANING

9 Look at the missing word for question 1. Is it a noun or an adjective? Does it have a positive or negative meaning?

10 Use the word given in capitals at the end of some of the lines to form a word that fits in the gap in the same line.

11 Work in pairs and discuss the questions.

1 How well do you know yourself?
2 Do you think your family knows you better than you do?

Multiple matching (Part 7)

▶ **EXAM** FOCUS p.187

1 Why do you think so many people follow in their parents' footsteps and end up doing a similar job?

2 You are going to read an article in which people talk about how their parents' careers have influenced their own career decisions. Read the text quickly and find out whether the people

1 are doing similar work to their parents.

2 are happy with the career they have chosen.

EXAM TIP

Underline the key words in the options and then read through the texts quickly to find a similar word or expression which says the same thing in a different way.

3 Look at the underlined words in Activity 4, question 1. Read text A and find matching words/phrases.

4 For questions 1–10, choose from the sections A–D. The sections may be chosen more than once.

Which person states the following?

As a child, I <u>always imagined</u> I would <u>follow in my parents' footsteps</u>.	1 *A*
I wasn't able to support myself doing the job I'd originally hoped to do.	2
My parents were initially unhappy about my choice of career.	3
Working in the family business when I was a child was very useful.	4
My parents didn't try to improve my chances when I was getting started.	5
I'm glad that I don't have to work as hard as my parents.	6
I've benefited from doing a variety of jobs.	7
My background gave me the confidence to enter a competitive field.	8
I've inherited some of the skills I need to do my job.	9
It took me a while to realise that having a parent in the same business was an advantage.	10

5 Would you consider doing the same job as one of your parents? Why/Why not?

Should you follow in your family's footsteps?

A Lauren Hill

Both my parents are doctors – my mum's a GP and my dad's a surgeon. So, as a child, I think it seemed natural to me that I too would study medicine at college, and go on to have a career as a doctor. But my parents certainly never suggested that they would want me to <u>carry on</u> the family tradition, and I think they were secretly pleased when, after university, I wandered first into a university teaching job and then into company law. Things definitely <u>worked out</u> for the best because I wouldn't have coped with the unsociable hours my parents worked nor with the enormous responsibilities. There are times, though, when I wonder what being a doctor would have been like. If only so at parties I could receive admiration and respect, instead of being regarded as uninspiring and unimaginative.

B Zoe Mackintosh

My dad started his business back in 1980. He buys and sells fruit and vegetables – not to customers on the street, but to other traders. It's a business-to-business operation. When I was a student, I was broke, so my dad offered me a part-time job to help with my finances. I accepted. But it wasn't until I was in my mid-twenties that I decided to join the family business. After completing my degree, I worked in a number of PR firms in different roles for a while. I wanted to gain some experience in other fields first, and this has allowed me to bring a fresh perspective to the business. When I suggested joining the family company, my dad was really surprised. He actually tried to <u>put me off</u> at first – he knows more than anyone how much hard work is involved, not to mention the long hours, whereas my mum tried to <u>talk me into</u> a high-status career, such as medicine or accounting, like all my friends. They're both convinced I made the right decision now, though.

C Max Howard

For many people <u>breaking into</u> the desirable world of television can seem impossible and it can seem that there's no hope of ever getting an opportunity. But because I'd grown up with it, this world felt familiar and easily accessible. My father was a well-known television presenter and my mother made TV documentaries. They were determined, however, that I should <u>make it</u> on my own and deliberately avoided opening any doors for me. I studied journalism and had a brief spell as a TV news reporter on a local TV station. I now work as a producer for an independent TV production company. The world of media has changed enormously since my parents' day but their skill in finding the heart of an issue and presenting it as a compelling story is still very relevant. I've <u>taken after</u> my parents in that respect, as I seem to have a natural talent for this.

D Rob Wilson

My father is a private investigator, specialising in tracking down people selling fake designer goods. From the age of twelve, I was enlisted to make undercover buys from market traders. I would buy T-shirts and sunglasses and I would get paid for that. It seemed like the easiest way in the world to make money but it never occurred to me that this early training would be so valuable. My dream was to become a stand-up comedian, which I had some success at, but not enough to pay the bills. Through one of my dad's contacts I started working as a private investigator in the field of intellectual property and copyright. Eventually I <u>set up</u> my own business specialising in protecting the rights of musicians and other artists. At that time I didn't understand how important my father's reputation would be for my success – people trust me.

Vocabulary
phrasal verbs

6 Match the underlined phrasal verbs in the article to meanings 1–8.

1 persuade
2 establish/create
3 discourage
4 succeed
5 continue
6 be similar to
7 enter
8 develop/have a good result

7 Work in pairs and discuss the questions.

1 Do your parents expect you to make it on your own?
2 Which member of your family do you most take after?
3 Do you think it's important to carry on family traditions?
4 Do your family try to put you off doing things?
5 Have your parents ever talked you into doing something?

Adverbs and adjectives

▶ **GRAMMAR** REFERENCE p.142

1 Complete the text with the words in the box.

---
easily friendly hard hardly lonely wrong

I **(1)** .... know my brother because he's so much older than me. But I think he's actually quite a **(2)** .... person to get to know anyway. People think he isn't **(3)** .... but really he's quite shy and doesn't make friends **(4)** .... He always thinks he's done something **(5)** .... to upset people but the real problem is that he's uncomfortable in social situations. I used to worry that he was **(6)** .... because he spent so much time on his own. But actually he enjoys spending time on his own. He's the kindest person in the world and he'd do anything for you.

> **LANGUAGE TIP**
>
> Adverbs are used to modify verbs. *She won the game easily*. Some adverbs have the same form as adjectives. *It's a hard decision. They worked very hard.*

2 Look at the words in the box in Activity 1 and answer the questions.

1 Which are adjectives? Which are adverbs?
2 Which words can be used as both an adjective and an adverb? Which ones are irregular?

3 Choose the correct adverb in italics.

1 At home we were allowed to speak *free/freely* without anyone criticising us.
2 You don't need to pay for advice on relationships; you can get that *free/freely* from friends.
3 I try *hard/hardly* to get on with my brothers and sisters.
4 Because we're twins, it's *hard/hardly* surprising that we have a lot in common.
5 He's been feeling depressed *late/lately*.
6 My mother had children *lately/late* in life.
7 My parents live *closely/close* to me.
8 You need to watch young children very *close/closely*.

Extreme adjectives, modifiers and intensifiers

▶ **GRAMMAR** REFERENCE p.142

4 Think of some extreme versions of the adjectives.

1 big *enormous, huge*   6 attractive
2 good   7 bad
3 surprised   8 strange
4 angry   9 difficult
5 frightened

5 Replace the words in italics with the adverbs in the box. There may be more than one possible answer.

---
a bit absolutely completely fairly very
---

1 He's *quite* intelligent.
2 He's *really* cautious.
3 She's *really* impossible to get on with.
4 She's a *really* good person.
5 He's a *really* amazing person.
6 He can be *quite* difficult.
7 They're a *really* weird family.
8 She looks *really* exhausted.

6 Choose the correct adverb in italics to complete the rules.

1 *Really/Very* can be used with any adjective in order to intensify meaning.
2 'Completely', *absolutely/really* and 'very' are only used with extreme adjectives.
3 *Quite/A bit* is only used when making a criticism with adjectives with a negative meaning.
4 *Quite/Fairly* can be used with any adjective to modify meaning.
5 *Quite/Fairly* can be used with an extreme adjective in order to intensify meaning.

7 Complete sentences 1–3 with phrases A–C to make statements you agree with. Work in pairs and discuss your sentences. Do you agree?

1 It's fairly easy
2 It's quite hard
3 It's absolutely impossible

A to judge a person's character from their appearance.
B to get on with everyone in your family.
C for parents to treat all their children equally.

Multiple choice (Part 4)

▶ **EXAM** FOCUS p.189

1 **Discuss the questions.**

1 How important do you think it is to have brothers and sisters?

2 Do you agree that parents treat younger siblings differently to their oldest child?

3 What characteristics do you think are typical of oldest/middle/youngest/only children?

2 **You're going to listen to a radio interview with a psychologist called Max about birth order. Read the first question and options A–C in Activity 4 and underline the key words.**

3 ▶ 07 **Listen to the first part of the interview.**

1 Which key words, or words with a similar meaning to the statement and options, did you hear?

2 Which option correctly completes statement 1, according to the information you hear?

4 ▶ 08 **Read through questions 2–7 and underline the key words. Then listen and choose the best answer, A, B or C.**

> **EXAM TIP**
>
> Use the questions to help you follow the discussion so that you don't get lost. Remember you will hear the information twice.

1 According to Max, research shows that

  A oldest children are likely to be the most successful in the future.

  B middle children are more likely to be happier than their siblings.

  C the youngest child is likely to be the least independent.

2 According to Max, what is the reason for oldest children's results in intelligence tests?

  A Parents offer more support to the oldest child.

  B Oldest children spend more time alone.

  C The oldest child benefits from teaching younger siblings.

3 What typical characteristic of oldest children did Max share?

  A He enjoyed being competitive.

  B He experienced jealousy of a sibling.

  C He always wanted to please his parents.

4 Max says that youngest children can often

  A seem very confident with older children.

  B be curious and creative.

  C refuse to accept their role as the baby of the family.

5 What does Max say is likely to increase the 'birth order effect'?

  A a large age gap between siblings

  B families with three or more siblings

  C having siblings of the same sex

6 Max says that the best combination for a successful marriage is between people who are both

  A oldest children.

  B middle children.

  C third-born children.

7 Max says we should be cautious about the 'birth order effect' because

  A it may only play a small part in forming personality.

  B people usually behave differently when they are away from their families.

  C it discourages people from changing their behaviour when they grow up.

5 **Work in pairs and compare your answers. Then look at the audio script on page 207. Underline the sentences which give the correct answers.**

6 **Work in pairs and discuss the questions.**

1 Did you find any of the information in the recording surprising?

2 What impact has the 'birth order effect' had on your family or another family you know?

3 What do you think is the ideal number of children in a family? Why?

Verb patterns: *-ing* or infinitive

▶ **GRAMMAR** REFERENCE p.143

1 **Work in pairs and discuss the questions.**

Do you:

A spend less time than you used to with one relation?

B have a new person in your family you get on well with?

C dislike a member of your family?

2 ▶ 09 **Listen to five people talking about one of their relations. Match Speakers 1–5 to questions A–C in Activity 1. You can use the questions more than once.**

3 **Match 1–5 to A–E to make sentences. Then listen again to check.**

1 It took me ages to have the confidence

2 It's not worth

3 We both love

4 We'd like him

5 I've promised

A to give him tennis lessons.

B riding, so it's great to have something in common.

C to come and live nearer.

D to be on my own with him.

E talking to him really because he just disagrees with whatever anybody says.

4 **Which of the following verbs/expressions are followed by *-ing*, and which by the infinitive? Which can be followed by both?**

1 like, love, prefer

2 be keen on, can't stand, enjoy, hate, mind

3 hope, promise, try

4 expect, encourage, persuade + direct object

5 **Describe a relationship with a member of your family. Use some of the verbs/ expressions from Activity 4.**

LANGUAGE TIP

To form a negative of the gerund or infinitive, use *not* before the verb.
*I hate **not** going … He told me **not** to go …*

---

6 **Choose the correct option in italics for the pairs of sentences 1–5 and explain the difference in meaning between each pair.**

1 **A** My mother stopped *making/to make* lunch because the phone rang.

   B My mother stopped *making/to make* lunch because we were hungry.

2 **A** Dad tried *phoning/to phone* but nobody answered.

   B Dad tried *phoning/to phone* but he couldn't remember the number, so he gave up.

3 **A** The kids remembered *buying/to buy* grandma a present for her birthday.

   B The kids remembered *buying/to buy* grandma a present but couldn't find it again later.

4 **A** I regret *telling/to tell* you that all train services have been cancelled.

   B I regret *telling/to tell* you because now you're upset.

5 **A** I forgot *to give/giving* my sister an old dress, and then I found it in her wardrobe.

   B I forgot *to give/giving* my teacher my essay and she wasn't happy when I handed it in late.

7 **Complete the text with the *-ing* or the infinitive form of the verbs in brackets.**

DESTINY CALLS

Nadja Swarovski who, along with four cousins, runs the famous Swarovski crystal company based in Austria, is very proud of her family dynasty. As a child, she remembers her grandfather **(1)** .... (*tell*) her why Daniel Swarovski, her great-great grandfather, decided **(2)** .... (*set up*) the company. He hoped **(3)** .... (*sell*) jewellery that ordinary people could afford **(4)** .... (*buy*) because he understood that beautiful things make people happy. This made perfect sense to Nadja because she enjoyed **(5)** .... (*sew*) crystals from the factory onto her favourite jeans.

Nadja surprised her family when she chose **(6)** .... (*study*) art history instead of the traditional family subject of engineering. She was also keen **(7)** .... (*get away*) from the pressure of being a Swarovski, and so ended up **(8)** .... (*enrol*) at the university of Dallas, Texas. But she couldn't escape her destiny forever. When she became the only female member of the board, Nadja was able **(9)** .... (*see*) that they were missing an opportunity. Although she didn't want to give up **(10)** .... (*produce*) things like the popular small crystal animals, she believed fashion was the future. She managed **(11)** .... (*persuade*) her cousins to start **(12)** .... (*work*) with top fashion designers, such as Alexander McQueen. His 2009 collection inspired other designers **(13)** .... (*make*) fabulous creations with crystal and since then stars such as Beyoncé and Rihanna have gone on **(14)** .... (*perform*) in dresses covered in Swarovski crystal.

Collaborative task (Part 3)
agreeing and disagreeing

▶ **EXAM** FOCUS p.190

1 Look at the photos. Why do you think these kinds of relationships are important?

2 ▶ 10 Look at the exam task. Then listen to Alana and Federico. Which of the relationships do they discuss? Why do they think they're important?

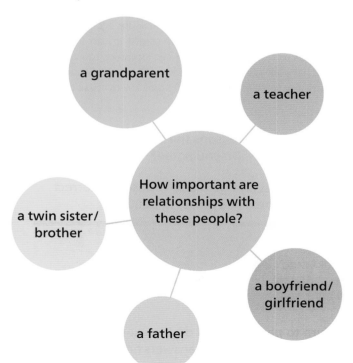

- a grandparent
- a teacher
- a twin sister/ brother
- **How important are relationships with these people?**
- a boyfriend/ girlfriend
- a father

3 Work in pairs. Add some expressions to the list. Practise saying them with the correct stress.

Agreeing: That's very true. Good point …

Partially agreeing: I see what you mean, but … I suppose so, but …

Disagreeing gently: I'm not sure about that. Well, actually …

Expressing strong disagreement: I have to disagree with you on that. I think the exact opposite.

Asking opinions: What's your view on that? Do you agree?

EXAM TIP

Give your opinions but make sure you also listen to your partner. Ask about his/her opinions and respond to what he/she says.

---

4 Work in pairs and do the exam task in Activity 2. Then decide which person might have the most influence on a young person's life.

5 Work in pairs and discuss the questions.

1 Which people do you think have had the most influence on different stages of your life?

2 In what way has an older relative been a good role model for you?

3 What are the advantages and disadvantages of belonging to a big family?

4 How easy is it to stay in touch with family members that live a long way away?

5 What kind of relationship do you have with your cousins?

Essay (Part I)
using linkers for contrast

▶ **WRITING** REFERENCE pp.166 and 167

1 Work in pairs. Read the exam task and essay title and think of some advantages and disadvantages of both situations.

> In your English class you have been discussing family relationships. Now, your teacher has asked you to write an essay.
>
> Is it better to have a small or a large age difference between siblings?
>
> **Notes**
>
> Write about:
>
> 1 competition
> 2 friendship
> 3 learning to share (your own idea)

Write an essay using all the notes and give reasons for your point of view. Write **140–190** words.

2 Match 1–6 to A–F to make sentences. Then work in pairs and decide which sentences you agree with.

1 Even though siblings who are close in age may argue,

2 Despite being born eight years apart,

3 I wish I had a much older brother to give me advice. On the other hand,

4 A small age gap between sisters can be a good thing, whereas

5 There is likely to be less competition between siblings born several years apart. However,

6 While having a sibling of a similar age may seem desirable,

A in my experience, boys may become too competitive.

B my younger brothers are happy to share a bedroom.

C they are more likely to grow up with many shared memories.

D forming a close bond depends much more on personality than age.

E they may find it difficult to develop a lasting relationship.

F I expect I'd get tired of him telling me what to do all the time.

3 In which of the sentences in Activity 2 is it also possible to use *although*?

4 Read the essay and find where the three points from the notes in Activity 1 are mentioned.

> Is it better to have a small or a large age difference between siblings? I think it's hard to say whether it's better to have siblings of a similar age or much older or younger because all families are different. We can't judge properly what it would be like to be in a different situation. **(1)** *However/Even though* we might like the idea of having a baby brother or sister, we can't judge what that would be like in reality.
>
> But I think the greatest advantage of having a small age gap is that when you're a child, you have someone to play with. As well as this, you have to learn to share your toys, instead of just keeping them to yourself. This makes playing with other children outside the family easier. **(2)** *Although/However*, there's likely to be much more competition between siblings who are close in age because they may be jealous of each other.
>
> The danger with having a large age gap is that you may not have a close relationship when you're grown up because you don't have the same shared memories. **(3)** *On the other hand/While* the age gap becomes less important as you get older, so it's always possible to make friends with your sibling as adults. Speaking from my own experience, having a sister who's only two years younger has been ideal. **(4)** *Whereas/Despite* being quite different, we've always got on and we're good friends now we're adults.

5 Underline the reasons the student gives for her point of view. Do you agree?

6 Read the essay again and choose the correct linking words or phrases in italics.

EXAM TIP

There are no right or wrong answers to the question. The important thing is to make sure you include all three points in your essay and explain your point of view.

7 Turn to page 139 and do the exam task. Try to give reasons for your answers and use some of the linking words.

1 Complete the second sentence so that it has a similar meaning to the first sentence, using the word given. Use between two and five words, including the word given.

1 I don't think parents should have to continue supporting their children when they're adults.

CARRY

I don't think parents should .... supporting their children when they're adults.

2 Everyone says Phoebe is very similar to her mother.

TAKES

Everyone says Phoebe .... her mother.

3 George's grandfather started his business when he was only eighteen.

SET

George's grandfather .... his business when he was only eighteen.

4 Seeing how hard my mother works has discouraged me from becoming a teacher.

PUT

Seeing how hard my mother works has .... from becoming a teacher.

5 Not many people become successful in the world of acting.

MAKE

Not many people .... in the world of acting.

6 My friends are trying to persuade me to have a party on Saturday.

TALK

My friends are trying to .... having a party on Saturday.

2 Correct the mistake in each of the sentences.

1 He's tried really hardly to get tickets for you.
2 The cinema is fairly closely to the station.
3 The football results were absolutely close.
4 She finished late and I was very furious with her.
5 They spoke free about their difficult childhoods.
6 It was hardly dark but he was completely frightened.
7 It would be a bit brilliant if we won the cup final.
8 She's been working very hardly lately.

3 Complete the sentences with the adjectives in the box.

cautious   confident   creative   independent
practical   sociable

1 Whereas I'm quite shy about speaking in public, my brother's always been ....
2 Even at the age of eighty-five, my gran never likes relying on other people. She's very ....
3 My husband's not very good at doing things with his hands. He's not at all ....
4 I prefer my own company but my sisters are the opposite; they're all really ....
5 My father paints and writes really well. He's always been really ....
6 I am not prepared to take risks anymore. I'm getting more and more ....

4 Complete the sentences using the correct form of the word in brackets.

1 My new car isn't as .... as I hoped it would be. (rely)
2 Molly's stories are very .... Her characters always have such exciting adventures. (drama)
3 My children will never try any new food. They aren't very .... (adventure)
4 I don't think you're being very .... about how much we can finish. (real)
5 I'm absolutely .... at languages. I just can't learn them. (hope)
6 I explained I'd been ill but the boss wasn't at all .... (sympathy)

5 Choose the correct option in italics to complete the sentences.

1 I regretted not *having/to have* a car to drive.
2 He'd like us *working/to work* late this evening.
3 I'm not very good at *running/to run*.
4 Have you remembered *locking/to lock* the door?
5 Melanie has promised *inviting/to invite* us to stay.
6 She stopped *working/to work* and had a rest.
7 The teacher made me *to finish/finish* my work before I left.
8 Jim asked me *not to/to not* speak.

3 Things that matter

1 What matters to you? Put the things in the box in order of importance.

education/career family friends interests money pets possessions places

Vocabulary
money

£230 million

2 Work in pairs. Discuss whether the items in the photos are:

A worth the money.   **C** a waste of money.

B good value for money.   **D** a bargain.

3 Work in pairs. Discuss what the expressions could mean. Do you have similar expressions in your language?

£15,000

1 He's got more money than sense.

2 Put your money where your mouth is.

3 I'm a bit short of money this month.

4 Money doesn't grow on trees.

5 She's got money to burn.

6 He's worth a fortune.

7 My mum always says she's not made of money.

8 Money makes the world go around.

£4,000

4 Complete the statements with the prepositions in the box. Which of the statements do you agree with? Discuss in pairs and give reasons.

away in of on to within

£65

1 It's difficult to live .... your means when you're a student.

2 You should always avoid being .... debt.

3 Having to live .... a tight budget is boring.

4 Very rich people should give most of their money ....

5 It's not a good idea to lend your credit card .... a friend.

6 Young people today have a higher standard .... living than their grandparents' generation.

Sentence completion (Part 2)

▶ **EXAM** FOCUS p.188

5 You're going to hear a multimillionaire called David Burton talking about his life. Read the gapped sentences (1–10). Which of the topics A–E do you expect to hear?

A how he made his fortune

B his attitude to money

C his typical working day

D what he spends his money on

E where he lives

6 ▶ 11 Listen and check.

7 Look at the gap (1–10) in each sentence. Which of the gaps, if any, may require

A an uncountable noun?

B a plural form?

C a number?

EXAM TIP

Usually, you only have to write one or two words or a number in each gap. Occasionally you may need to write three words.

8 Listen again and complete the sentences.

9 Work in pairs and compare your answers. Then look at the audio script on page 208 to check your answers. Make sure you have spelt the words correctly.

10 Work in pairs and discuss the questions.

1 Do you think money can make people happy?

2 Do you think it is better to win, inherit or earn money?

Giving it all away

David's early ambition was to be a **(1)** .... like his uncle.

His father was disappointed when he decided to leave **(2)** .... to start his own business.

David believes being able to manage **(3)** .... is essential to succeed in business.

David says he didn't feel much **(4)** .... at being able to buy expensive things.

His first charity project involved financing **(5)** .... for young people from disadvantaged backgrounds.

While he was travelling in India, David realised that the best way for people to get out of **(6)** .... was to set up a business.

The charity has provided more than **(7)** .... individuals with a loan.

David considers building a **(8)** .... in Malawi to be one of his greatest achievements.

David believes that people from a close **(9)** .... are happier than wealthy individuals.

According to David, money can give people **(10)** .... , although it may also cause problems.

Using modifiers for comparison

▶ **GRAMMAR** REFERENCE p.144

1 Look at the sentences from the listening on page 27 and complete them with the correct comparative or superlative form of the adjectives in brackets. Then look at the audio script on page 208 to check your answers.

1 In fact I was .... (*empty*) and .... (*lonely*) than before.

2 One of the things I'm .... (*proud*) of is being involved in a construction project for a new hospital in a small town in Malawi.

3 Being part of a community makes people .... (*content*) than becoming a millionaire.

4 Having too much money isn't .... (*difficult*) .... not having enough money.

2 Decide which pairs of sentences have a similar meaning, and which have a different meaning.

1 **A** My car was by far the most expensive thing I've ever bought.

B My car was a lot more expensive than anything else I've ever bought.

2 **A** My grandfather is one of the most generous people I know.

B There aren't many people who are as generous as my grandfather.

3 **A** Money doesn't make you nearly as happy as you think.

B Money makes you a lot less happy than you think.

3 Complete the second sentence so that it has a similar meaning to the first, using the word given.

Example: *A scooter isn't nearly as expensive as a sports car.* **FAR**

A sports car is far more expensive than a scooter.

1 Our standard of living is a bit lower than it was. **QUITE**
Our standard of living is not .... it was.

2 There aren't many cities which are as exciting as Rio de Janeiro. **ONE**
Rio de Janeiro is .... exciting cities.

3 She doesn't have nearly as much free time now. **LESS**
She has .... free time than before.

4 Not many people earn such a high salary as he does. **THAN**
His salary is .... most people's.

5 He's almost as wealthy as she is. **BIT**
She's .... him.

6 It's getting much more difficult to get a bank loan. **AS**
It is .... to get a bank loan now.

Comparing quantities

4 Use the table to make six sentences that are true about you.

I spend	most	of my money on …
	a large amount	
	quite a lot	
	hardly any	of my time -*ing*.
I don't spend	much	
	any	

5 Compare your answers in groups and write a paragraph about how your group spends time and money.

Example: *The thing we spend most/least time/money on is …*
More/Less than half of us spend a large amount on …

Long turn (Part 2)
comparing

▶ **EXAM** FOCUS p.190

1 **What do these photographs have in common? Choose A or B.**

   A They show things which are important to people.

   B They show people in unusual situations.

2 **Make a list of the similarities between the two photographs.**

3 **Read the sentences about the photographs. Where can you add the words in brackets to the sentences? There may be more than one possibility.**

1 The photographs show an achievement. (*both*)

2 The man looks happy. (*also*)

3 The man looks as if he's enjoying himself. (*too*)

4 ▶ 12 **Listen to a student comparing the two photographs. Does she mention any of the points on your list?**

speculating

5 **Complete the sentences with *like* or *as if/as though*. In which sentences is it only possible to use *like*? Why?**

1 It looks .... a graduation ceremony.

2 The man looks .... he's very proud of his car.

3 It looks .... hard work.

4 He looks .... he's a bit obsessive.

5 She looks .... she's having more fun than the man.

contrasting

6 **Look at sentences A and B and answer questions 1–3 about *whereas* and *while*.**

A While the man may have a passion for his car, it's probably not something he'll own for his whole life.

B The first picture is celebrating an achievement, whereas the second picture shows someone who values an important possession.

1 Which sentence is making a comparison and showing how the two things are different?

2 In which sentence is it possible to use both *whereas* and *while*?

3 In which sentence could you use *although* instead of *while/whereas*?

EXAM TIP

Don't describe what's in the photographs. Focus on the main topic and compare the main similarity and any differences between the pictures.

7 **Work in pairs. Student A: Look at the photos on page 134. Student B: Look at the photos on page 136. Take turns to compare your photos. Try to use expressions for comparing, contrasting and speculating.**

8 **Work in pairs and discuss the questions.**

1 What achievements do you feel proud of?

2 Which events do you think are important to celebrate with friends and family? Why?

Multiple choice (Part 5)

▶ **EXAM** FOCUS p.187

1 **Work in pairs and discuss the questions.**

1 How interested are you in sport?

2 Do you find any sports boring?

3 Does it matter to you if a particular team or player wins or loses?

2 **Read the title and first paragraph of the article and guess what it will be about. Then read the rest of the article and check.**

3 **Read the questions/stems in Activity 4 and underline the key words. Skim the text and highlight the part which answers each question.**

EXAM TIP

Always read the text quickly to get an idea of what it is about before you try to answer any of the questions.

4 **Read the article again carefully. For questions 1–6, choose the answer (A, B, C or D) which you think fits best according to the text.**

1 What is the writer's attitude towards football fans attending matches?

    A She's impressed by their behaviour.

    B She's surprised by how much money they spend.

    C She's embarrassed by how irresponsible they are.

    D She's sympathetic to their feelings.

2 The writer mentions people who live 'in a dream state' in order to

    A give an example of people who have uncontrollable emotions.

    B criticise people who have unrealistic expectations.

    C contrast different types of emotional attachments.

    D explain why passions can be more important than real relationships.

3 The writer thinks having a passion is a good thing because

    A it helps people learn how to express their emotions.

    B it encourages more considerate behaviour.

    C it gives people an opportunity to act like a different person.

    D it makes everything else in life seem unimportant.

4 What does the writer mean by 'thin on the ground' in line 30?

    A something which is easily forgotten

    B something which occurs infrequently

    C something which takes place only once

    D something which is unexpected

5 The writer mentions Wimbledon to show that

    A some sports are less likely to inspire strong feelings.

    B some passions last for many years.

    C sports fans can behave uncharacteristically.

    D people often behave strangely to get on TV.

6 What was the writer's purpose in writing this text?

    A to encourage people to talk about their passions openly

    B to convince the reader that sports fans are normal human beings

    C to explain why the excitement of winning is worth the disappointment of losing

    D to argue that a passion for sport provides an opportunity to experience highs and lows

ALL YOU NEED IS LOVE
(AND A SCARF)

Grown men with their faces buried in each other's shoulders or hidden behind shaking hands. Young mothers shouting in triumph. These are familiar sights at football grounds all over the world. But why do the fans care so much and what does this kind of passion do to people?

While the extreme emotions on display seem alien to those who don't share a passion for football, for dedicated fans, it's a perfectly normal way to behave. They would be prepared to go to almost any lengths to get their hands on a ticket for a crucial match and many would turn up anyway, even without one. It might sound like madness, but as someone who once sold a car to finance a trip to see Arsenal play Barcelona, I completely understand their desperate desire to be part of it all.

This kind of passion should not be confused with an obsession which can be self-destructive. There are those who live in a dream state, passionately in love with a famous actor or singer, someone they know they will never get the chance to meet in real life – and this inhibits their ability to form real relationships. However, there are also ordinary people – sensible parents, husbands, employees and employers – whose interests are much more healthy and straightforward. Their emotions are also linked to forces they cannot control, but far from causing damage, their passion is a positive one.

Maybe some people are incapable of finding a passion, but if so, they are missing out. Passions are deep, full of joy and pain, teaching you how to sob when you feel hurt, how to react to a disappointment, how to sing with enthusiasm in public. Because of them you might end up hugging a complete stranger or making new friends. They help you to feel part of a community and have something to tease your neighbour about. They are a great way for families to bond together; many dads claim that they are only spending their time fishing or playing chess because their child is keen, when, actually, they are delighted to share an activity which is removed from home, job or money worries.

Explosions of joy are normally thin on the ground. The birth of your child, your wedding day, a pay rise are all lovely and a reason to do something special, but they do not happen every week. If you happen to follow a football or rugby team, there are celebrations all the time.   *line 30*

For some, a passion can be switched on and off – which is better than not having a passion at all, I suppose. Witness the behaviour that tennis brings about at the annual two-week UK tennis tournament at Wimbledon. Calm, controlled middle-aged women are suddenly prepared to camp overnight on damp pavements in London and squeal encouragement. Otherwise cool, fashionable students are happy to wave at the TV cameras while wearing silly hats and sunglasses that spurt water.

In the end, what defines us as human is not only language. It is the ability to care about something that does not directly affect our health, or wealth, or importance. Passions are a rehearsal for life, a distraction from boredom and, most of all, they are fun – even when they let you down.

5 Do you agree with the writer that having a passion for something is positive?

-ed adjectives and prepositions

6 Choose the correct prepositions in italics. Then ask your partner the questions.

1 What sports do you get excited *with/about*? What sports do you find exciting?

2 Do you ever get frustrated *on/with* a sportsperson/team? Which person/team do you find frustrating?

3 Who are you impressed *by/for*? Who do you find impressive?

4 Who or what do you get annoyed *of/by*?

5 What do you sometimes feel embarrassed *in/by*? Who do you find embarrassing?

Present perfect and past simple

▶ **GRAMMAR** REFERENCE p.145

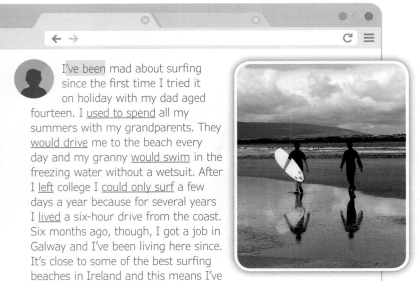

I've been mad about surfing since the first time I tried it on holiday with my dad aged fourteen. I used to spend all my summers with my grandparents. They would drive me to the beach every day and my granny would swim in the freezing water without a wetsuit. After I left college I could only surf a few days a year because for several years I lived a six-hour drive from the coast. Six months ago, though, I got a job in Galway and I've been living here since. It's close to some of the best surfing beaches in Ireland and this means I've been able to go surfing every weekend, which is fantastic. I met my girlfriend in the sea and we've been together for three months now. Since April I've been having lessons to become a surfing instructor – so far I've had four, which I've really enjoyed. When I qualify, I'm hoping to start my own surfing school with some friends. I've never entered a surfing competition and that's also something I'd like to do one day.

1 **Read Liam's blog about his passion for surfing. Answer questions 1–4.**

1 How long has Liam loved surfing?
2 Does he still spend his summers with his grandparents?
3 When did he move to Galway?
4 How often does he go surfing now?

2 **Look at the underlined verb forms in the text. Which ones describe**

1 completed actions in the past?
2 past habits which are now finished?

3 **Look at the highlighted example of the present perfect simple in the blog. Circle five more examples.**

4 **Match 1–3 to uses of the present perfect A–C.**

1 I've been able to go surfing every weekend.
2 I've never entered a surfing competition.
3 I've been mad about surfing since the first time I tried it.

A began in the past and is still continuing
B has recently happened and is relevant to the present
C refers to indefinite time in the past

5 **Look at the sentences. Which of the time expressions underlined refers to a period of time and which to a point in time?**

1 I've been mad about surfing <u>since</u> the first time I tried it aged fourteen.
2 We've been together <u>for</u> three months.

6 **Work in pairs and answer the questions.**

1 Which of these time expressions are usually used with the past simple/the present perfect?
2 Which time expression can be used with both the past simple and present perfect?

ago already at lunchtime in 2010
just last month never once so far
this month yet

Present perfect simple or continuous?

7 **Match the sentences from the blog to the uses of the present perfect (A and B).**

1 I've been having lessons.
2 I've had four [lessons].

A a completed activity
B an activity over a period of time (which may or may not be finished)

8 **Complete the sentences with the correct form of the verbs and phrases in brackets. There may be more than one possibility.**

1 I .... (*ride*) a motorbike since I was seventeen.
2 I .... (*once witness*) a crime.
3 I .... (*live*) abroad when I was a child.
4 I .... (*have*) an operation a few years ago.
5 I .... (*never go*) camping.
6 I .... (*just win*) a competition.

9 **Work in pairs. Ask and answer questions with *Have you ever … ?* and *How long … ? * Use the ideas in Activity 8 to help you.**

Example: *Have you ever ridden a motorbike? How long have you been riding motorbikes? When was the last time you rode a motorbike?*

Open cloze (Part 2)

▶ **EXAM** FOCUS p.186

1 **Work in pairs and discuss the questions.**

1 What do you do to cheer yourself up when you're depressed?

2 What makes you really happy?

2 **Read the text and discuss the questions.**

1 What is 'hygge'?

2 How can it make people feel happier?

3 **Look at the example (0). What part of speech is it? Now look at gaps 1–8. What kind of word do you need to write in each gap (preposition/ noun/time expression/pronoun, etc.)?**

4 **Complete the text with one word in each gap.**

EXAM TIP

Read the whole sentence, especially the words before and after each gap. Think about what kind of word is missing (e.g. a preposition, pronoun).

5 **Work in pairs. Compare your answers and say why you chose them.**

as and *like*

▶ **GRAMMAR** REFERENCE p.146

6 **Complete the sentences with *as* or *like*.**

1 Was that film .... all his other ones?

2 Shall we still have lunch together, ... we said yesterday?

3 I've always regarded you .... a friend.

4 A job .... that one takes a long time to finish.

5 He's working .... a waiter in the holidays.

6 Please do it carefully .... I asked you.

LANGUAGE TIP

as + noun for a role or purpose:
*She works as **a musician**. I use that room as **a study**.*
as + noun clause for manner:
*I treated him as **my son**.*
like + noun for comparison:
*You're just like **Tony**. Like **Jane**, I love jazz.*
like + noun for informal examples:
*Food like **that risotto** is worth waiting for.*

Hygge: the art of simple pleasures

The Danes are famous for **(0)** _being_ one of the world's happiest nations. One possible reason **(1)** .... this could be the untranslatable concept of 'hygge'. Hygge has already gained a lot of publicity outside Denmark. This is thanks to a stream of recently published self-help books, **(2)** .... all urge us to embrace hygge in order to improve our sense of well-being and happiness.

Writer, Helen Russell, who moved to Denmark several years **(3)** .... , is a hygge enthusiast. She has been fascinated by the idea ever **(4)** .... she arrived. Her book, *The Year of Living Danishly: Uncovering The Secrets of the World's Happiest Country*, makes it easy to understand **(5)** .... Helen and her family are still living **(6)** .... Helen says 'hygge' can be defined **(7)** .... 'the absence of anything annoying or emotionally overwhelming'. It's all about being kind to yourself and celebrating the simple things in life, **(8)** .... spending time with friends and family, or eating ice cream. So find your inner Dane – and do what makes you happy without feeling guilty about it.

Article (Part 2)
engaging the reader
▶ **WRITING** REFERENCE p.171

1 **Read the exam task and answer the questions.**

1 What kind of style will you write the article in? How do you know?

2 What information do you need to include?

> You see this advertisement in a magazine for young people.
>
> ## WHAT I'D SAVE IN A FIRE
>
> Write us an article describing something you own and explaining why it's important to you.
>
> The best article will be published in the magazine next month.
>
> Write your article in **140–190** words.

2 **Look at opening paragraphs A and B. Which one is most effective? Think about**

1 how appropriate the style is.

2 how varied the language is.

3 whether it engages the reader.

A What I'd save in a fire

Have you ever thought about which possession you'd choose to save if your house was on fire? Well, for me it would definitely be my tablet. Obviously, I'd rescue my family and pets first but after that I'd grab my tablet and my phone.

B What I'd save in a fire

My tablet is very important to me and I would be very upset if it got lost or damaged. I spend hours every day using my tablet and I would be lost without it. I think most people feel the same way about their laptops or tablets.

3 **Look at notes A–H and choose whether to include them in paragraph two (a simple description of the object) or paragraph three (the reasons why it's special to you).**

A	birthday present from parents
B	not expensive and very ordinary to look at
C	two years old
D	used to have to carry my laptop everywhere
E	can watch films on it and play games anywhere
F	made by Samsung
G	user-friendly
H	useful for studies

EXAM TIP

Try to make the reader feel you are 'speaking' directly to him/her. You can do this by asking the reader a question and making your tone chatty rather than formal.

4 **Work in pairs. Write paragraphs two and three, using the ideas in Activity 3.**

5 **Look at possible concluding sentences A and B. Which one would have the most positive effect on a reader?**

A	So for all these reasons, the first thing I would think of taking with me is my tablet.

B	The main reason I'd grab my tablet first in a fire is because it would be like losing my right hand if I had to be without it.

6 **Make notes on your own response to the advert. Choose a favourite possession and divide your notes into four paragraphs:**

1 Introduction (to get the reader's attention)

2 Background (a description of the object)

3 Opinion (the reasons why it is important to you)

4 Conclusion (a brief summary)

7 **Write your article in 140–190 words. Then check it for spelling and punctuation. Write another draft if necessary.**

8 **Read other students' articles and choose which ones to include in the magazine.**

1 Choose the correct option (A, B, C or D) to complete the sentences.

1 A .... standard of living is important to me.
   A tall   B big   C great   D high

2 The house they live in must be worth a ....
   A treasure   B fortune   C resource   D wealth

3 When I was at college I had to learn to live ....
   a budget.
   A on   B in   C from   D at

4 I'm afraid I can't come because I'm .... of money.
   A low   B lacking   C short   D tight

5 She is always .... debt at the end of the term.
   A on   B at   C with   D in

6 I'm still learning to live .... my means.
   A between   B within   C under   D at

2 Complete the second sentence so that it has a similar meaning to the first sentence, using the word given. Use between two and five words, including the word given.

1 Rebecca started living here five years ago.
   FOR
   Rebecca .... five years.

2 I last saw Mike in 2006.
   SINCE
   I .... 2006.

3 This is my first visit to India.
   TIME
   This is the first ....
   to India.

4 I don't spend much money on clothes these days.
   ANY
   I .... money on clothes
   these days.

5 This hotel isn't nearly as expensive as the other one.
   FAR
   The other hotel is ....
   this one.

6 Both Tom and Zak are equally friendly.
   JUST
   Tom is .... Zak.

7 There aren't many designer brands that are as expensive as Prada.
   ONE
   Prada is .... designer brands.

3 Complete the sentences with the correct form of the word in brackets.

1 I haven't got much money but I'm not .... about it. (worry)

2 Golf is not a very .... sport to watch on TV. (interest)

3 Having a passion can make life more .... (excite)

4 I'm really .... by my obsession with that actor. (excite)

5 What is the most .... film you have ever seen? (frighten)

6 I'm .... that the cup final is over at last. (relief)

4 Complete the text with one word in each gap.

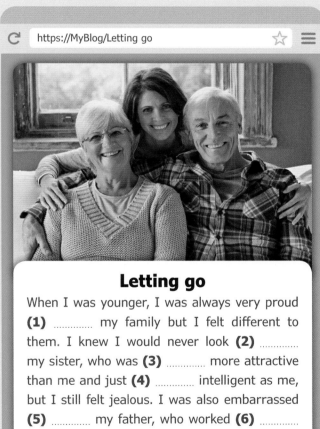

https://MyBlog/Letting go

Letting go

When I was younger, I was always very proud **(1)** .... my family but I felt different to them. I knew I would never look **(2)** .... my sister, who was **(3)** .... more attractive than me and just **(4)** .... intelligent as me, but I still felt jealous. I was also embarrassed **(5)** .... my father, who worked **(6)** .... an actor, instead of having a 'normal' job. But now I'm older, none of those negative feelings matter anymore. I've always **(7)** .... very close to **(8)** .... of my parents and know I'm very lucky to have them.

Multiple-choice cloze (Part 1)

1 For questions 1–8, read the text below and decide which answer (A, B, C or D) best fits each gap. There is an example at the beginning.

Happy families

It came as no surprise to me when a newspaper article I read **(0)** *B, recently* claimed to prove that the happiest children tend to be **(1)** .... children.

When I was younger, I used to **(2)** .... having a brother because I thought that parents with just one child were bound to **(3)** .... them more attention and love them more.

My most unhappy childhood memories involve my older brother, Thomas. I didn't get **(4)** .... with him at all and, because he was much bigger than me, he would always **(5)** .... any fights we had. My parents took the view that they should not interfere in our arguments, and made us sort them **(6)** .... ourselves, which meant that Thomas could do whatever he wanted.

However, the good news about siblings is that as they get older, they seem to start valuing each other more. In fact, nowadays Thomas and I are quite **(7)** .... I suppose this is not surprising, since we share a history that goes back a long way. It's special for us but no one else is very **(8)** .... in our past.

0	**A** lately	**B** recently	**C** currently	**D** presently
1	**A** only	**B** single	**C** unique	**D** individual
2	**A** miss	**B** hope	**C** wish	**D** regret
3	**A** pay	**B** make	**C** allow	**D** provide
4	**A** on	**B** by	**C** round	**D** away
5	**A** win	**B** beat	**C** succeed	**D** overcome
6	**A** of	**B** over	**C** out	**D** through
7	**A** near	**B** close	**C** familiar	**D** attached
8	**A** concerned	**B** caring	**C** interested	**D** knowledgeable

Open cloze (Part 2)

2 For questions 9–16, read the text below and think of the word that best fits each gap. Use only one word in each gap. There is an example at the beginning.

Why trees matter

Everyone knows that trees are important **(0)** *for* the environment and human health. In cities, trees improve air quality and they absorb pollution. They remove dangerous gases **(9)** .... CO_2 and nitrogen oxide from the air and release oxygen back into the environment. Trees can help in the fight against climate change **(10)** .... they are known to significantly reduce temperatures by providing shade and also by releasing water vapour through their leaves.

But trees have many other practical benefits, which are **(11)** .... just related to physical health but also to mental health and well-being. People who live in areas where there are lots of trees feel happier and healthier **(12)** .... those living in very built-up urban areas. In the past, architects and town planners didn't **(13)** .... to understand the effect that trees have on people, which **(14)** .... why many urban environments lack enough green spaces. Now things are changing as so many studies **(15)** .... shown that trees can make a real difference to people's lives. **(16)** .... of the most surprising findings is that people in hospital have quicker recovery times if they are able to see trees.

Word formation (Part 3)

3 For questions 17–24, read the text below. Use the word given in capitals at the end of some of the lines to form a word that fits in the gap in the same line. There is an example at the beginning.

A worthwhile challenge

Most people agree that learning to play a **(0)** _musical_ instrument is one of the most worthwhile things they have ever done but also one of the hardest. A lot of children are very **(17)** .... when they first take up an instrument, but don't realise how much practice will be involved. Sadly, they quickly start to lose interest as they find the technical skills **(18)** .... difficult. If they feel they are not making enough progress, young people often give up having lessons after two or three years, only to regret it when they are older. But those who have enough talent and **(19)** .... and are willing to put in the effort it takes to reach a reasonable standard, can rightly feel a strong sense of **(20)** ....

Apart from acquiring a lifelong hobby and a **(21)** .... skill, playing an instrument for pleasure is beneficial in less obvious ways too. Learning a new piece of music requires a huge amount of **(22)** .... Although it may not seem like it, this is an **(23)** .... way of reducing stress because your brain is completely focused on the music, which means **(24)** .... about anything else is impossible.

MUSIC

ENTHUSIASM

INCREASE

DETERMINE

ACHIEVE

VALUE

CONCENTRATE
EFFECT

WORRY

Key word transformation (Part 4)

4 For questions 25–30, complete the second sentence so that it has a similar meaning to the first sentence, using the word given. Do not change the word given. You must use between two and five words, including the word given.

Example:

Conor has a natural ability for music like his parents.

AFTER

Conor _takes after his parents_ in his natural ability for music.

25 Julia can sing much better than me.

WELL

I can't .... Julia.

26 My dad has a beautiful voice but he hates performing.

DESPITE

My dad hates performing .... a beautiful voice.

27 I don't know my sister very well because she's so much older than me.

HARDLY

I .... because she's so much older than me.

28 It's been ages since I saw James.

NOT

I .... ages.

29 I think I forgot to lock the door.

REMEMBER

I don't .... the door.

30 My mother started her own business when she was forty.

SET

My mother .... her own business when she was forty.

4 Forces of nature

1 You are going to read an article about superhumans. Look at the photo on the left and read the title and introduction to the article. Work in pairs and discuss the questions.

1 Why do you think many people are so keen on films about people with special powers, like *X-Men*?

2 What are some of the special powers often shown in films and comic books?

Multiple matching (Part 7)

▶ **EXAM** FOCUS p.187

2 Read the article quickly. Which 'superpowers' are mentioned?

3 Read the questions in Activity 4. Then underline the key words and scan the article to find ideas which have the same meaning.

4 For questions 1–10, choose from the sections A–D. The sections may be chosen more than once.

EXAM TIP

Be careful! There might seem to be similar information in more than one text. Make sure the word or expression you choose has the same meaning as in the question, even though it will be expressed differently.

Which person's superpower

may be shared by other people who don't realise they have it?	1
is beneficial for the person's mental and physical health?	2
could potentially affect a person's mental development?	3
requires theoretically impossibly quick reactions?	4
may have inspired the story of a legendary character?	5
may help give an insight into curing certain illnesses?	6
was eventually discovered by chance?	7
is believed by the person to be a question of mind over body?	8
could be acquired by whoever is prepared to believe in it?	9
cannot be explained by scientists?	10

X-MEN: THE REAL-LIFE SUPERHUMANS

Disappointingly for comic-book fans, there is no equivalent to X-Men in the real world. But there are a surprising number of people who – by way of genetic mutation – have acquired abilities that could comfortably be classed as superhuman.

A Liam Hoekstra

Born prematurely, it was feared that Liam Hoekstra would be in poor health as he grew up. If anything, the opposite was true and despite initial problems with his heart and kidneys, it was apparent by the age of only five months that Liam was developing superhuman strength. He was diagnosed with a rare condition characterised by an absence of myostatin. This is a protein which regulates muscle development, a lack of which leads to the kind of physical attributes that athletes can only dream about: 40 percent more muscle than normal, breathtaking strength and speed and almost no body fat. It is possible that the myths about the Greek hero Hercules were based on individuals with this condition. There are no negative side-effects; the only possible drawback was that without adequate body fat, brain growth in childhood could be restricted. Thankfully, Liam seems unaffected. His condition is more than a medical rarity; it could help scientists unlock the secrets of muscle growth and deterioration and lead to new treatments for diseases which cause weakness, such as osteoporosis.

B Wim Hof

One of the original characters in the *X-Men* was Bobby Drake, otherwise known as Iceman. As far-fetched as it sounds, in the real world there is a real-life Iceman, called Wim Hof. He may not be able to turn everyday objects into ice, as Bobby Drake did, but he holds 20 world records related to resisting the cold, which he says is the result of meditation practices. Among Hof's achievements are standing submerged in an ice bath for one hour and 44 minutes and running a marathon in the Arctic Circle wearing only shorts. Over a period of 20 minutes in the ice bath his temperature and heart rate remained completely normal.

Scientists have confirmed that Hof is indeed able to regulate his body functions; by controlling cell production he gains improved immunity and better cognitive performance. Hof believes the skill is attainable by anyone who can convince themselves they can do it.

C Dean Karnazes

Dean Karnazes's muscles have extraordinary properties. Most people suffer intense fatigue and are forced to give up when too much exercising causes lactic acid to build up in their muscles. Not so Karnazes: his body clears the acid with such extraordinary efficiency that he can remain hydrated and functional for remarkably long periods during feats of endurance. His 22-year career includes running 350 miles in 80 hours and 44 minutes without sleep, completing a 135-mile ultra-marathon in Death Valley, California, in temperatures of 49C and a marathon in each of the USA's 50 states on 50 consecutive days. Unaware of his 'gift' until he took part in a scientific study at the age of 30, he is convinced that there are people like him everywhere who have no idea they have this ability.

D Isao Machii

The scientific world is totally confused by Isao Machii, a Japanese practitioner of Iaido, the art of the samurai sword, who is the holder of several world records involving fast sword cuts. For one title he had to cut through a tennis ball travelling at 440 miles per hour. His most impressive feat was when an airgun fired a 5mm plastic pellet at Machii at a speed of 200mph. At this speed it is not likely that the human eye could track an object of this size and unimaginable that human reflexes could respond. Yet he was able to draw his sword and slice it in two when it was in mid-air. A psychologist who observed the experiment said "He was expecting it before it happened – a unique form of anticipatory awareness, sort of like Spiderman."

---

5 Work in pairs and discuss the questions.

1 Which of these superpowers do you find most fascinating? Why?
2 What are the potential dangers of having one of these 'gifts'?
3 If you could choose any superpower, what would it be? Why?

Vocabulary
compound words

6 Read the sentences and think of another way of expressing the words in italics.

1 She was wearing *ordinary* clothes when I saw her.
2 The *disadvantage* of going by train is the time it takes.
3 The view from my window was absolutely *incredible*.
4 The story was so *unlikely* that everyone just laughed.
5 Taking the pills had a negative *impact* so I stopped taking them.

7 Match 1–5 to A–E to make compound words from the article.

1	breath	A	day
2	side	B	fetched
3	draw	C	back
4	far	D	taking
5	every	E	effect

8 Match the compound words in Activity 7 to the words in italics in Activity 6.

9 Work in groups and discuss the questions.

1 What are the drawbacks to being a student?
2 What is the most breathtaking view you have ever seen?
3 Which everyday activities do you find most tedious?
4 What is the most extraordinary thing that has ever happened to you?
5 What is the most far-fetched story you have ever heard?
   Example: *One of the drawbacks to being a student is not having enough money to go out.*

Articles
definite, indefinite and zero articles

▶ **GRAMMAR** REFERENCE p.146

1 In the article on page 39, Wim Hof showed an amazing ability to resist cold conditions. Complete the sentences about Wim Hof with *a/an, the* or – (zero article). Then check Text B.

1 [Hof] may not be able to turn .... everyday objects into ice, …

2 Among Hof's achievements are standing submerged in .... ice bath for one hour and 44 minutes.

3 [He also ran] .... marathon in .... Arctic Circle wearing only .... shorts.

4 Over .... period of 20 minutes in .... ice bath his temperature and heart rate remained completely normal.

5 Hof believes .... skill is attainable by anyone who can convince themselves they can do it.

2 Complete the rules about articles (1–3) with the uses (A–E). Some rules match more than one use.

1 We don't use an article

2 We use *a/an* (the indefinite article)

3 We use *the* (the definite article)

A when there is only one of something.

B when we want to talk about people or things in general.

C when we want to talk about something which has been mentioned before.

D when we mention something for the first time, or when it is not important which one.

E when we use plural, uncountable and abstract nouns.

3 Match the examples from Activity 1 with the uses in Activity 2. There may be more than one example of each use.

4 Think of any other examples or rules you know for articles and check the Grammar Reference.

5 Discuss the kinds of weather conditions which pilots may experience. Then complete the gaps in the story with *a/an, the* or – (zero article).

PROFILE PHOTOS UPDATES

A pilot's story

As pilots, we have to get used to **(1)** .... storms and **(2)** .... severe weather, and we are obviously prepared for **(3)** .... emergencies. However, sometimes they can take you by **(4)** .... surprise. A year ago, I was flying to **(5)** .... USA and we were over **(6)** .... Atlantic Ocean when a ball of lightning struck **(7)** .... aircraft I was flying. Within seconds, **(8)** .... bright blue ball of light with **(9)** .... yellow tail filled **(10)** .... windscreen and there was **(11)** .... loud bang. My colleague said it felt as if **(12)** .... cat had brushed against his leg as **(13)** .... lightning struck. Fortunately, after a lot of violent shaking, **(14)** .... things soon returned to **(15)** .... normal.

6 Work in pairs and compare your answers. Say why you chose them, referring to the rules in Activity 2.

7 Work in groups. Discuss what types of weather conditions you like/dislike.

Example: *I'm quite scared of storms but I love snow.*

8 Find someone who has had one of the following experiences.

1 been afraid of a storm

2 been snowed in

3 had heatstroke

4 been in a flood

5 skidded on a patch of ice

6 seen lightning strike

7 lost their way in fog

8 been in or on a rough sea

9 Tell the class about the experiences you found out about.

Word formation (Part 3)

▶ **EXAM** FOCUS p.186

1 Look at the photo and the title of the article below. What kind of place do you think Death Valley is? How do you think it got its name?

2 Look at each gap and decide what part of speech is missing. Read the whole of the surrounding context before you make a choice.

3 Use the word given in capitals at the end of some of the lines to form a word that fits in the gap in the same line. Which word needs a negative prefix?

EXAM TIP

You may need to add a suffix (e.g. -ness/-ous) to change the word to another part of speech, (e.g. -y luck – luck**y**); or a prefix (e.g. un-/dis-) to change the meaning (e.g. lucky – **un**lucky).

Death Valley

Death Valley got its name in 1849 when a group of **(0)** unlucky miners made the mistake of passing through it on their way to California. Temperatures can rise above 120 degrees Fahrenheit in Death Valley, but having no **(1)** .... of conditions there, the miners nearly died of heatstroke.

LUCK

KNOW

Despite its name, more than 1.3 million **(2)** .... still go there every year. It is likely, however, that many of them have absolutely no idea how **(3)** .... such a hot, dry climate can be. **(4)** .... walkers often do not drink nearly enough water or wear the **(5)** .... clothes that are required in this extreme heat.

VISIT

DANGER
EXPERIENCE

SENSE

Heatstroke often occurs when the body is unable to control its temperature. **(6)** .... signs of this are high body temperature, red dry skin, very bad headaches and feeling dizzy. All this is also often accompanied by **(7)** .... If heatstroke is suspected, the person should get out of the sun at once and receive urgent medical **(8)** .... , otherwise they have only a 20 percent chance of surviving.

WARN

SICK

ASSIST

---

4 What advice would you give to someone going to a very hot or cold climate?

Examples:

You should (drink) … Make sure you (wear) …
Avoid (sitting in the sun). Don't (ignore) warning signs.

Vocabulary

negative prefixes with adjectives

5 Choose the prefix in italics which makes the adjective negative.

1 The miners' trip through Death Valley was *in/un*successful.

2 Death Valley is a very *in/un*hospitable place.

3 The group on the expedition became *un/dis*trustful of each other.

4 It's *im/in*possible to know how people can survive in such extreme conditions.

5 The instructions on how to get there were *il/un*logical.

6 Some people think it is *ir/in*responsible to risk getting heatstroke.

LANGUAGE TIP

The prefixes *un-*, *in-* and *dis-* can be used to make adjectives negative.

(Note: *in-* becomes *im-* before 'm' or 'p', *ir-* before a word beginning with 'r' and *il-* before a word beginning with *l*).

Un- and *dis-* can also be used with verbs and nouns (**un**tie, **dis**appear/**dis**appearance).

---

6 Add a negative prefix to the underlined adjectives.

1 One <u>advantage</u> of winter is how much we spend on heating our homes.

2 I think it is <u>legal</u> to speak on a hands-free mobile while driving.

3 It's <u>likely</u> that we'll be able to have a barbecue unless it gets much warmer.

4 I've noticed that people get <u>patient</u> when they're driving during hot weather.

5 It was a great job despite the <u>regular</u> working hours.

6 I'd be <u>capable</u> of surviving in low temperatures even if I had the right equipment.

7 Work in pairs. Discuss something

1 which is unusual about you.

2 which has made you indecisive.

3 which makes you impatient.

1 **How much do you know about Antarctica? Do the quiz. Then turn to page 139 and check your answers.**

1 Antarctica has the world's largest
   A volcano.
   B desert.
   C mountain range.

2 Has Antarctica always been cold?
   A No, it used to be tropical.
   B Yes, it's always been covered in thick ice.
   C Yes, but the ice used to be a lot thinner.

3 Which of these animals do you NOT get in Antarctica?
   A penguins
   B seals
   C polar bears

4 Who led the first team to reach the South Pole in 1911?
   A Roald Amundsen
   B Robert Falcon Scott
   C Ernest Shackleton

5 Why is Ernest Shackleton's 1908 expedition famous?
   A Everyone except Shackleton survived the trip.
   B The men survived but they didn't get to the South Pole.
   C All the men died on the way back from the South Pole.

Multiple choice (Part 4)

▶ **EXAM** FOCUS p.189

2 **You are going to hear an interview with Leo Stone, who describes his expedition to the South Pole in the steps of the explorer, Shackleton. Before you listen, read the questions and options in Activity 3 and underline the key words.**

EXAM TIP

The interviewer's questions will help you to locate the questions you are listening for. The information on the recording is in the same order as the questions 1–7.

3 ▶ **13** **Listen to the interview and answer questions 1–7. Listen out for paraphrases or synonyms of the words you underlined in Activity 2.**

1 What was unusual about Leo's team?
   A They were all descendants of Ernest Shackleton.
   B They all had a personal link with the 1908 trip.
   C They'd all attempted to reach the South Pole before.

2 What does Leo say was the hardest thing for the team before the expedition?
   A organising the finance
   B preparing mentally
   C getting physically fit

3 What does Leo say was easier for the 21st-century expedition than for Shackleton's expedition?
   A planning their daily route
   B doing the cooking
   C carrying their equipment

4 What problem did both expeditions experience?
   A running out of food
   B a serious illness
   C bad weather

5 How did Leo feel when he was crossing the Antarctic plateau?
   A He hadn't expected it to be so difficult.
   B He was worried they wouldn't reach the South Pole.
   C He doubted his skills as a leader.

6 The part of the trip Leo enjoyed the most was when they
   A reached the South Pole.
   B reached the same point that Shackleton had got to.
   C reached home safely.

7 What does Leo admire about Shackleton?
   A his determination
   B his ambition
   C his bravery

4 **Check your answers. What words or phrases did you hear to justify choosing A, B or C for each question? Listen again and check the audio script on page 209.**

5 **Discuss the questions.**

1 What would you find hard about a trip like this?
2 Shackleton is considered a hero and a role model by many people. Who are your heroes and role models?
3 Which part of the world would you most like to explore? Why?

Vocabulary
idioms: the body

6 **Match the underlined idioms 1–10 to their meanings A–J.**

1 The hardest part was getting their heads around doing a 900-mile journey.
2 When he came face to face with conditions there, Shackleton began to doubt he'd ever reach the Pole.
3 He's always putting his foot in it. He just doesn't know when to keep his mouth shut.
4 My father and I don't see eye to eye. Perhaps our relationship will improve when I leave home.
5 Something in the distance caught my eye.
6 I must keep an eye on the time. I don't want to be late.
7 It was really difficult to keep a straight face; he looked so silly.
8 I'm beginning to get cold feet about the whole idea.
9 I can't face going to work. I feel terrible.
10 You need to put your foot down. Don't agree to working late every evening.

A pay attention to
B look serious
C attract your attention
D change your mind
E get on with each other
F feel unable to
G have direct experience (of something)
H say the wrong thing
I say no to something
J understand/accept an idea

7 **Work in pairs. Tell your partner the last time you did the following things. Your partner should take notes.**

1 put your foot in it
2 couldn't face doing something
3 put your foot down
4 couldn't keep a straight face
5 got cold feet about something
6 came face to face with something strange

8 **Change partners and tell him/her what your first partner said. Are there any similarities?**

Narrative forms
past simple, past continuous and past perfect

▶ **GRAMMAR** REFERENCE p.148

1 You are going to read a story about a man who was buried in an avalanche on a mountainside. Read paragraph 1 and predict what happens next.

The avalanche <u>struck</u> without warning. I <u>had been putting up</u> a snow shed 12,000 feet up in the Colorado mountains that morning and when it <u>happened</u> I <u>had just stopped</u> for a break. One minute I <u>was eating</u> my lunch and the next I <u>found</u> myself under 50 feet of snow.

2 Which of the underlined forms

1 refer to a finished event in the past?
2 refers to something which happened before a point in the past?
3 describes an action already in progress when one or more events happened?

3 What are the names of the verb forms in Activity 2? How are they formed?

4 Read the rest of the story below quickly. Don't worry about the gaps yet. How well did you predict the ending?

5 Complete the story with the correct form of the verbs in brackets.

I **(1)** .... (have) a mouth full of snow and it **(2)** .... (be) totally dark. To begin with I **(3)** .... (think) I **(4)** .... (already die). Then I **(5)** .... (notice) that tears **(6)** .... (run) diagonally across my face and I **(7)** .... (realise) I **(8)** .... (lie) upside down. As soon as I **(9)** .... (free) my upper body I **(10)** .... (start) to dig. After many hours I finally **(11)** .... (see) the first little chink of light. When rescuers finally **(12)** .... (arrive), I **(13)** .... (be) on the mountain for nearly 48 hours.

past perfect simple and past perfect continuous

6 Complete the sentences with the past perfect simple or past perfect continuous form of the verbs in brackets. Then match the examples with one of the statements, A or B.

1 Since I .... (finish) my homework, I decided to go round to a friend's house.
2 Andy's leg .... (hurt) for ages before he went to the doctor.
3 We .... (never see) a glacier before we went to Antarctica.
4 I .... (not hear) the news until Sophie rang me.
A Only the simple form is possible here.
B It is more natural to use the continuous form here because the action continues over a period of time.

> ### LANGUAGE TIP
>
> If the time sequence is clear or there are time linkers such as *before* and *after*, it is not necessary to use the past perfect. *I went for a run* **before** *I had lunch* OR *I had been for a run* **before** *I had lunch.*
>
> BUT sometimes the past perfect is necessary to emphasise the order of events.
>
> *When Tim arrived the party started.* (it started after Tim arrived)
>
> *When Tim arrived the party had started.* (it started before Tim arrived)

7 Complete the sentences so that B has the same meaning as A. Sometimes more than one form is possible.

1 A Jack was hoping to compete in the Olympics. Then he hurt his back.
  B Before he .... (hurt) his back, Jack .... (hope) to compete in the Olympics.
2 A Luke spent six months in hospital. He studied to be a lawyer during this time.
  B While Luke .... (recover) in hospital, he .... (study) to be a lawyer.
3 A During his swim to the island, Lewis cut his knee badly on a rock.
  B Lewis .... (swim) to the island when he .... (cut) his knee badly on a rock.
4 A Frances and Tom went out together for two years. Then they split up.
  B Before they .... (split up), Frances and Tom .... (go out) together for two years.
5 A It wasn't necessary for me to buy any food. Karen did it earlier in the day.
  B I .... (not/need) to buy any food because Karen .... (already/do) it earlier in the day.

Ranking

1 Imagine you were on a desert island. Look at the diagram and discuss which of the skills you'd find easy or hard. Put them in order of difficulty. Use some of the language below to give opinions.

For me, it'd be … that would be hardest.

I don't think I'd be able to …

What I'd find easy would be …

To be honest, the only thing I could do would be …

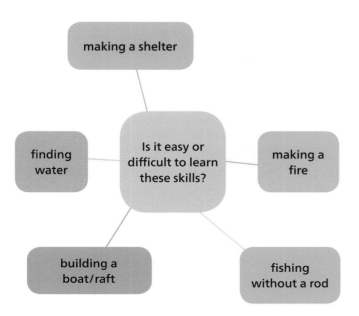

Collaborative task (Part 3)

▶ **EXAM** FOCUS p.190

2 Work in pairs. Look at the examiner's instructions and underline the two things you have to discuss.

> Here are some survival skills that people sometimes need to learn. Talk to each other about whether it would be easy or difficult to learn these skills.
>
> (after a two-minute discussion) Thank you.
>
> Now you have about a minute to decide which two survival skills would be the most useful to learn.

3 ▶ 14 Listen to students doing the second part of the task. Do you agree with their opinions?

4 Complete the sentences, then listen again to check your answers.

1 .... of the .... for me would be finding water.

2 I'd .... making a fire .... making a shelter.

3 I think learning to make a fire would be the .... for me.

4 So .... skills, making a fire and finding water would be the most useful.

5 Change the sentences in Activity 4 so that they have the opposite meaning.

6 Do the task in Activity 2, choosing from the survival skills in the diagram. You have two minutes for the first part and one minute to make the decision.

7 Compare your decisions in groups. Did you agree?

8 Work in pairs and discuss the questions.

1 What kind of person do you need to be to survive on a desert island?

2 How important is it for people to know how to survive in the wild?

3 Do you think most people today have lost touch with nature?

4 In what ways can the natural world be a threat to humans?

5 In what ways can humans be a threat to the natural world?

Essay (Part 1)
expressing and supporting ideas
▶ **WRITING** REFERENCE pp.166 and 167

1 Work in pairs. Read the essay title and discuss whether you agree or disagree with the idea of adventure tourism.

> In your English class you have been talking about extreme environments. Now, your English teacher has asked you to write an essay.
>
> Do you think 'adventure tourism' in unexplored parts of the world should be encouraged?
>
> **Notes**
> Write about:
>
> 1 negative effects of tourism
> 2 personal risk
> 3 .... (your own idea)
>
> Write an essay using **all** the points and give reasons for your point of view. Write **140–190** words.

2 Match the ideas 1–4 to notes 1 and 2 in Activity 1. Decide whether the writer is agreeing or disagreeing with the essay title in each case.

> 1 If people train and prepare for expeditions, there's a good chance they'll be safe.
> 2 The problem is that beautiful places will get spoilt if too many people go there.
> 3 As long as people respect the environment, there should be very little damage.
> 4 In my view, anything too dangerous should be left to the professionals.

3 Match the reasons A–D to the points 1–4 in Activity 2.

> A An increased number of tourists will lead to more building development.
> B If people don't know what they're doing, it can endanger their lives and the lives of others.
> C It requires people to be responsible and avoid leaving rubbish around.
> D These days, there is a lot of equipment to help people.

4 Think of some more points and supporting information (examples or reasons) for notes 1 and 2 in Activity 1. Compare your ideas with a partner.

> EXAM TIP
>
> Remember to clearly state your main point in the form of a summary sentence for each note. Support it with a reason or example if there is space.

5 Work in pairs to think of any connecting words you can use to link the supporting information to the main points.

Examples: *Reasons: because (of), due to*
Examples: An example of this is, Take, for example
Adding reasons/examples: In addition, As well as this

6 Think about what your own point will be for note 3 in Activity 1 and compare your idea with a partner. There are some suggestions below. Remember to give a reason for the point you choose.

local job opportunities   personal development
knowledge about the world

7 Read the essay title and task and plan how you will answer it. Use the guidelines 1–4 below.

> In your English class you have been discussing the importance of nature. Now, your teacher has asked you to write an essay.
>
> Many people think living in the countryside provides a better way of life. To what extent do you agree?
>
> **Notes**
> Write about:
>
> 1 health
> 2 day-to-day life
> 3 .... (your own idea)
>
> Write an essay using all the notes and give reasons for your point of view. Write **140–190** words.

1 Read the question and underline the key points.
2 Brainstorm ideas around the topic. What will your own idea be?
3 Make notes on the positive and negative points. Do you agree or disagree, or can you see both sides?
4 Plan how many paragraphs you will have and decide which notes you will include in each one.

8 Check what you have written and make sure you have not included the same mistakes that you made in your last piece of writing.

1 Complete the article with *a/an*, *the* or – (no article).

Record-breaking WALK

After **(1)** .... incredible 859 days and 6,000 miles, British explorer Ed Stafford became **(2)** .... first man to walk **(3)** .... entire length of **(4)** .... Amazon. He finally reached **(5)** .... Atlantic in **(6)** .... Brazil two and a half years after he started his epic adventure in **(7)** .... jungles of Peru.

The final leg proved one of **(8)** .... most challenging, with Mr Stafford collapsing **(9)** .... few hours before reaching his final destination.

Mr Stafford fell out with his original walking partner Luke Collyer, 37, **(10)** .... outdoor activities instructor, and after only three months, Mr Collyer returned to **(11)** .... UK. Mr Stafford advertised for **(12)** .... new walking partner and was joined by Sanchez Rivera, **(13)** .... Peruvian forestry worker. Living off **(14)** .... piranha and rice, they made their way through Peru, Colombia and Brazil. Mr Stafford said on Monday, 'All I want now is **(15)** .... portion of fish and chips and **(16)** .... nice cold beer.'

2 Complete the sentences with the correct form of the word in brackets.

1 I am .... of skiing. I'm too scared. (capable)
2 His approach to the problem is emotional and .... (logic)
3 The project was .... despite all the investment in it. (success)
4 My mother is .... with my younger brother. She never explains things properly. (patience)
5 That is an extremely .... way to behave. You should be trying to set a good example. (responsibility)
6 Some celebrities are .... when journalists start asking them personal questions. (trust)

3 Match 1–8 to A–H to make sentences.

1 I always *put my foot in it* when I'm nervous and
2 His explanation is rather *far-fetched*, which means
3 I can never *keep a straight face* so
4 I'm *getting cold feet* about the cycling race because
5 If I'm told there will be *side effects*,
6 Tom and I don't *see eye to eye* about many issues so
7 My parents want me to *keep an eye* on my brother so
8 If something in a shop window *catches my eye*,

A I'm useless at telling jokes.
B I say really embarrassing things.
C I won't be able to go out tonight.
D I can't resist going in to look at it.
E I find it difficult to believe.
F I don't think I've trained enough.
G I can't see our relationship lasting.
H I prefer to avoid taking it.

4 Complete the second sentence so that it has a similar meaning to the first sentence, using the word given. Use between two and five words, including the word given.

1 I lived in London until I got married last year.
BEEN
I .... in London until I got married last year.
2 It took three days for us to walk there.
WERE
We .... three days.
3 I couldn't remember the way there, so I got a taxi.
FORGOTTEN
I .... get there, so I got a taxi.
4 It was three years since I'd visited Peru.
NOT
I .... to Peru for three years.

5 Eat your heart out

Vocabulary
food

1 Work in pairs. Look at the photos of daily diets from around the world and discuss the questions.

1 Which diet looks the most appealing?
2 Which diet looks the most similar to your own?
3 What can we tell about the countries by looking at these people's diets?

2 Find out as much as you can about your partner's diet. Does your partner

1 snack between meals?
2 eat fast food regularly?
3 drink a lot of tea and coffee?
4 eat plenty of fresh fruit?
5 prefer to eat organic food?
6 avoid certain foods?

3 Complete the phrases with the words in the box.

balanced fat free low vegetarian vitamins

1 a high-............. diet
2 a strict .... diet
3 a diet rich in ....
4 a well-............. diet
5 a ....-salt diet
6 a dairy-............. diet

4 Use the phrases in Activities 2 and 3 to describe the diet most people have where you live. How healthy is it? Which phrases would you use to describe the diet you should have?

Expressions of quantity

▶ **GRAMMAR** REFERENCE p.149

5 How healthy do you think a Japanese sumo wrestler's diet is compared to other athletes?

6 Choose the correct option(s) in italics. Sometimes both options are possible.

1 Japanese sumo wrestlers consume *an enormous amount of/a great deal of* calories – ten times more than the recommended daily intake for an average man.

2 Sumo wrestlers eat *very few/very little* eggs.

3 Sumo wrestlers drink *a great deal of/an enormous amount of* beer.

4 A sumo wrestler's diet only contains *a little/a few* salt.

7 Work in pairs and discuss the questions.

1 Which of the expressions in the box can be used instead of the expressions of quantity in italics in Activity 6?

a bit of   a lot of   hardly any

2 Which expressions of quantity in Activity 6 and in the box above can be used with countable/uncountable nouns? Copy the table and complete it. Some can be used with both.

Countable	Uncountable

8 Turn to page 149 for more practice with countable and uncountable nouns.

9 What is the difference in meaning between these examples?

1 **A** The shop sells a few cakes.
  B The shop sells very few cakes.

2 **A** There's a little cheese left.
  B There's very little cheese left.

10 Work in pairs. Ask and answer questions based on the sentences in Activity 9.

Subject/Verb agreement

▶ **GRAMMAR** REFERENCE p.149

11 Work in pairs. Choose the correct option in italics and explain your choices.

1 Not many people *like/likes* raw fish.

2 Two thousand five hundred calories per day *is/are* enough for the average man.

3 Everyone *need/needs* to eat a balanced diet.

4 Eating a lot of fresh vegetables and cheese *is/are* good for you.

5 There *is/are* a lot of advice on the internet about eating a healthy diet.

6 Most of my family *eat/eats* meat but I'm a vegetarian.

12 Complete these sentences about eating habits so that they are true for you. Then compare with a partner.

1 Most of my family …

2 Both of my parents …

3 One of my friends …

4 No one in my house …

LANGUAGE TIP

Don't get confused between *a few* and *few*.

The party was OK; there were a few people I knew there. (a few = some)

The party wasn't a success; few people turned up. (few = hardly any). N.B. *hardly any* is more natural in spoken English.

Open cloze (Part 2)

▶ **EXAM** FOCUS p.186

1 **Work in pairs and discuss how far these statements are true for you.**

1 I can't stand the taste of chilli. It's too hot.

2 I love food which has lots of spices and different flavours.

3 I am addicted to caffeine – I drink at least four cups of coffee a day.

2 **Read the text opposite quickly and choose the correct words in italics.**

1 The writer *likes/doesn't like* chilli.

2 Chilli *can be/isn't* very addictive.

3 **Look at the gaps in the text. In which four gaps should you put an expression of quantity? Give reasons for your answers.**

> **EXAM TIP**
>
> In Part 2 you need to use a variety of grammatical forms, such as pronouns (*he, them*), prepositions (*at, about*), articles (*a, the*), auxiliaries (*do, are*), linking words (*although, next*), comparisons (*than, as*) and quantifiers (*any, many*).

4 **Now think of the word which best fits each gap. Use one word in each gap. There is an example at the beginning.**

5 **Look at the expressions of quantity from the text. What other ways are there to say the same thing?**

1 very few people

2 does not seem to have any addictive qualities

3 a large quantity of

4 lots of our favourite dishes

6 **Work in pairs and discuss the questions.**

1 What do children generally dislike eating?

2 What foods did you hate at first, but enjoy now?

3 Is there any food that you refuse to eat? Why?

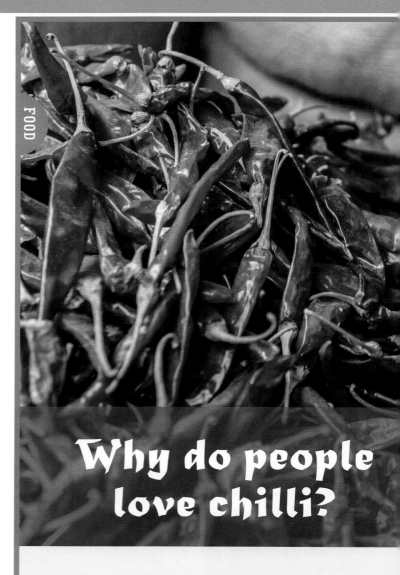

FOOD

Why do people love chilli?

People don't wash their eyes in lemon juice or pour boiling hot tea over themselves, so why are we prepared to go through so **(0)** much pain for the sake of chilli?

Chilli is not the only strange thing that people seem to enjoy. For example, very **(1)** .... people like the bitter taste of coffee to begin with but soon most of us **(2)** .... used to it. But coffee contains caffeine, which has some addictive qualities, and this explains **(3)** .... it is so popular. But capsaicin, the ingredient which makes chillies hot, does not seem to have **(4)** .... addictive qualities whatsoever. **(5)** .... we consumed a large quantity of it, it would kill us. And yet chillies have **(6)** .... used in cooking in almost **(7)** .... culture for thousands of years. Today, a third of the world's population eat chilli at least once a day. Lots of our favourite dishes just wouldn't taste right **(8)** .... it.

Sentence completion (Part 2)

▶ **EXAM** FOCUS p.188

1 Do most people still cook traditional dishes in your country? What new foods have become popular recently?

2 Look at question 1 in the text below. What kind of information do you think is missing? Give reasons for your answers.

- **A** a meal
- **B** a type of food
- **C** an animal

3 Underline the key words in the text below and make sure you understand what each sentence means.

4 ▶ 15 You will hear a food writer called Sarah Willis talking about the history of cooking. Follow the steps in Activity 2 for each answer, then listen and complete the sentences.

> **EXAM TIP**
>
> You may hear more than one number/noun/adjective/verb that will fit grammatically. But only one of these will fit the meaning.

5 Read through your answers to check they make sense grammatically.

6 Work in pairs and discuss the questions. Give reasons for your answers.

1 How much raw food do you eat?

2 Do you think people should eat less meat?

3 What would you like to eat more or less of?

THE IMPORTANCE OF COOKING

Sarah says about 60 percent of a chimpanzee's diet consists of a mixture of **(1)** ....

There is no **(2)** .... in a large percentage of the plants that chimpanzees eat.

The size of the human **(3)** .... makes it difficult for people to eat large quantities of plants.

Before they discovered cooking, it could take a minimum of **(4)** .... for people to eat their food.

One benefit of cooking was that **(5)** .... could be kept until the following day.

Some scientists think cooking resulted in an increase in the size of the **(6)** ....

The idea of sharing a **(7)** .... with the whole family probably started when people began to cook.

The risk from **(8)** .... meant that female cooks needed protection.

New evidence from Africa shows that **(9)** .... could have been used earlier than scientists previously thought.

During the last ice age the extra **(10)** .... provided by cooked food helped people to survive.

Multiple choice (Part 5)

▶ **EXAM** FOCUS p.187

1 **Discuss the questions and give reasons for your answers.**

1 If you lived on your own, would you bother cooking?
2 Would you ever replace a meal with an energy drink or smoothie?

2 **Read the article quickly to find out three pieces of information about a food product called Soylent. Then compare with a partner.**

EXAM TIP

Remember, when you are looking for the answers in this part, the questions will follow the order of the text. Always check your answers very carefully.

3 **For questions 1–6, choose the answer (A, B, C or D) which you think fits best according to the text.**

1 Why did Rob Rhinehart initially create Soylent?

   A He saw it as a way of earning money to support his new company.
   B He felt that cooking was taking up too much of his time.
   C He wanted to live on a diet of nutritious food.
   D He thought that he would be able to live more cheaply.

2 Following the interest in his blog, Rhinehart

   A couldn't keep up with the demand for Soylent.
   B had to choose which of his businesses to close.
   C improved the recipe for Soylent.
   D started producing big quantities of Soylent.

3 The writer was surprised by the public reaction to Soylent because

   A liquid food has always been associated with ill health.
   B people were already familiar with the idea of liquid meal replacements.
   C there are lots of similar products available.
   D astronauts stopped using liquid food a long time ago.

4 What does Rhinehart say about people's eating habits in the future?

   A They will feel less hungry at meal times.
   B They will prefer eating liquid food.
   C They will only cook when they feel like it.
   D They will appreciate eating out more than people do now.

5 What point is made in the fifth paragraph?

   A Most of our food has been altered in some way.
   B Food production needs to get more efficient.
   C People are reluctant to eat food products they consider unnatural.
   D Plants which are easy to grow will soon replace more popular vegetables.

6 In the final paragraph, the writer expresses

   A doubt that Soylent is only suitable for one group of people.
   B hope that Soylent may be a solution to a serious problem.
   C surprise about the predicted demand for Soylent products.
   D disagreement that products like Soylent are a risk to family life.

4 **Work in pairs. Check your answers by matching key words in the options to what is stated in the text.**

5 **Work in pairs and discuss the questions.**

1 Would you consider trying Soylent? What do you think are its advantages and disadvantages?
2 What would you give up if you wanted to save money?

   A buying snacks   D your phone
   B going out   E your car
   C buying presents   F something else?

6 **Match the underlined phrases in the article to their meanings 1–6.**

1 refuse to accept
2 remove the need for
3 discover by accident
4 no longer possible to continue
5 be limited to
6 spread quickly on the internet

7 **Work in pairs and decide whether both or only one of the verbs in italics collocates with the noun. Then check the meaning in a dictionary.**

1 Their crop of soya beans has *doubled/expanded* in size.
2 The business *expanded/grew* rapidly.
3 They *raised/grew* a huge family on very little money.
4 No one *raised/introduced* any objections to the plan.
5 The company had to *raise/increase* production to meet demand for the product.

8 **Use the verbs in Activity 7 to talk about changes in your town/city, your workload and the cost of transport.**

THE DEATH OF COOKING?

Rob Rhinehart's idea for Soylent (the name is a hybrid of *soybeans* and *lentils*) dates back to when he was living on his own in San Francisco and struggling to build a wireless networking business. Desperate to preserve his rapidly declining funds, he identified food as one of his biggest costs and <u>hit upon</u> a novel way to economise. After researching the essential nutrients required for maintaining human health, he ordered the ingredients from the internet and blended them together to make a liquid concoction that would <u>do away with</u> the bother of cooking.

In a blog post entitled *How I Stopped Eating Food*, he wrote about how the idea of food was outdated. The posting <u>went viral</u> and, when his original wi-fi business finally <u>reached the end of the line</u>, Rhinehart decided to put all his energies into making Soylent a success. He raised money by getting small sums from hundreds of online investors. This enabled him to start producing Soylent on a large scale. Last year the company was said to be valued at $100m. Now, the ready-to-drink version – Soylent 2.0 – is packaged in attractive white bottles and shipped across the USA and Canada and to other markets. More than 25m servings have been shipped since May 2014.

The public reaction which greeted Soylent was a little surprising, given that the idea of liquid food is nothing new. In hospitals it has been used for decades to feed patients that are too weak to digest solid food. Liquid meal replacements are also a regular feature of the diet industry and have been sold to people hoping to lose weight as a miraculous way of both satisfying hunger and minimising calorie intake. The concept of liquid food first caught the public imagination following the early expeditions into space when astronauts survived on packets of powdered dried food, which had to be dissolved in hot water. These days, liquid meal replacements are no longer considered rocket science but what is new is the suggestion that these products should become a normal part of our everyday diet.

Rhinehart is convinced that we will start to abandon three meals a day and instead rely on meal replacement drinks which meet our dietary requirements. 'We don't work on farms, we don't work on assembly lines and I don't think we should eat like we do. I think people will switch to eating when hungry rather than eating on a schedule.' He stresses this does not mean the end of cooking or eating for pleasure; people will only cook when they have time or are in the mood, and will continue to enjoy socialising with friends in restaurants.

One of the ingredients for Soylent is oil from seaweed, which Rhinehart considers a wonder plant because it is both extremely nutritious and fast-growing. He believes that one day we will all cultivate seaweed or other forms of algae in our gardens. The main ingredients for Soylent are extracts from soya, lentils and beetroot, plants which are known to be beneficial for health. Despite this, Rhinehart's product has drawn plenty of criticism from nutritionists, who say something is lost when giving up eating food in its natural state. Soylent's creator is <u>having none of it</u>. He argues that humans have always interfered with nature and that all of the crops that we produce have gradually been modified and adapted for human consumption over time.

Another objection to Rhinehart's theory about the future of food is that its appeal may <u>be confined to</u> single young people. The idea of families sitting around drinking from their individual Soylent bottles seems quite chilling as it reduces the traditional shared meal to a cold functional experience. But there are others who argue that meal replacement drinks like Soylent could be used in the battle against childhood obesity. According to Rhinehart, children love Soylent and he is considering bringing out flavoured versions which would appeal to them. Perhaps an unintended benefit of products like Soylent is that they could, with any luck, be a way to control our ever-increasing addiction to salt and sugar.

Passive forms

▶ **GRAMMAR** REFERENCE p.150

1 Read the sentences about celebrations. Decide whether it is better to use the active (sentence A) or passive (sentence B) form of the verb and say why.

1 A At weddings in Italy, *they often give* sugared almonds to guests.
   B At weddings in Italy, sugared almonds *are often given* to guests.

2 A Some people hate surprise parties that *people give* them on their birthdays.
   B Some people hate *being given* surprise parties on their birthdays.

3 A *We must make* a decision soon about which restaurant we should book for mum and dad's wedding anniversary.
   B A decision *must be made* soon about which restaurant we should book for mum and dad's wedding anniversary.

4 A *We will provide* flowers on all the tables at the wedding reception.
   B Flowers *will be provided* on all the tables at the wedding reception.

5 A I was really thrilled when *my sister asked me* to give a speech at her wedding.
   B I was really thrilled *to be asked by my sister* to give a speech at her wedding.

2 Read the text about a celebration. What is unusual about it?

At the end of November an annual feast **(1)** .... in Lopburi, Thailand. An enormous amount of fruit and vegetables **(2)** .... by local people. Chefs **(3)** .... to prepare a wonderful meal. Not so unusual, perhaps, except that the 3,000 guests are all monkeys! Monkeys **(4)** .... everywhere in this jungle town and monkeys **(5)** .... to bring wealth, in the form of tourism. The feast **(6)** .... in 1989 by a local businessman as a way of saying thank you to them.

3 Complete the text with the verb phrases in the box.

are believed   can be seen   have been invited
was started   will be donated   will be taking place

4 Work in pairs. Think of popular celebrations in your country. What food is typically eaten and how is it made? Try to use passive forms.

Passive reporting verbs

5 Look at sentences A, B and C. Which sentence(s) avoid(s) saying *who* believes? What is the difference in form?

A Thai people believe that monkeys bring wealth.
B Monkeys are believed to bring wealth.
C It is believed that monkeys bring wealth.

6 Complete the second sentence so that it has a similar meaning to the first sentence, using the word given.

1 People expect tourists to carry sticks to protect themselves from curious monkeys.
   ARE
   Tourists .... sticks to protect themselves from curious monkeys.

2 Most people think monkeys are a huge tourist attraction.
   BE
   Monkeys .... a huge tourist attraction by most people.

3 Newspapers claim that twenty top chefs have been invited to prepare the meal.
   BY
   It .... newspapers that twenty top chefs have been invited to prepare the meal.

4 The tourist office has estimated that over 10,000 visitors watch the feast.
   BEEN
   It .... that over 10,000 visitors watch the feast.

5 Everyone says monkeys can be very aggressive around food.
   TO
   Monkeys .... be very aggressive around food.

7 Work in pairs. Discuss stories which have been reported recently online or on TV.

Example: *The prime minister/president is said to be …*
A new film about … has been made recently.

A

B

Long turn (Part 2)
comparing and giving a reaction
▶ **EXAM** FOCUS p.190

Both these photos show people eating out in restaurants. Compare the photos and say why the people might choose to eat in places like these.

EXAM TIP

Listen carefully to the question and make sure you answer it. There are usually two parts to the question.

1 Look at the photos and the exam task, and tick the statements you agree with. Can you think of any other points of comparison between the photos?

1 Although the food in an expensive restaurant may be wonderful, the atmosphere isn't as friendly as in fast-food restaurants.

2 In expensive restaurants you often have to have full meals, whereas you can usually just get a snack in fast-food places.

3 While fast-food restaurants are quick and cheap, they usually serve unhealthy junk food.

4 Both formal and fast-food restaurants are popular with young people.

2 Underline the linking expressions in Activity 1 which are used to compare and contrast.

3 Work in pairs. Match the sentences 1–6 to the types of restaurant in the photos, A and B.

1 You don't have to dress up.
2 You can't hear yourself speak.
3 It's overpriced.
4 They're good for special occasions.
5 The atmosphere is more casual.
6 The food's a bit basic.

4 ▶ 16 Listen to Danuta doing the task and answer the questions.

1 What differences does she mention between the photos?

2 How does she respond to the second part of the question?

5 Look at the audio script on page 211. What adjectives does Danuta use?

6 Work in pairs. Turn to page 134 and complete Task 1. Then turn to page 136 and swap roles for Task 2.

Describing a personal experience

1 Read the restaurant review and tick the things that are mentioned.

- staff
- writer's expectations
- location
- décor
- other diners
- experience
- prices
- food

2 Work in pairs and discuss the questions.

1 Would you go to Franco's after reading this review?

2 Do you prefer to read restaurant reviews or to get personal recommendations from friends before going to a new restaurant?

3 How good do you think the restaurants are where you live? Which ones would you recommend to a visitor to your town/city?

4 Have you ever been disappointed or pleasantly surprised by a meal in a restaurant?

3 In which paragraph(s) does the writer

A give details about the food?

B say who she recommends the restaurant for?

C describe her experience?

D express negative points?

LANGUAGE TIP

Recommend can be followed by *-ing* or a clause.

I would strongly recommend booking/that you book in advance.

---

4 Copy the table and complete it with words/phrases from the review.

food	staff	experience
best pizza in the city, …		

5 Underline examples in the text where the writer uses

A adverbs for emphasis.

B the passive.

C expressions for giving opinions.

Franco's

Franco's on Canal Street is said to be the best pizza restaurant in the city but I'd always avoided going there because of their no-bookings policy; there's nothing I hate more than having to queue for ages. But last week a friend insisted on taking me there and although we did have to wait about 20 minutes for a table, it was definitely worth it.

There are only six pizzas on the menu, which may disappoint some who expect to have a wider selection on offer, but for me it's the quality of the ingredients that counts – not the size of the menu. The pizzas here actually taste authentically Neapolitan, which isn't that surprising given that the owner is from Naples and had the wood-fired pizza oven specially designed there.

The service was very efficient – but not too efficient. We didn't get the impression that the waiters were under pressure to serve us quickly so that they could squeeze in more customers. In fact, they couldn't have been friendlier or more helpful.

The only downside was that it was extremely hot as we were given a table quite close to the pizza oven. But on the whole, it was a first-rate experience – so much better than going to one of the characterless pizza chains. I'd strongly recommend going to Franco's. It's a great place for a top-quality, affordable meal out with friends.

Review (Part 2)

▶ **WRITING** REFERENCE p.172

6 Read the exam task and write a review, using some of the ideas and language from the review of Franco's. You should write 140–190 words.

You see this advertisement in the local paper.

WANTED: RESTAURANT CRITICS!

Have you tried a new restaurant in your area recently? We'd like to know your opinion, not only of the food but also the staff, the atmosphere and the prices. Tell us whether you would recommend the restaurant to other people.

The best review will be published in next week's paper.

Write your **review**.

EXAM TIP

You should include both positive and negative comments but don't forget to state your overall opinion.

1 Choose the best answer (A, B, C or D) to complete the sentences.

1 He snacks a lot .... meals.
   A besides   B on   C between   D from

2 It's important to eat a diet .... in vitamins.
   A rich   B high   C full   D plenty

3 People would be healthier if they ate less .... food.
   A fast   B quick   C hurried   D speedy

4 Never add salt to any dish without .... it first to see if it's needed.
   A tasting   B cooking   C flavouring   D pouring

5 Some cultures are known .... their spicy food.
   A by   B for   C about   D with

6 What .... are needed to make that dish?
   A parts   B items   C ingredients D pieces

7 A lot of children are addicted .... sugar.
   A for   B on   C to   D by

8 The price of coffee .... by more than 20 percent last year.
   A raised   B increased C expanded   D doubled

2 Complete the sentences with one word.

1 We've got very .... cheese left. Can you go to the shops for me?

2 I don't eat .... eggs these days; just two a week.

3 There's only a tiny .... of cake left. Who's eaten it all?

4 She eats .... any chocolate these days.

5 Eating .... of fruit is very good for you.

6 There are only a .... calories in a strawberry.

7 There's a great .... of salt in this dish.

8 We cooked an enormous .... of food for the party.

3 Choose the correct word in italics to complete the sentences.

1 A high percentage of people *is/are* allergic to nuts.

2 Both coffee and tea *contain/contains* a lot of caffeine.

3 Only one of my brothers *is/are* a good cook.

4 Neither of my parents *eat/eats* meat.

5 The government *has/have* introduced new rules about food labels.

6 Information on ways to improve your diet *is/are* available on the website.

7 The Spanish *eat/eats* a lot of fish.

8 Four hundred pounds *is/are* an awful lot of money to spend on one meal.

4 Complete the sentences with the correct passive form of the verb in brackets.

1 Children .... (*teach*) about healthy eating in many schools.

2 This restaurant .... (*review*) in six newspapers recently.

3 The onions must .... (*fry*) until they are soft.

4 That chef .... (*say*) to be extremely talented.

5 All the cake .... (*eat*) last night.

6 Only fifty people .... (*invite*) to their wedding, which is on Saturday.

6 In the spotlight

1 **Work in pairs and discuss the questions.**

1 What kinds of live performances do you enjoy?

2 Do you ever give money to street performers? Why/Why not?

3 What are the best/worst street performers you have seen?

2 **Choose the word/phrase in italics which does NOT fit in phrases 1–5.**

1 The *main/most obvious/highest/key* (dis)advantage of (being a street performer) is …

2 *Another/One further/One different/An additional* (dis)advantage of … (working in X) is …

3 … is a *huge/considerable/major/large* (dis)advantage.

4 It would be *great/good/no/big* fun to …

5 … would probably *need/take/use/require* a lot of time.

3 **Work in pairs and discuss the advantages and disadvantages of being a street performer. Use phrases from Activity 2 and the ideas in the box.**

interest   pay   practice   risk of injury   stress of performing   travel   working hours

Discussion (Part 4)

▶ **EXAM** FOCUS p.190

4 **Work in pairs and discuss the first question.**

1 Which do you think you need more of to succeed in the arts: luck or talent?

2 How important do you think it is for schools to offer art, dance and drama classes to all students?

3 What has your experience been of art, dance or drama classes at school?

4 What do you think of people who take part in TV talent shows?

5 In which area of the arts would you most like to excel?

6 Which painter, dancer, writer, musician, etc. do you most admire? Give reasons.

5 ▶ 17 **Listen to two students, Roberto and Beata, answering question 1. Do you agree with their opinions?**

6 **What language did Roberto/Beata use to**

1 ask his/her partner a question?
2 summarise his/her partner's opinion?
3 accept his/her partner's argument?

7 **Look at the audio script on page 211 and check your answers.**

8 **Do you think Roberto and Beata answered the question well? Why/Why not? In what ways, if any, could they improve their answers?**

9 **Work in pairs. Discuss the other questions in Activity 4. Try to expand your answers as much as you can.**

EXAM TIP

Say as much as possible but try to include your partner in the discussion and listen to what he/she says.

Vocabulary
the arts

10 **Complete the sentences with the words in the box.**

abstract blockbusters cast contemporary gallery productions

1 I'm not convinced I like all classical ballet but I love .... dance.
2 I sometimes nip into an art .... or exhibition during my lunch break.
3 I prefer landscapes or portraits to more .... paintings.
4 I'll often go to a play more than once if there's a different .... performing.
5 I tend to go for original theatre .... by controversial directors.
6 I'm a keen film-goer but I usually avoid ....

11 **Work in pairs.**

1 Rewrite the sentences in Activity 10 so they are true for you. Say the sentences to a partner, giving reasons. Try to use some of the language from Activity 2.
2 Take turns to describe a live performance you have seen.
3 Find out as much information as you can about your partner's favourite painting, dance production, play, music, etc.
   Example: *It was … by … I saw/heard.*
   It makes me feel …
   I was really impressed by …

Multiple choice: short extracts (Part 1)

▶ **EXAM** FOCUS p.188

1 ▶ 18 **You will hear people talking in eight different situations. First, underline the key words in question 1. Then listen and choose the best answer, A, B or C.**

1 You hear a woman talking about a play. What did she dislike about it?

    A the lighting   **B** the music   **C** the costumes

2 **Work in pairs and answer the questions to check. Then listen to question 1 again.**

1 Was the information in the recording in the same order as options A, B and C?

2 Did you hear any of the key words in options A, B or C?

3 Does the woman make negative comments about all the options, A, B or C?

4 Which words did you hear that refer to lighting, music and costumes?

5 Which words signal what the woman disliked about the play?

3 ▶ 19 **Underline the key words in questions 2–8. Then listen and choose the best answer, A, B or C.**

> **EXAM TIP**
>
> Don't worry if you don't understand every word. Just focus on choosing the best option to answer the question.

2 You hear a man and a woman talking about a visit to the theatre. How does the woman feel about the arrangements?

    A annoyed that the play finishes so late

    B worried about when they're going to eat

    C confused about what time the play starts

3 You hear part of a radio programme. What kind of programme is it?

    A a celebrity interview

    B a film review

    C a news show

4 You hear a woman giving some information on the radio about a comedy festival. Why is it going to be different this year?

    A The tickets will be more expensive.

    B It will be held in a smaller venue.

    C It will be on different dates.

5 You hear a man interviewing a ballet dancer on the radio. Why has she decided to retire later this year?

    A She is worried about getting injured.

    B She no longer enjoys performing.

    C She wants to make her family the priority.

6 You hear a man and a woman talking on the radio about a new art exhibition. What do they agree is special about it?

    A the variety of genres

    B the unusual location

    C the famous artists

7 You hear an actress being interviewed on the radio. What is she doing?

    A giving her opinion about the topic of the play

    B describing her relationship with the director

    C stating a wish to direct a play herself

8 You hear a man and a woman talking. Who is the man?

    A her brother

    B her teacher

    C her friend

4 **Work in pairs and discuss the paraphrases you heard which helped you to choose your answers. Then check the audio script on page 211.**

5 **Work in pairs and discuss the questions.**

1 How often do you go to the theatre/the cinema/art galleries?

2 Do you think the government should subsidise the arts so that the average person can afford to go to more live performances, art exhibitions, etc.? Give reasons.

3 Have you ever appeared in a play or other live performance? If not, would you like to? Give reasons.

Future forms

▶ **GRAMMAR** REFERENCE p.151

1 **Decide which of the underlined verbs are examples of the present continuous, present simple, *will, going to* or modal verbs.**

A: So, who do you think will get the main part?

B: I expect **(1)** <u>it'll be</u> Zoe. She's probably the best singer and dancer although my dad thinks it **(2)** <u>could be</u> Molly. Mr Paton says **(3)** <u>he's going to tell</u> us in our next drama class.

A: When **(4)** <u>are you starting</u> rehearsals?

B: On Friday. **(5)** <u>It's going to be</u> really hard work because the show **(6)** <u>opens</u> in three weeks' time. In fact I think **(7)** <u>I'll go</u> and start reading the script now.

A: **(8)** <u>I'll help</u> you learn your lines, if that's any help.

2 **Match the numbered future forms in the dialogue to their uses A–H.**

A an offer
B a fixed arrangement
C a timetabled event in the future
D an intention – something that someone has decided to do in the future
E a prediction based on a belief or opinion
F a prediction based on fact
G a future possibility
H a spontaneous decision

3 **What words can you use instead of *could* for example 2 in Activity 1?**

4 ▶ 20 **Complete the dialogues with the correct future form of the verbs in brackets. Then listen and check.**

will/present continuous

A: What **(1)** .... (*do*) this weekend?

B: I **(2)** .... (*go*) to the dance festival in the park. It's on all weekend.

A: Oh, I'd really like to go but my brother **(3)** .... (*move*) house and I have to help him.

B: That's a shame!

A: Never mind. I'm sure you **(4)** .... (*enjoy*) it.

B: Yes. It should be fun, especially as I think the weather's going to be good.

going to/*will*/present simple

A: Hi, Ben! Are you going to the film festival at the weekend?

B: Yes, on Saturday. I **(5)** .... (*buy*) the tickets online this afternoon.

A: How much are they?

B: Only £15. I **(6)** .... (*get*) you one if you like.

A: That would be great. What time **(7)** .... (*start*)?

B: At 7.30. But I **(8)** .... (*leave*) home early, at six o'clock because of the traffic. I'll pick you up on my way if you want.

as soon as, until, when, before, after

5 **Look at the examples and answer the questions.**

• ***As soon as*** *the film* ***ends***, *we'll call a taxi.*
• *We'll have dinner* ***when*** *she* ***arrives***.

1 What form of the verb follows a future time expression?

2 Is the clause with the time expression referring to the present or the future?

3 Is the time clause at the beginning or the end of the sentence?

4 What is the difference in meaning between *as soon as* and *when*?

6 **Choose the correct option in italics.**

Laura is hoping to go to drama college after she **(1)** *will leave/leaves* school. As soon as she **(2)** *is finishing/finishes* her exams, she's going to research the best places to study. When she **(3)** *finds/is going to find* somewhere that she can do both drama and dance, she'll apply to go there. But first she wants to take a year out and work in a supermarket or as a waitress until she **(4)** *will have/has* enough money to contribute towards her college fees. Before anywhere **(5)** *is offering/offers* her a place, though, she'll need to have an audition.

7 **Complete these sentences about your life and then discuss them with a partner.**

1 As soon as .... , I ....
2 Before .... , I ....
3 After .... , I ....
4 I won't .... until ....

8 **Tell your partner about**

1 something you intend to do later today.
2 an arrangement for next weekend.
3 a hope for the future of your country.
4 a prediction about the world in the next ten years.

Gapped text (Part 6)

▶ **EXAM** FOCUS p.187

1 **Work in pairs and discuss the questions.**

1 What are the reasons for using different kinds of social media? Which ones are more popular? Why?

2 What kinds of people use social media most? Think about age, type of job, personality type, etc.

3 Do you think people who use social media a great deal are narcissistic (interested in themselves and the way they appear to other people)?

2 **Read the text quickly and answer questions 1 and 2.**

> **EXAM TIP**
>
> Make sure you read the whole text quickly before trying to answer the questions.

1 How does the writer explain *narcissism* in the first paragraph?

2 Complete this sentence to summarise the writer's main point.

Socal media encourages people to

A get a false impression of the celebrities they follow.

B have unrealistic hopes for their own futures.

C become too focused on the opinion others have of them.

3 **Look at the text around the first gap and at the list of options in Activity 4.**

1 Predict what kind of information you think is missing from the gap.

2 Which of the missing options links back to the topic of the paragraph?

3 Underline the words and phrases which link the option to the missing information.

4 **Follow the procedure in Activity 3 for the rest of the gaps (2–6) and choose the sentence that fits each gap. There is one extra sentence which you do not need to use.**

A Such increases pre-date social media but they have clearly worsened since its arrival.

B Furthermore, the need to be appreciated is a crucial part of psychological wellbeing, unless it is taken too far and becomes a nonstop search to be valued by others.

C However, the danger is when these efforts to compensate are supported and rewarded by others.

D Then came reality TV, which turned the attention back to ourselves.

E New 'self-help' mathematical formulas could be built into Facebook, Twitter and Instagram.

F The explanation for this is that narcissistic individuals are much more likely to use social media to portray an enviable, if unrealistic, self-image, broadcasting their life to an audience and gaining many virtual friends.

G Interestingly, what they all seem to have in common is digital attention seeking.

5 **Work in pairs and discuss the questions.**

1 Is it true to say that many people these days expect to become famous without needing to put in the effort?

2 Which social media do you enjoy using most? What do you use it for?

3 What, if any, concerns do you have about the use of social media?

4 Are there any issues in the article which you strongly agree or disagree with?

Sharing the (self) love: the rise of the selfie and digital narcissism

Welcome to the age of digital narcissism. We can all name celebrities who are keen users of social media and who we suspect have the following things in common: a desire to be noticed, a self-important view of themselves, superficial personalities and shameless self-publicity. In that sense, they are just like millions of their Facebook and Twitter fans around the world, except successful.

Until the 90s, the media provided an escape from reality by transporting viewers to the fictional universe of situational comedy and soap operas. [1] It did this by broadcasting the allegedly genuine and ordinary lives of everyday people and making them into cultural blockbusters. However, in the past decade, social media appears to have enabled everybody to make their life public and be the star of their own 24/7 show.

There are now many mega-successful apps and websites. [2] It all began with MySpace, a list of hopeful future pop stars and DJs. Then came Facebook, the choice of the average person. YouTube gave everybody their own TV channel, Blogger and Tumblr made us all creative writers. Twitter brought in loads of followers and LinkedIn encouraged us to give each other approval of our professional skills. Instagram made 'selfie' the word of the year, while Tinder and Snapchat made Facebook look intellectual.

Unsurprisingly, narcissism levels have been rising for decades. [3] At the same time, the advent of Facebook and Twitter has brought with it a steep decline in generosity and levels of sympathy. We are now more connected than ever, but also less interested in other people, except when it comes to finding out what they think about us. It is as if being closer to others made us more antisocial.

Needless to say, most social media users are not narcissistic. Yet the more narcissistic you are, the heavier your social media use. Indeed, scientific studies have shown that the number of status updates, attractive selfies, followers and friends are all positively linked to narcissism. [4]

The big problem with the rise of digital narcissism is that it puts enormous pressure on people to reach unachievable goals, without necessarily putting in much effort. Wanting to be Beyoncé or Jay Z is hard enough already, but when you are not prepared to work hard to achieve it, you are better off just being less ambitious. Few things are more destructive than the belief that you have the right to something, combined with a lazy work ethic. Ultimately, online evidence of narcissism may be little more than a way of making up for a low and fragile self-esteem. [5] In this case, reality is misinterpreted and narcissistic fantasies are strengthened.

Perhaps it is time to turn social media into a therapeutic tool, at the service of the public and society. Examining the rise of narcissism could be done both at an individual and population level. [6] The aim of this would be to make users aware of their excessive self-promotion, uncontrollable self-love and even signal when an entire population might be at risk of becoming too self-obsessed for its own sake. Or is it too late?

Vocabulary
word formation

6 Work in pairs. Student A: make adjectives from the words in the first box. Student B: make nouns from the words in the second box.

Adjectives from nouns/verbs

achieve (v)   ambition (n)   culture (n)
destroy (v)   excess (n)   hope (n/v)
intellect (n)   science (n)   therapy (n)

Nouns from adjectives/verbs

approve (v)   believe (v)   choose (v)
evident (adj)   generous (adj)
promote (v)   real (adj)

7 Compare answers and check with the underlined words in the article.

8 Complete the sentences with the correct form of the words in brackets. Then work in pairs and discuss whether you agree with the statements.

1 I don't always feel very .... (hope) about the impact of technology on our lives.

2 I think I am probably more of a .... (create) than a .... (science) person.

3 Very .... (ambition) people are more likely to be disappointed in life.

4 I think everyone should have the .... (choose) of what to study at school.

5 It's important for children to get a lot of parental .... (approve) when they're growing up.

6 There is no .... (evident) that sugar is bad for you.

Future perfect and continuous

▶ **GRAMMAR** REFERENCE p.152

1 Read part of an article in which a film director gives his views about the future of cinema. Do you agree with what he says?

I'm sure that I'll still <u>be making</u> films for the cinema <u>in</u> thirty years' time. After all, the cinema offers a group experience that is sociable and is not at all the same as watching a film on the small screen at home. Although some directors <u>will be experimenting</u> with interactive techniques in 2050, many others <u>may have come</u> to the conclusion that the reason most people like going to the cinema is the opportunity to be passive for a change. Things <u>will have changed</u> a lot though <u>by then</u>. Many cinemas <u>might have already closed down</u> and those which remain <u>will be charging</u> much more for the experience.

2 Read the extract again. Which of the underlined forms is

1 a future continuous form?
2 a future perfect form?
3 a time linker connected to the future?

3 Complete the rules.

- Future continuous: *will/may/might* + ... + *-ing*
- Future perfect: *will/may/might* + ... + ... participle

4 Which verb form is used

1 for an action which began before a specific time in the future and will probably continue after it?
2 for an action which is already finished by a specific time in the future?

> ### LANGUAGE TIP
> The future continuous is also used to talk about things you expect will happen because they usually do.
> *Do you think you'll be going to Spain again this summer?*

5 Read the rest of the article and choose the correct option in italics.

I think by 2050 we'll (**1**) *be watching/have watched* an increasing number of 3D films. Film-makers may even (**2**) *be finding/have found* a way to project our faces onto the characters on the screen by that time. I think here in Hollywood we will still (**3**) *be making/have made* films – I don't think any other country will (**4**) *be replacing/have replaced* us as the film-making centre of the world.

6 Complete the sentences with the future continuous or future perfect form of the verbs in brackets.

By 2050 …

1 most young people .... (*stop*) going to the cinema.
2 everybody will .... (*use*) surround sound systems with their TVs.
3 we may .... (*choose*) from a huge cyber library whatever television programme we want to watch.
4 we'll .... (*interact*) with the screen when we move and speak.
5 they might .... (*invent*) contact lenses with a chip inside so that we can watch the screen in 3D.
6 holographic TV screens will .... (*project*) images around our rooms at home.

7 Tick the sentences you agree with in Activity 6. Then work in pairs and discuss your opinions. Use the expressions from Activity 2 on page 58.

8 Work in pairs. What do you think the world will be like in 2050? What will have changed and what will be happening? Use the ideas in the box to help you.

the environment family friends food leisure time medicine and technology travel work

Vocabulary
expressions with *get*

1 *Get* has a variety of different meanings. Replace *get* in questions 1–6 with one of the verbs in the box. Then work in pairs and ask each other the questions.

---

become have move/travel persuade receive understand

---

1 Was there a subject at school that you really didn't get?

2 What techniques do you use to get people to do what you want?

3 When do you normally get the time to relax?

4 In which situations do you get angry?

5 How do you get from one place to another?

6 How many texts do you get in an average day?

Multiple-choice cloze (Part 1)

▶ **EXAM** FOCUS p.186

2 Read the text quickly. What did science fiction get right and wrong when it predicted the future? What did it not predict?

EXAM TIP

Part 1 tests language (focusing on vocabulary) such as
- phrasal verbs (e.g. *get away*).
- collocations (e.g. *do your homework*).
- words with similar meanings (e.g. *travel, trip, journey*).
- linking words (e.g. *although*).
- set phrases (e.g. *on purpose*).

---

3 Read the text again and decide which answer (A, B, C or D) best fits each gap.

0	A say	B call	C tell	D name
1	A true	B right	C exact	D correct
2	A got	B arrived	C reached	D appeared
3	A instead	B rather	C sooner	D except
4	A drive	B travel	C voyage	D journey
5	A for	B to	C in	D against
6	A up	B off	C over	D down
7	A make	B do	C get	D take
8	A end	B effect	C result	D solution

4 Work in pairs. Compare your answers and explain why you chose them.

5 Do you agree with the writer about the importance of the computer? What other inventions do you think have had a huge impact on our lives?

Unbelievable! H.G.WELLS' MIRACLE SHOW! Wondrous!

AN ALEXANDER KORDA SPECTACLE

THINGS TO COME

SEE – THE BIRTH OF SUPERMAN!
SEE – THE GLASS CITIES!
SEE – 1000 PASSENGER AIR LINERS!
SEE – ROCKET SHIP TO THE MOON!

WOMAN OF TOMORROW – WILL SHE BE SADIST! BEAST! BARBARIAN! BEAUTY! WILL HER KISSES KILL!

RAYMOND MASSEY · RALPH RICHARDSON
SIR CEDRIC HARDWICKE · MARGARETTA SCOTT
AND A CAST OF 20,000   A FILM CLASSICS INC. RELEASE

FROM FICTION TO REALITY

Science-fiction films have promised us many exciting gadgets. We have seen hoverboards, domestic robots and flying cars, to **(0)** D, name just a few, but most of these predictions have not come **(1)** .... yet. Take, for example, the way I **(2)** .... to the office this morning: I came by bike **(3)** .... than on a hoverboard.

Not much has changed there, then – the bicycle was invented in the nineteenth century! Almost the whole **(4)** .... was on a form of Tarmac, also invented that same century. Also, **(5)** .... some people's surprise, robots haven't taken **(6)** .... either the home or the workplace yet.

On the other hand, in 1987 it was predicted in the TV series *Star Trek* that we would be using touch-screen technology before too long. So perhaps fiction doesn't always **(7)** .... it wrong after all. Maybe the most astonishing development has been the microchip and its place in computers. The **(8)** .... on our lives has been amazing, and this was never really predicted.

Report (Part 2)
text organisation

▶ **WRITING** REFERENCE p.170

1 Read the report which a teacher was asked to write for the director of her language college. Answer the questions in pairs. Give examples.

1 What was the purpose of her report?
2 What is her recommendation?
3 Is it written in an informal or a formal style?

Report on suggestion for a college cinema

(1) ....

The aim of this report is to outline the advantages and potential problems of investing money in a small cinema, and make recommendations. In order to do this, both students and staff were consulted.

(2) ....

It was generally believed that a college cinema could have wide-reaching benefits for both students and teachers. It was suggested that films in other languages as well as English could be shown, which would widen the appeal, and that the cinema might also be used for conversation classes.

(3) ....

The main concerns that were raised are as follows:

1 It would be expensive to set up and run.
2 Since many students watch films on their laptops, they might not be prepared to pay to watch films at a cinema.
3 Only big cinemas have access to blockbusters when they first come out.

(4) ....

I am concerned that the cinema may not pay its way at first. However, all things considered, the benefits outweigh the disadvantages. I would therefore recommend going ahead with the project.

---

2 Give each of the four sections of the report a heading, so that it is easier to read. Choose from the headings in the box.

Advantages   Introduction   Potential problems
Recommendations

3 Look at the underlined phrases in the text. Find examples of the following and discuss why they are commonly used in reports.

1 passive forms/reporting verbs
2 linking words
3 clauses of purpose

4 Read the exam task and underline the key words.

> The director of your college has asked you to write a report on a visit you made to a self-study centre at a local university. You should explain how successful it has been and recommend whether or not your college should have one.
>
> Write your **report** in **140–190** words in an appropriate style.

5 Divide these points into the advantages and disadvantages of the study centre you saw.

1 It is under-used at weekends.
2 People from the community use the facilities, which helps to fund it.
3 Many students still prefer to study in their own rooms.
4 The worksheets provided give extra practice of classroom work.
5 A full-time assistant has to be on duty even if the centre is empty.
6 The facility helps to attract potential students to the college.
7 It cost a lot to set up because of all the computers, etc.
8 Writing materials for the centre is time-consuming for the teachers.

6 Write your report for the task in Activity 4. You can use some of the points in Activity 5 as well as your own ideas.

EXAM TIP

Organise your report under clear headings and include numbers or bullet points to make your points clearly.

1 Complete the sentences using the correct form of the word in brackets.

1 Some people think that new technology will lead to the .... of the film industry. (destroy)

2 An .... amount of practice can lead to more injuries for dancers. (excess)

3 There is no .... as yet that robots will be a serious threat to jobs. (evident)

4 The film is a .... account of a great painter's life. (fiction)

5 I sometimes like to escape from .... by going to a musical. (real)

6 We wanted to see a film, but there wasn't much .... (choose)

2 Complete the sentences with the words in the box.

away   down   into   over   round   through

1 The only way I can get .... to my cousin is by talking about dance.

2 *City Lights* is on TV tonight. I never got .... to seeing that at the cinema.

3 It took him ages to get .... the disappointment of not being in the play.

4 If I stay in every night watching TV, it gets me ....

5 Comedians can't get .... with simply repeating the same jokes at every performance.

6 Everyone says it's a really good series, but I just can't get .... it.

3 Complete the sentences with the future continuous or future perfect form of the verbs in brackets.

1 I think I'll still .... (*learn*) my lines until just before the play starts.

2 The film may already .... (*start*) by the time we get there.

3 I hope they'll .... (*show*) his still lifes at the exhibition.

4 We might .... (*use*) the same costumes in our next production.

5 People will probably still .... (*watch*) live theatre in fifty years' time.

6 I think people will .... (*lose*) interest in computer games a long time before 2025.

4 Choose the correct option, A, B or C.

1 Sorry, I can't come on Saturday. I .... an old school friend for lunch.

   A meet
   B am meeting
   C will meet

2 As soon as she .... , will you text me?

   A phones
   B will phone
   C will be phoning

3 I .... my drama course by the end of next year.

   A will be completing
   B will have completed
   C am completing

4 This time tomorrow, I .... in front of hundreds of people.

   A will dance
   B will be dancing
   C dance

5 Don't worry, I haven't forgotten. I .... to him later.

   A speak
   B will have spoken
   C am going to speak

6 I'll meet you after I .... work.

   A finish
   B am finishing
   C will finish

7 Don't be nervous. I'm sure you .... really well tomorrow.

   A do
   B are doing
   C will do

8 Let's hurry! They .... the theatre doors at 7.30 and then you have to wait until the interval to go in.

   A close
   B are going to close
   C are closing

Multiple-choice cloze (Part 1)

1 For questions 1–8, read the text below and decide which answer (A, B, C or D) best fits in each gap. There is an example at the beginning.

Graffiti: Art or crime?

The **(0)** _C, term_ 'graffiti' was originally used by archaeologists to describe the words and pictures scratched on walls by the Greeks and Romans. However, graffiti took **(1)** .... a new meaning in the mid-1960s when it was used as a means of political communication and resistance. Since then many countries have made graffiti – which can **(2)** .... a lot of time and money to remove from buildings – illegal.

More recently, though, urban art is **(3)** .... recognition as a form of cultural expression. Walking through the streets of Barcelona, to **(4)** .... just one of many cities, the graffiti there immediately **(5)** .... your eye. **(6)** .... , some cities, such as Buenos Aires, take advantage of the interest in graffiti by organising a **(7)** .... for tourists around its colourful streets.

Graffiti artists are now being encouraged to display their work in galleries, which is **(8)** .... people ask themselves whether graffiti, when it is legal, should be renamed street art.

0	**A** title	**B** label	**C** term	**D** phrase
1	**A** on	**B** over	**C** in	**D** round
2	**A** need	**B** take	**C** use	**D** want
3	**A** gaining	**B** gathering	**C** collecting	**D** having
4	**A** say	**B** name	**C** tell	**D** call
5	**A** takes	**B** pulls	**C** catches	**D** interests
6	**A** Nonetheless	**B** In fact	**C** Otherwise	**D** After all
7	**A** journey	**B** travel	**C** tour	**D** voyage
8	**A** making	**B** forcing	**C** causing	**D** starting

Open cloze (Part 2)

2 For questions 9–16, read the text below and think of the word that best fits each gap. Use only one word in each gap. There is an example at the beginning.

The coldest city on earth

Although the remote region of Yakutsk in Siberia covers more than a million square miles, it is home to **(0)** _fewer_ than one million people and has hardly any large towns. In January the temperatures are -45°C, causing the metal on people's spectacles to stick to **(9)** .... cheeks.

Locals claim there are **(10)** .... lakes and rivers in the region for each inhabitant to have one. According **(11)** .... legend, when the god of creation arrived in Yakutsk, he got **(12)** .... cold that his hands were frozen and he dropped all the natural resources there. The capital of the region, also called Yakutsk, is six time zones away from Moscow.

There's no railway, so travellers have the option of a 1,000-mile boat ride up the Lena river during **(13)** .... few months of the year when it isn't frozen, or they have to use the 'Road of Bones', **(14)** .... was built by prisoners and can only be used in winter, when the rivers freeze over. Truck drivers bringing supplies to remote villages go in pairs and never turn their engines **(15)** .... during the two-week drive. **(16)** .... they break down on the little-used road, it means almost certain death.

Word formation (Part 3)

3 For questions 17–24, read the text below. Use the word given in capitals at the end of some of the lines to form a word that fits in the gap in the same line. There is an example at the beginning.

Anyone for bugs?

In the kitchen of the Archipelago restaurant in London, the head chef is making final **(0)** ...preparations. to one of the salads that has helped to make his restaurant so famous. Taking a wok off the stove, he spoons a **(17)** .... red sauce onto a bed of salad leaves. At first **(18)** .... , this could be any other Thai salad, with its chilli, garlic and many other **(19)** .... ingredients. But it's not long before you can recognise the shape of an insect – the thin legs, huge eyes and long tail of a locust. The less **(20)** .... among us would not be too keen on eating insects such as locusts and crickets but they are, in fact, **(21)** .... tasty. Many people find the idea of eating insects **(22)** .... However, for around 2.5 billion of the world's population, insects like these form part of their **(23)** .... diet. This is very **(24)** .... as they are low in fat, high in protein and full of vitamins as well as being energy efficient.

PREPARE

SPICE

SEE

COLOUR

ADVENTURE

SURPRISE

FASCINATE

DAY

FORTUNE

Key word transformation (Part 4)

4 For questions 25–30, complete the second sentence so that it has a similar meaning to the first sentence, using the word given. Do not change the word given. You must use between two and five words, including the word given.

Example:

I don't think John has got his father's musical talent.

AFTER

John doesn't appear to take after *his father as far as musical talent is concerned.*

25 You will get the results by Friday.

GIVEN

I .... you the results by Friday.

26 A fast-food chain has taken over two of our local restaurants.

BY

Two of our local restaurants .... a fast-food chain.

27 Nearly all the shops in this town are expensive.

HARDLY

There .... shops in this town.

28 Many people believe that too much sugar is bad for your health.

TO

Too much sugar .... bad for your health.

29 George hadn't finished doing his homework when I went to pick him up.

STILL

George .... when I went to pick him up.

30 My brother often arrives unexpectedly.

TURNING

My brother is .... unexpectedly.

7 A place to live

1 You are going to read an article about young people who live with their parents. Read the title and discuss the questions.

1 What do you think 'fly the nest' means?
2 When do young people in your country typically leave home?

Multiple matching (Part 7)
▶ **EXAM** FOCUS p.187

▶ **EXAM** FOCUS p.187

2 Read the texts quickly. The general attitude of the four people to living with their families is that it's

a) convenient.　　b) extremely difficult.　　c) great.

3 In questions 1–10, underline the key words and look for synonyms and paraphrases in the texts.

4 For questions 2–10, choose the best answer from the people A–D.

Which person says that

a family member disapproves of her lifestyle choice?	1	C
a few people she knows pity her for the situation she is in?	2	
her parents have mixed feelings about her being at home?	3	
she doesn't expect her parents to do everything for her while she's living with them?	4	
her living arrangements are a good solution for a short period?	5	
there are potential health implications of being out of work?	6	
some young people these days have little control over their lives?	7	
she would prefer to change the surroundings that she lives in?	8	
she was encouraged to lead an independent life while still a teenager?	9	
the lack of privacy means she is sometimes reluctant to entertain at home?	10	

5 Work in pairs and discuss why you chose the answers you did.

EXAM TIP

In this part of the reading test the focus is on scanning for information. Skimming for gist first will give you an idea of the overall content but must be done quickly.

The struggle to fly the nest

Four young people explain what it's like to go back and live with their parents.

A Maria, 28, Ireland

The only way I could afford to train to be a teacher as a mature student was to move back home, as I couldn't pay the high rent for university accommodation. On an everyday basis it's fine as it's not a long-term commitment and I <u>get on</u> well with my parents. Having said that, as soon as I'm qualified and working, I'll <u>move out</u> and get my own place. The benefits are mainly financial although it's nice to have supportive parents around after a bad day. It's weird, though, that the general reaction is to feel sorry for me. Various friends and colleagues think it must be awful, even though I tell them it's by choice and I'm lucky to have the option. There are no ground rules but I try to be quiet when I get in late or leave early. And it hasn't had too much impact on my social life, although at times it does <u>put you off</u> having people over when you know your mum might pop in at any moment!

B Gaia, 26, Italy

At nineteen, my dad told me to explore the world and stand on my own feet. I spent two years in the USA as part of my first degree and then I did a Master's degree in Florence in international relations. I also had a wonderful year working for the United Nations Development Programme in Brazil and a few months in Brussels. But despite all this, I'm back in the city where I was born and living with my parents again. The fact that you don't have to worry about housework means you can concentrate on your life. I do make an effort not to take my parents for granted, though, so I share the cooking, for example. I have different volunteer activities but my main focus is looking for a real job. I don't want to be rich but I think our generation is suffering because if you don't have a job, you aren't empowered and can't lead your own life. And that is so important.

C Nicole, 24, Sweden

I've studied in Rome, Stockholm and Warsaw but after I came back to Malmö I wanted to do a degree in journalism so I decided to stay with my father. He doesn't charge me anything for rent or food so right now I'm saving a lot of money and I can do whatever I want – even have parties. But it still doesn't feel like my home so it's not ideal. If I could, I'd paint and decorate the house and <u>throw</u> stuff <u>out</u>.

Everyone thinks it's cool that I live with my dad, apart from my sister, who I think is convinced that I'm lazy and spoiled and that it's time for me to move out. I'm the only one I know who lives at home – it's the social norm in Sweden to be independent. If I <u>took out</u> a student loan, I could afford to rent a flat by myself but that would imply that I was staying here and when I finish my degree I want to move to Stockholm. I think you have a better chance of finding a job there, even though it's so expensive.

D Daniela, 22, UK

After I graduated, I ended up spending six months unsuccessfully looking for work. During this period my parents <u>let</u> me <u>off</u> paying rent even though they are also finding it tough financially at the moment. I've now managed to find some part-time bar and waiting work. Mum and Dad like having me around and know being back home makes sense but they're worried about me and are aware that it is important for me to spread my wings. I read somewhere that long-term unemployment can make people stressed and anxious and I myself spent a couple of months really struggling before I was able to <u>build up</u> my confidence and feel happy again. The problem is that people are retiring later and, as a result, there are not as many jobs free higher up. I'd love to move out – I particularly miss not being able to have my mates round to stay – but I don't have the money or job security to make that financial commitment.

Vocabulary
phrasal verbs

6 Complete the sentences with the words in the box. You can use the words more than once. Then check with the underlined words in the article.

off   on   out   up

1 I get .... well with my parents.
2 As soon as I'm qualified and working, I'll move .... and get my own place.
3 It does put you .... having people over when you know your mum might pop in at any moment!
4 If I could, I'd paint and decorate the house and throw stuff ....
5 If I took .... a student loan, I could afford to rent a flat.
6 My parents let me .... paying rent.
7 I myself spent a couple of months really struggling before I was able to build .... my confidence.

7 Match the phrasal verbs in Activity 6 to their meanings A–G. Check the context in the text.

A give permission not to do something
B leave the house you are living in in order to live somewhere else
C get rid of something by putting it in a bin or giving it to someone
D have a good relationship
E increase
F make you not want to do something
G borrow money (from a bank or institution)

8 Work in pairs. Choose three phrasal verbs each and write a sentence for each one about your life. Your partner should ask you questions to find out more information.

Example: A: *I'm hoping to take out a loan to buy a car.*
B: *That's great. When did you pass your test?*

9 Work in groups and discuss the questions.

1 What will you miss or did you miss most about your home when you move(d) out?
2 How difficult is it for young people in your country to find somewhere to buy or rent?
3 What more do you think your country could do to help young people?

Modal verbs
possibility and certainty
▶ **GRAMMAR** REFERENCE p.153

1 Do you think this newspaper headline could be true/must be true or can't be true? Give reasons.

> **Life expectancy to reach 100 years globally within 10 years**

2 Underline a modal verb of possibility or certainty in each sentence. The first one is done for you.

1 His German <u>must</u> be very good after ten years in Berlin.
2 You can't be serious about driving in this fog. It's dangerous.
3 He may decide to live at home after all. He keeps changing his mind.
4 He couldn't have been staying with his brother. They don't get on at all.
5 That could be Steve over there on the right. Or it might be Andy.

3 Complete the gaps in rules A–C with the underlined modal verbs.

A When we are sure something is true, we use ....
B When we are sure something is not true, we use .... or ....
C When we think something is possibly true we use ...., ... or ....

4 Which verb form do we use after the modal in a) the present? b) the past?

> **LANGUAGE TIP**
> Use the weak form of *have* /həv/ in past modals.
> *She must have /mʌstəv/ missed the bus.*

ability

5 Look at sentences A–E and underline a modal of ability. The first one is done for you. Then match sentences 1–5 in Activity 2 to A–E.

A He <u>couldn't have found</u> a flat he wants to rent.
B Maybe he was able to find a room at a friend's instead.
C You won't be able to see a thing.
D I can't see very well without my glasses.
E But he couldn't speak a word before he went.

6 Which of the phrases you underlined in Activity 5 refers to

1 general ability in the past?
2 ability in the future?
3 ability in the present?
4 ability on a particular occasion in the past?
5 things which were possible but didn't happen?

7 Choose the best alternative in italics. Explain your choices.

1 He *might/must* be here somewhere because he promised to meet me.
2 After we'd tried everything, we *could/were able* to get the computer to work at last.
3 I hope *can/to be able* to finish this work today.
4 Surely they *couldn't have been playing/may have been playing* football all that time!
5 Sam *couldn't have been/wasn't able to have been* driving the car. He was at home with me.

8 Work in pairs. Take turns to use the cues in brackets to make responses to the statements. Remember to use the weak form of *have* /həv/ for past forms.

1 **A:** James looks very relaxed these days.
   B: .... (*must/give up/work*)
2 **A:** I think that's Alfie who's running towards us.
   B: .... (*can't/never take/any exercise*)
3 **A:** Florence keeps checking her phone.
   B: .... (*may/expect/a message*)
4 **A:** Is that your mother in front of us in the queue?
   B: .... (*couldn't/get here/before us*)
5 **A:** I can't understand where the cat is in all this rain.
   B: .... (*could/hide/in the shed*)

9 Complete the sentences with expressions of ability so that they are true for you. Use the ideas in the box to help you.

> cook   play a musical instrument   run a marathon
> ride a motorbike/horse   speak a language fluently

Example: *I used to be able to run a marathon when I was fitter.*

1 I used to …
2 Once, I …
3 One day, I hope …
4 I've never …
5 It would be nice …
6 If my life had been different, …

Long turn (Part 2)
stating preferences and speculating
▶ **EXAM** FOCUS p.190

1 Work in pairs and compare the photographs. Use some of these expressions of certainty, probability and doubt.

They seem/appear (to be) …
It looks like/as if (they are) …
It must/could/may/can't (be/have been) …
I'd imagine (that they are) …
I'm fairly/absolutely certain (they are) …
As far as I can see, (they are) …
I suppose (they are)…
They are definitely …

2 ▶ 21 **Read the exam task. Then listen to a student doing it. Which place did he choose?**

> Look at the photos, which show unusual places to stay. Compare the photographs and say which of the places you think would be more enjoyable to stay at.

3 Complete these sentences, which focus on expressions of speculation. Then listen again and check.

1 I'm not absolutely .... what the place on the right is.
2 It .... be an underwater hotel.
3 The other one .... to have been built in the trees.
4 The underwater hotel .... quite luxurious.
5 The treehouse .... to be more basic.
6 It would .... be less expensive to stay at.
7 It .... be an interesting experience to stay at both of them.
8 I'd .... the treehouse might not be such fun in bad weather.

4 ▶ 22 **Listen again to the sentences from Activity 3 and underline the words which are stressed. Practise saying them with the same 'certain' or 'uncertain' intonation.**

EXAM TIP

In the first part, summarise the main similarity and difference. Mention any other similarities and differences if you have time. Don't describe one picture in detail.

5 Work in pairs. Turn to page 135 and complete Task 1. Then turn to page 137 and swap roles for Task 2.

Vocabulary
describing places

1 What is your idea of a paradise on earth? Think about the landscape, the people and the way of life.

2 Look at the photograph of a place in Tibet. Which of these adjectives could you use to describe it?

bustling   cosy   inspiring   magnificent
mysterious   peaceful   polluted   remote
run-down

3 ▶ 23 Underline the stressed syllable in each adjective in Activity 2 and then listen and check. Practise saying the words.

4 Match some of the adjectives in Activity 2 to the groups of adjectives in italics which have the same meaning.

1 The most *dramatic/stunning/splendid/impressive* view I've seen is …
2 A/An *isolated/secluded/inaccessible/out-of-the-way* place I've been to is …
3 I find … a *tranquil/calm/soothing/relaxing* place to be.
4 I think … has a *weird/strange/curious/unusual* atmosphere.
5 Visiting … was an *uplifting/moving/stimulating/ spiritual* experience.

5 Complete the sentences in Activity 4 so that they are true for you. Then discuss in groups which view sounds the most dramatic, which place was the most isolated, etc.

Multiple choice (Part 4)
▶ **EXAM** FOCUS p.189

6 You will hear a journalist interviewing a travel writer called Olivia Rees about Shangri-La. Read the questions and options and underline the key words. Discuss other ways you could say these words.

7 ▶ 24 Listen and choose the best answer, A, B or C.

1 Olivia believes that the novel *Lost Horizon* was popular in the 1930s because
  A people needed an escape from reality at that time.
  B the film adaptation made it a household name.
  C it took place somewhere that very few travellers had visited.

2 In Olivia's opinion, people can still relate to the novel because
  A it involves choices which are relevant to us all.
  B adventure stories never go out of fashion.
  C family disagreements are always interesting.

3 The people of Shangri-La were considered to be unusual because of their
  A high level of educational achievement.
  B indifference to acquiring money.
  C ability to avoid ever looking older.

4 Olivia found it interesting that the author, James Hilton,
  A was influenced by Buddhist beliefs.
  B had only made one trip to Tibet.
  C got all his information from books and magazines.

5 Olivia says the similarities between the stories of Shambhala and Shangri-La show that Hilton
  A took an interest in Tibetan culture.
  B believed such a society could really exist.
  C was unable to think of original ideas.

6 Olivia says that the county of Zhongdian
  A was originally called Shangri-La.
  B is recognised as the setting for the novel.
  C has found a new source of income.

7 Olivia says the reaction of people who visit modern-day Shangri-La may be
  A surprise at the number of tourists who go there.
  B disappointment because it is different from the book's description.
  C dissatisfaction that the scenery is not beautiful.

8 Listen again and check your answers to question 1 in Activity 6. The audio script on page 213 will help you.

1 Which words from options A, B and C are mentioned in the recording?

2 Which words are a paraphrase of the correct answer?

3 Which words show why the wrong options are wrong?

9 What places in your country or elsewhere in the world

1 have a relaxed pace of life?

2 have/haven't lived up to your expectations?

3 are cut off from the outside world?

Vocabulary

travel: collocations and phrasal verbs

10 Choose the word in italics which does NOT collocate with the noun.

1 a *domestic/direct/long-distance/seasonal* flight

2 a *season/direct/one-way/open/return* ticket

3 a *sightseeing/package/round/guided* tour

4 a *package/camping/shopping/tourist* expedition

5 a *tourist/weekend/long-distance/sightseeing* excursion

6 a *business/coach/day/round/direct* trip

11 Have you ever almost missed a flight? What happened? Compare your experience with the text above.

Topic ▾	Posts ▾	Latest Post ▾
Family Trip	1	04 September

Last year we decided to **(1) get away** without the rest of the family as a birthday treat. My sister, who lives near the airport, offered to **(2) put us up** for the night and the next morning we **(3) set off** in plenty of time to drive to the airport. Even though the snow **(4) held** us **up** for a little while, the trip was fine and we got there in plenty of time.

My husband **(5) dropped** me **off** in front of the departures gate and he went to park the car while I joined a queue to **(6) check in** our bags for the flight.

However, ninety minutes later, the final call for our flight was being announced and my husband still wasn't back. I waited. Eventually, he **(7) turned up**, very stressed, and we arrived at the departure gate with only a few minutes to spare. Apparently he **(8) had left** his coat **behind** in the car after he'd parked and had to go back to get it because his passport was in the pocket. Unfortunately he'd also forgotten where he'd parked it!

12 Match the phrasal verbs (1–8) in the text to their meanings A–H.

A take (somebody/something) to a place and leave there

B register

C provide a bed

D leave

E have a holiday

F not remember to bring

G arrive

H delay

13 Work in pairs and describe a trip you have been on. Use some of the expressions in Activity 12 to describe the journey and place itself. Think about, for example:

- when you left home.
- how you got to your destination.
- who went with you.
- any problems during your journey.
- your reaction to the place when you got there.

Relative clauses

▶ **GRAMMAR** REFERENCE p.154

1 Read the text and guess which place is being described.

2 Decide which lines contain

A a defining relative clause (provides essential information).

B a non-defining relative clause (adds extra information).

3 In which line(s) could the relative pronoun (and preposition, if there is one)

A be replaced by *that*?

B be left out?

C be replaced by *where?*

4 Join these pairs of sentences using relative clauses. Add commas where necessary. There may be more than one possibility.

1 The nearest town is 5km from here. It doesn't have a train station.

2 Many local people now work in tourism. They used to work in the fishing industry.

3 Where's the bus? It goes to the beach.

4 This hotel belongs to a woman. She's not here at the moment.

5 In summer the water is always warm. You can go swimming.

6 That man is a tour guide. I met him yesterday.

7 The road takes you to the top of the mountain. It's very steep.

8 The place is very beautiful. We stayed there last summer.

5 Describe one of the most popular places in your country and why people go there. Use the phrases below.

It's a place which …

It's somewhere that …

The people who live there …

One reason why people like it is …

THE LAND OF ICE AND FIRE

The island, which is bigger than Ireland, has a population of only 370,000. Around two thirds of people live in the southwest of the country, where the capital Reykjavík is situated. In recent years the island, whose main attraction is its abundance of volcanoes and geysers, has become increasingly 5 dependent on tourism. It's easy to understand why most tourists who come to the island choose to come in summer, when there are over twenty hours of daylight. But although it's known as 'the land of ice and fire', winter temperatures, which average about −1° C, are not as cold as you might expect. One 10 of the places which tourists most want to go to is the Blue Lagoon, a naturally heated pool of seawater in the middle of a lava field, in which you can bathe all year round.

so, such, too, enough, very

▶ **GRAMMAR** REFERENCE p.155

6 Look at the underlined examples with *so/such/enough* and *very* and match 1–5 to A–C to make rules about how they are used in a sentence. Some letters are used more than once.

It rained <u>so heavily</u> and the roads were <u>so dangerous that</u> I decided not to go.

It takes <u>too long to walk</u> there and a taxi will cost <u>too much</u>.

He was in <u>such a temper that</u> we couldn't argue with him.

She didn't have <u>enough money to buy</u> the coat she wanted.

He's <u>clever enough to find</u> the solution if he concentrates.

<u>Very few people</u> have been there and yet there are <u>so many wonderful places to visit</u>.

1 *so* is used

2 *enough* is used

3 *such* is used

4 *too* is used

5 *very* is used

A before a noun/after an adjective.

B before a noun (+ adjective).

C before an adjective/adverb/determiner (e.g. *much/many/few*).

1 Complete the sentences with *enough*, *so*, *such*, *too* or *very*.

1 He was .... surprised that he went to check.

2 My brother isn't practical .... to put up a shelf.

3 Isn't your car .... old to drive all that way?

4 There aren't .... many people who could do that.

5 We had .... a good time that we decided to stay for longer.

6 Is that fruit ripe .... to eat yet?

7 He did .... well in his exams that nobody believed him at first.

8 It's a .... interesting book.

2 Complete the sentences so they are true about you. Then work in pairs and compare.

1 I haven't got enough time …

2 It's such a wonderful opportunity …

3 It's so exciting …

4 I don't think I'm old enough …

5 I have very few …

6 It's too expensive …

it is, there is

▶ **GRAMMAR** REFERENCE p.155

3 Choose the correct pronoun in italics.

(1) *It/There* is very expensive to take a taxi in some countries and **(2)** *it/there* is always the problem of whether and how much to tip the driver. In some countries **(3)** *it/there* is not customary to tip them at all so **(4)** *it/there* doesn't seem to be a general rule. For that reason **(5)** *it/there* is a good idea to find out what the customs are before visiting a country otherwise **(6)** *it/there* might be misunderstandings. And **(7)** *it/there* is no point offending people unnecessarily these days when it is so easy to find out if **(8)** *it/there* is a difference in social customs.

4 Complete these sentences with *it* or *there* and a form of *be* if necessary.

1 .... not unusual to have dinner at 10.30p.m.

2 .... common for men to greet each other with a kiss on the cheek.

3 .... might sometimes be applause when a guest arrives.

4 .... no need to tip waiters in restaurants.

5 Make sentences with *it* and *there* to describe customs in your own country.

Key word transformation (Part 4)

▶ **EXAM** FOCUS p.187

6 Complete the second sentence so that it has a similar meaning to the first sentence, using the word given. Do not change the word given. You must use between two and five words, including the word given.

1 It was too foggy for us to ski.
SO
It was .... not ski.

2 He couldn't afford a taxi, so he went by bus.
ENOUGH
He .... for a taxi, so he went by bus.

3 There was so much traffic that we missed the show.
SUCH
There was .... that we missed the show.

4 I had a wonderful time and I really enjoyed seeing everyone again.
GREAT
I had a wonderful time and .... everyone again.

5 He said I didn't need to make an appointment.
NEED
He said .... for me to make an appointment.

6 I think that taking your coat is unnecessary.
POINT
I think that .... taking your coat.

Essay (Part 1)
including a range of structures
▶ **WRITING** REFERENCE pp.166 and 167

1 Discuss whether you agree or disagree with the statements about travel and say why.

1 It broadens the mind.
2 It is better to spend money on possessions.
3 You don't need to travel because you can experience what countries are like online.
4 Travel develops skills such as self-reliance.
5 Travel is good for your CV.

2 Look at the essay title and think of points for and against. How would you organise the essay?

> Some people argue that travelling abroad is a valuable part of every young person's education. To what extent would you agree with this opinion?
>
> **Notes**
>
> Write about:
>
> 1 the cost
> 2 being independent
> 3 job advantages (your own idea)

3 Read the model essay opposite. What are the main points and the supporting information in each paragraph?

4 Complete the sentences with the linking words/phrases in the box.

even if   if   so that   this   unless   which

1 .... you apply for a programme .... provides accommodation, you still have to pay for the flight.
2 Many young people work in a restaurant .... they can save enough for the air fare.
3 You don't gain independence from going abroad .... you learn the language. .... allows you to mix with the people.
4 .... you spend most of your time with people of your own nationality, it can turn out to be just like an extended holiday.

Some people argue that travelling abroad is a valuable part of every young person's education.
To what extent would you agree with this opinion?

In some parts of the world, travelling abroad before starting university or finding a job is seen as a very useful experience to have.

However, obviously not everyone can afford it. Even if you apply for a volunteer programme which provides food and accommodation, you still have to find the money to travel there. Many young people work in a shop or restaurant so that they can save up enough for the air fare.

In addition, it could be argued that you don't necessarily gain independence from going abroad unless you learn the language. This allows you to mix with the people living there. If you spend most of your time with people of your own nationality, it can turn out to be just like an extended holiday. You may not learn a lot from it.

On the positive side, having lived in another country is often an advantage when applying for jobs because it shows you have experienced other cultures and developed some life skills.

Personally, I think the ideal time to travel is when you are young and have no commitments. Having said that, it is not practical for everyone.

5 Work in pairs. Turn to page 139 and follow the instructions.

EXAM TIP

Include a range of simple and complex sentences to make your essay more effective.

LANGUAGE TIP

Try to include adverbs which show your attitude, such as *personally*, *obviously* and *unfortunately*.

6 Exchange essays with another student and think about the questions.

1 Have you included all the information required?
2 Have you organised the essay into paragraphs?
3 Have you included linking words?
4 Are your main points backed up with supporting detail?
5 Have you included a mix of simple and complex sentences?

1 Complete this story about Mothman, using the correct form of the modal verbs in brackets.

Mothman

Many years ago a strange creature was spotted in West Virginia in the USA. It looked like a man with wings and most witnesses claim it **(1)** .... (*must/be*) nearly two metres tall; others say it **(2)** .... (*may/have*) eyes in its chest. Nobody is very sure what this creature **(3)** .... (*could/be*). Some people today think these witnesses **(4)** .... (*might/mistake*) big owls flying around for the creature. Others feel it **(5)** .... (*must/be*) a UFO because there were also strange lights around it. And even people who think there **(6)** .... (*can/be*) such things as a Mothman enjoy watching the films about it or visiting the four-metre sculpture in West Virginia.

2 Complete the text with the correct relative pronoun in each gap.

Cape Cod

Cape Cod, **(1)** .... is referred to locally as 'the Cape', is famous around the world as a summer playground for the rich and powerful, **(2)** .... own charming seafront summer houses there. But it is also the destination of choice for many East-Coast middle-class families **(3)** .... come to enjoy the relaxing pace of life. It's a place **(4)** .... people come to fish, sail and generally get in tune with nature. It is hard to overestimate the Cape's stunning beauty. The coast, **(5)** .... faces the Atlantic, amounts to one long, awesome beach, **(6)** .... is backed by giant sand dunes and protected from development. The towns and villages are very attractive, with pretty cottages and clapboard houses, **(7)** .... were built by sea captains 200 years ago.

However, unlike other US beach destinations such as Florida or California, **(8)** .... it is consistently hot, Cape Cod can be misty and even chilly occasionally during the summer season.

3 Choose the correct option (A, B, C or D) to complete the sentences.

1 The fishing village was .... far away to visit for one day.

   A so   **B** very   **C** too   **D** enough

2 I need to get a .... ticket because I am coming back this evening.

   A round   **B** return   **C** package   **D** direct

3 There's no .... buying a car if you're never going to drive it.

   A reason   **B** need   **C** point   **D** objective

4 It was .... a beautiful place that they decided to stay there longer.

   A so   **B** enough   **C** really   **D** such

5 It's a very .... location, cut off from the outside world.

   A alone   **B** far   **C** remote   **D** unconnected

6 You can't just turn .... like this, unexpectedly, and expect me to be free.

   A on   **B** up   **C** in   **D** off

8 Moving on

Multiple matching (Part 3)

▶ **EXAM** FOCUS p.189

1 You will hear five different people talking about the future of their profession. What do you think these jobs involve?

Example: *I think a robotics engineer spends a lot of time designing software systems for robots.*

robotics engineer   social-networking counsellor   spaceship pilot
vertical farmer   virtual lawyer

2 ▶ 25 Listen and choose from the list A–H what each speaker says their job will involve in the future. Use the letters only once. There are three extra letters which you do not need to use.

A working with new employees	Speaker 1 ☐
B getting new qualifications	Speaker 2 ☐
C spending less time travelling	Speaker 3 ☐
D enabling a service to be provided at a lower cost	Speaker 4 ☐
E being available on demand	Speaker 5 ☐
F designing new products	
G working longer hours	
H making better use of power resources	

3 Work in pairs and compare your answer for Speaker 1. Then look at the audio script on page 214. Underline the part of the text that gives the correct answer.

4 Now listen to Speakers 2–5 again. Identify the key phrases that give the answers. Check with a partner and then look at the audio script on page 214.

5 Work in pairs and discuss the questions.

1 Which of the jobs would you most like to have? Why?

2 Which of the jobs wouldn't you consider doing? Why?

3 Which of the jobs do you think is the most: worthwhile? highly skilled? stressful? physically demanding?

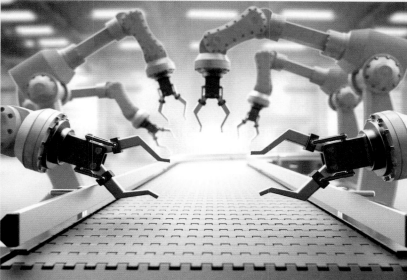

Vocabulary

collocations and phrasal verbs with *work*

6 Choose the correct word in italics. Then work in pairs and decide if you agree with the statements.

1 Helping people gives me a lot of *work/job/employment* satisfaction.
2 I expect there isn't much *job/work/career* security in counselling.
3 Until quite recently, engineering used to be seen as a male *employment/occupation/work*.
4 People who work in the medical *profession/career/occupation* need complete dedication.
5 A good place to look for a job is through a(n) *work/profession/employment* agency.
6 It's important to look for a job that offers good *work/career/profession* opportunities.

7 Match the phrasal verbs in italics to the definitions A–F.

1 We finally *worked out* how much tax we would have to pay.
2 Things *worked out* really *well* for him after he moved abroad for his job.
3 I *get worked up* about things too easily at work, especially if a customer is rude or difficult.
4 I *work out* at the gym three or four times a week during my lunch hour.
5 We need to *work out* who would be the best person to talk to the boss.
6 If the meeting is cancelled, we'll just have to *work around* it and sort the problem out ourselves.

A do exercise
B become angry or upset
C have a (good/bad) result
D calculate
E manage a situation
F plan/decide

8 Write questions using the phrasal verbs in Activity 7. Then ask your partner.

Example: *What do you get worked up about?*
Do you think working out at the gym is the best way to keep fit?

LANGUAGE TIP

When a phrasal verb has two different meanings, they may use different grammatical structures. For example *work out* (solve) takes a direct object.

*I **worked out** the problem.*
*I **worked** the problem **out**.*

But *work out* (take exercise at the gym) does not.

*I **work out** every day.*

Collaborative task and discussion (Parts 3 and 4)
agreeing and disagreeing

▶ **EXAM** FOCUS p.190

1 **Look at the examiner's instructions and the diagram and underline the key words.**

> Here are some different jobs that college students can choose for a career and a question for you to discuss. First you have some time to look at the task.

accountant

social worker

Are these jobs difficult?

taxi driver

dentist

hairdresser

2 **Look at the statements made by some students. For each one, mark whether you agree (✓), disagree (✗) or are not sure (?).**

1 Being a dentist is difficult because you have to concentrate all the time. If you make a mistake, you could really hurt your patient.

2 I think hairdressing is difficult because people may get upset if they don't like their new haircut. It's a big responsibility.

3 Taxi drivers have to work long hours and sitting in traffic is stressful – so for me that would be a difficult job.

3 ▶ **26** **Listen and copy the intonation patterns in these phrases for agreeing and disagreeing.**

1 Actually, I'm not sure about that.
2 I agree up to a point but …
3 I suppose so.
4 That's just what I was going to say!
5 That's a good point.
6 Really? That's not how I see it.

4 **Work in pairs. Complete the statements with your own ideas. Then take turns reading them aloud. Use the phrases in Activity 3 to agree and disagree with each statement.**

1 The best/worst thing about being an accountant …
2 The most/least rewarding thing about being a social worker …
3 I would hate to be a/an … because …

EXAM TIP

Try to discuss each prompt in the exam task without spending too long on any one of them.

---

5 **Do the speaking task in Activity 1.**

6 **Work in pairs. Decide which of the jobs would be the most difficult. You have a minute to do this.**

7 **Discuss the questions.**

1 Do you think people should be paid more for doing a dangerous job?
2 Would you want to have the same job/career for your whole life?
3 Do you think it's possible for anyone to become a police officer?

1 Have you ever had an interview for something? How did you feel?

2 ▶ 27 You will hear people talking in three different situations. For each question, choose the best answer, A, B or C.

1 You hear a manager talking to an employee. What is he doing?
   A requesting some information
   B advising her about a problem
   C explaining how to do something

2 You hear part of a radio programme on the subject of job interviews. What does the presenter recommend?
   A doing research about the company
   B asking lots of questions
   C repeating key information

3 You hear a discussion between two colleagues. What is the woman doing?
   A reminding the man to do something
   B accusing the man of not telling her something
   C denying she had forgotten to do something

Reporting verbs

▶ **GRAMMAR** REFERENCE p.156

3 Complete the reported statements with the correct form of the verbs in brackets.

1 'Everyone should find out as much as possible about their prospective employer.'
The presenter .... (advised)

2 'You forgot to give me the message.'
Mike's boss .... (accused)

3 'I didn't take any calls from the customer.'
Mike .... (denied)

4 'I can find out what went wrong.'
Mike .... (offered)

5 'Why don't you apply for the job?' said Joe.
Joe .... (suggested)

6 'Ella, please help me with this report. I can't do it,' said Jack.
Jack .... (persuaded)

7 'You need to fill in the form in black ink, Ruby.'
Ruby's manager .... (explained)

4 Look at the examples in Activity 3 and match the reporting verbs in the box to the patterns. For some verbs more than one pattern is possible.

accuse advise deny explain offer suggest
persuade

A verb + object + infinitive, e.g. *remind*, …
B verb + infinitive
C verb + *-ing*
D verb + object + *of* + *-ing*
E verb + *that* + clause

say, speak, talk, tell

5 Complete the sentences with the correct form of the verbs in the box. You can use the verbs more than once. In which sentences is it possible to use more than one of the verbs?

say   speak   talk   tell

1 Your manager shouldn't .... like that to you!

2 Everyone .... I'm very lucky to have such a good job.

3 Don't .... me you haven't filled in the application form yet!

4 Why don't you just .... there's been a misunderstanding?

5 That was a very silly thing to .... to a customer.

6 Our manager .... to everyone in the team about applying for the new post.

6 Work in pairs. Read the problem and the advice. Which advice do you agree with? Explain your answer.

7 Report the advice given to Sophie using suitable reporting verbs.

Example: *Tim reminded Sophie that it was her manager's responsibility to manage staff.*

Problems at work – solved

I work as a marketing assistant for a media company. I only joined the company a year ago and I'm really enjoying working there. My problem is that whenever our manager is out of the office, one of my co-workers takes an extended coffee or lunch break, or leaves work at least 30 minutes early. I don't like having to cover for him and I don't know whether I should say anything to my manager.

Sophie

Advice:

Tim: Don't forget it's your manager's responsibility to manage her staff properly, not yours.

Elena: I wouldn't tell your manager or you'll get a reputation for telling tales.

Rory: Why don't you have a coffee with your co-worker and explain your concerns?

Maia: Ignore what your co-worker does. It's actually none of your business and he may be dealing with personal problems that you aren't aware of.

Rick: Your manager may react badly when she finds out what's been going on and that you haven't done anything about it – she may feel she's unable to trust you.

Anna: Explain to your co-worker that his behaviour is making you feel uncomfortable and that if things don't change, you will be forced to report him to your manager.

Multiple matching (Part 7)

▶ **EXAM** FOCUS p.187

1 You are going to read an article about five people whose work involves them living and working abroad. Work in pairs and answer the questions.

1 Why do some people choose to go to work in another country?

2 What do you think the disadvantages of living abroad would be?

3 Which countries would you like to go to work in? Why?

4 How easy do you think it is for migrant workers to work in your country? Explain your answers.

2 Read questions 1–10 and underline the key words and phrases. The first one is done for you.

> **EXAM TIP**
>
> The information in the text may not come in the same order as in the questions.

3 For questions 2–10, choose the best answer from the people A–E.

Which person mentions

having always had a <u>passion to see the world</u>?	1	B
wanting work to be more of a challenge?	2	
deciding to live abroad because it was less expensive?	3	
taking a while to adapt to a new way of living?	4	
finding the ideal job by accident?	5	
discovering unexpected things about living in a place?	6	
regularly travelling long distances to do a specific job?	7	
sacrificing career opportunities in order to live abroad?	8	
appreciating the long holidays which the job makes possible?	9	
living in a wild and uninhabited environment?	10	

Vocabulary

linking words and expressions

4 Look at the linking expressions underlined in the text. Which are used to

1 give extra information?

2 express reason/result?

3 express a purpose for doing something?

4 contrast information?

5 Look carefully at how the linking expressions are used in context, including the punctuation. Complete the sentences with the linking words or phrases in the box.

---
although   as well as   despite   however
in order to   so   that's why   too
---

1 I applied for the job. .... , I didn't get it, unfortunately.

2 .... I am more than qualified for the job, I didn't even get an interview.

3 I love travelling. .... the work was perfect for me.

4 I think the reason I didn't get the job was my poor Spanish, ... I have enrolled on a beginners' course.

5 I am trying to improve my French, ... learning Spanish.

6 .... improve my vocabulary, I am watching French films.

7 .... the high salary I was offered, I decided to turn down the job.

8 I enjoyed my time at the law firm. I made a lot of friends there ....

6 Write sentences that are true for you, using the linking words in Activity 5.

7 Work in pairs and discuss the questions. Try to use expressions from Activities 4 and 5.

1 Which of these jobs would you find the most interesting? Why?

2 Which do you think is more important: the job you do or the place where you live? Why?

To the ends of the earth

Five people tell us how they've found success living and working in exotic locations.

A **Emma** <u>While</u> I enjoyed my job at a busy surgery in Oxford, checking people's blood pressure wasn't really stretching me enough, <u>so</u> I applied for and got a job with the Flying Doctor service in Australia. We doctors are dropped off by plane at remote houses in the bush hundreds of miles from the town where we're based. We use the houses for our clinics. Common problems we have to treat are injuries after falls from horses, farm accidents, snake bites, <u>as well as</u> having to attend road accidents in the middle of nowhere.
I wanted a job which would enable me to experience a different kind of life, and this job certainly does that.

B **Holly** I've had the travel bug ever since I was very young. As soon as I left university, where I studied journalism, I got myself an administrative job and saved up enough money to go backpacking to New Zealand. When I got back, I started job-hunting <u>so that</u> I could save money for another big trip, which is when I stumbled across an advert for a job with a publisher of travel guides. When I was offered the job and was sent to South Africa <u>to</u> write a blog, I could have burst with excitement. The best part of my job is being able to take time off to go travelling for a couple of months. <u>Although</u> I travel for work, it's not the same as a holiday, when I can switch off and don't have deadlines. <u>Still</u>, I can't think of any job I'd rather be doing.

C **Jonathan** I'm a graphic designer, and when I was made redundant I decided to set up my own business with my wife. The only problem was meeting the same standard of living – apartment, car, meals out. <u>That's why</u> I hit on the idea of moving somewhere in the world where you can enjoy the same lifestyle for far less. <u>In order to</u> help us make the decision, we made contact through Facebook and Twitter with other people who have done the same thing.

D **Annie** I was on a business trip to Buenos Aires for a couple of weeks when I met an Italian who became the love of my life. <u>Since</u> I was freelance and he was a TV producer in Argentina it made sense that I would be the one to move. <u>Despite</u> this, the decision was agonising <u>as</u> I was building a career as a newspaper correspondent and all my contacts were in London. There was <u>also</u> the issue of leaving my family, friends and home but I knew if I didn't give it a try, I'd regret it forever. Fede took time off to help me settle in, but then I began to realise the enormity of what I'd done. <u>Because</u> I didn't speak Spanish very well, I felt frustrated and stupid but four months on I don't regret a thing.

E **James** As an engineer, I happily accepted an invitation to build a scientific research centre in Antarctica. Apart from scientists and explorers, this place has been untouched by civilisation, which means we have only the basic requirements for human survival. From the moment you arrive you are faced with danger, whether it is landing in a plane on an ice runway or travelling across sea ice. <u>However</u>, seeing giant icebergs for the first time blew my mind. There are lots of surprises <u>too</u>, such as suffering from sunburn and the twenty-four hours of sunlight a day which makes it difficult to sleep <u>even though</u> you are exhausted.

1 ▶ 28 You'll hear part of a job interview with Lauren. Listen and underline eight factual mistakes in Lauren's email to her mum.

Hi Mum,

The interview for the job in Greece went well, I think. First the interviewer asked me how I'd heard about it. I told her I'd spotted the advert in a local newspaper and thought it was something I'd enjoy doing.

Then she said the job would involve looking after young teenagers and asked me whether I'd had much experience of doing this. So I told her that I look after Nancy and Harry now and again and that I was taking them camping the next day. She said I might be unlucky, as she'd heard it was going to snow. Then she told me to enjoy the weekend and said she'd phone soon. She told me not to worry if I didn't hear anything for a few weeks.

Fingers crossed, Lx

2 Work in pairs. Correct the incorrect details. Then listen again and check your answers.

Example: *I told her I'd spotted the advert on the internet.*

Reported statements

▶ **GRAMMAR** REFERENCE p.156

LANGUAGE TIP

You don't need to change the tense if the situation remains the same and it is clear from the context. *She said she looks after Nancy and Harry.* (and she still does)

3 Turn to page 158 and follow the instructions for Exercises 2 and 3.

4 Complete the table to show how direct speech changes to reported statements. Use the audio script on page 215 to help you.

Direct speech	Reported statements
past simple	past perfect
present perfect	
present simple	
will	
present continuous	
be going to	
would, might	

Reported questions and imperatives

▶ **GRAMMAR** REFERENCE p.157

5 How did the interviewer say sentences A–D in direct speech?

A She asked me how I'd heard about the job.

....

B She asked me whether I'd had much experience of doing this.

....

C She told me to enjoy my weekend.

....

D She told me not to worry.

....

6 Look at the things that Lauren's friend Jack asked or said after she started the job. Change them to reported speech, using *tell, ask,* etc. or a reporting verb.

1 'Do you get paid well?'
2 'Let me know if there are any more job vacancies!'
3 'Who are you going to be working with next week?'
4 'What did you do yesterday?'
5 'Don't forget to take some photos.'
6 'We'll email you if we come over to Greece.'

LANGUAGE TIP

Remember to change pronouns, e.g. *I → she; me → her.*
Time expressions may change, e.g. *yesterday → the day before.*

7 Work in pairs and follow the instructions.

1 Tell your partner four things about yourself. One of them should be false.
2 Join up with another pair. Tell the others what your partner told you.
3 Guess which of the four things they tell you is untrue.

Concrete and abstract nouns

1 Which word in each pair is a concrete noun such as a person and which is an abstract noun?

engineering/engineer   journalist/journalism
music/musician   visitor/visit

2 What suffixes do you often add to a word to make a concrete noun? Complete the table. Add some more words with the same suffixes to the list.

	Abstract noun	Concrete noun
1	creation	*creator*
2	advice	
3		employer/employee
4	tourism	
5		applicant
6		representative
7	childhood	
8		politician

3 Decide if the words are verbs or adjectives. What is the abstract noun for each?

angry arrive behave confide difficult friendly
know permit progress sad short strong

4 Complete the sentences with the noun form of the words in brackets. Add *a/an* if necessary.

1 The school won't give us .... (*permit*) to take a week off during term time.

2 I'm finally beginning to make .... (*progress*) with my maths and science.

3 She had .... (*difficult*) understanding what I wanted her to do.

4 We're going on .... (*visit*) to Rome next week.

5 I can't carry this any further, I haven't got the .... (*strong*)!

6 Cara and I have .... (*friend*) built on respect and trust.

Word formation (Part 3)

▶ **EXAM** FOCUS p.186

5 Use the word given in capitals at the end of some of the lines to form a word that fits in the gap in the same line.

> **EXAM TIP**
>
> Read the text first to see what it is about and try to predict some of the missing words.

The video game designer

At the office where video games are designed, everyone is working hard on the **(0)** production of their latest game. The licence for the game cost millions of dollars – so there's no room for any mistakes. **PRODUCE**

However, despite the time pressures and **(1)** .... working hours, everyone seems surprisingly calm. A man called Tim, **REGULAR**

who has overall **(2)** .... for the design, **RESPONSIBLE**

explains why over 100 people are involved in the **(3)** .... of just one video game. **CREATE**

Apparently it's because of the complex **(4)** .... which is involved. He himself is **TECHNIQUE**

not actually **(5)** .... involved in doing **PERSON**

any of the drawings. That job is done by the team of **(6)** .... which he employs **ART**

to work for him. Neither is he involved in the computer side of the games. What he has to do is to make all the plans and **(7)** .... One would imagine this is **DECIDE**

not always totally straightforward! But Tim claims to find his work **(8)** .... and **ENJOY**

appears to welcome the challenges he must have to face every day.

6 Would you like to do this job? Why/Why not?

1 Read the letter of application. What job is Magda applying for? Is she qualified for the job?

Dear Sir Madam,

Following your recent advertisement in *The Traveller*, I would like to apply for the **(1)** *job/position* of hotel receptionist.

(2) *Right now/At present* I am completing my second year at Poznań University, where I have been studying Spanish. I would now like to spend some time developing my confidence in spoken Spanish.

As well as Polish and Spanish, I also speak fluent English. I **(3)** *got/obtained* the diploma you **(4)** *require/want* three years ago and I have worked in hotels **(5)** *on a number of occasions/lots of times*.

(6) *In addition/Also*, **(7)** *I possess/I've got* the energy and good communication skills which you are looking for.

I would be grateful if you could send me further details of the job, including the salary. I enclose my CV and I **(8)** *look forward/am looking forward* to hearing from you **(9)** *soon/in the near future*. I have only three weeks **(10)** *left/remaining* of my university year. After that time, I will be **(11)** *free/available* if **(12)** *I am required/you need me* to come for an interview.

Yours faithfully,

Magda Koblewska

2 Choose the most suitable options in italics in the letter. Explain your choices.

3 In which paragraph is Magda

A saying why she wants the job?
B explaining why she is suitable for the job?
C saying when she can meet her possible employers?
D asking for information?

4 Look at the letter again and find fixed phrases for 1–5.

1 to say where you heard about the job
2 to say which job you're interested in
3 to give details of your qualifications
4 to ask for further information
5 to explain what you are sending with the letter

Letter of application (Part 2)
using formal language

▶ **WRITING** REFERENCE p.169

5 Read the exam task and the advertisement. Underline the important information in the advertisement.

> You have seen a job advertisement on the internet and have decided to apply for it. Read the advertisement and write your **letter** in **140–190** words.

Home | **About us** | **Activities** | **Jobs**

Wanted

Young people of 18+ to become activity instructors with an international summer school. Experience is not important, as training will be given. Love of sport, energy, enthusiasm and an ability to relate to young people is essential.

6 Read the exam task again. Make a detailed plan about what will be in each paragraph of your letter. Follow the structure of Magda's letter and use some of the fixed phrases and expressions.

EXAM TIP

If you begin the letter with the name of the person you are writing to, end the letter *Yours sincerely*. If you start with *Dear Sir/Madam*, end with *Yours faithfully*.

7 Write your letter. When you have finished, check your work using the checklist on page 165 to help you.

1 **Choose the correct option (A, B, or C) to complete the sentences.**

1 I'm happy at my place of work but there aren't many .... opportunities.

A profession   B work   C career

2 Have you managed to work .... how much overtime we've earned this week?

A out   B in   C up

3 I enjoy working there, ... there's a lot of pressure at times.

A although   B despite   C however

4 I have an interview next week. .... I'm going to get something smart to wear.

A That's why   B So   C In order to

5 Can I borrow your computer .... I can do my CV?

A so that   B to   C in order

6 There is a problem with staffing at the moment but we'll have to work .... it.

A for   B around   C over

2 **Complete the sentences with the correct form of the verbs in the box. You can use the verbs more than once.**

---
say speak talk tell
---

1 He really .... a lot of rubbish sometimes.

2 She's very quiet and never seems to have much to .... for herself.

3 Sorry I can't understand you. Please .... more slowly.

4 I think most people .... to themselves; they just won't admit it!

5 We're very honest with each other. I can .... anything to her.

6 Everyone gets a bit nervous when they have to .... in public.

7 Don't .... me you've never had a job!

8 Why don't you just .... your boss you need a day off?

3 **Complete the second sentence so that it has a similar meaning to the first sentence, using the word given. Use between two and five words, including the word given.**

1 'Make sure you lock up when you leave the office tonight,' Jake told his colleagues.
REMINDED
Jake .... lock up when they left the office that night.

2 'Carol, why not take a break while things are quiet?' the manager said.
SUGGESTED
The manager .... take a break while things were quiet.

3 'It was Anna who lost the contract,' said Jon.
ACCUSED
Jon .... losing the contract.

4 'You mustn't talk to the press about the incident,' the boss said to us.
WARNED
The boss .... talk to the press about the incident.

5 'I'm really sorry that I didn't meet the deadline,' said Joanna.
APOLOGISED
Joanna .... meeting the deadline.

6 'I'm going to hand in my notice tomorrow,' said Alfie.
THE
Alfie decided to hand in .... day.

7 'If I were you, I would look for another job,' said Max.
RECOMMENDED
Max .... for another job.

8 'I didn't break the photocopier,' said Maria.
DENIED
Maria .... the photocopier.

9 Lucky break?

1 Discuss the questions.

1 Do you tend to make decisions only after careful consideration or quickly, without much thought?

2 In which important situations have you found it easy or difficult to decide on a course of action?

3 What are the most important life decisions? Would you ever leave these to instinct or chance? Give reasons.

Gapped text (Part 6)

▶ **EXAM** FOCUS p.187

2 Read the title and the first paragraph and guess why the writer of the article recommends taking a chance. Then read the article quickly to see if you were right.

3 Six sentences have been removed from the article. Choose from the sentences A–G the one which fits each gap 1–6. There is one extra sentence which you do not need to use.

A These results probably indicate that the changes that were made were long overdue.

B This isn't to say that everyone considering a drastic change in life should leap into action.

C They did not enjoy the experience but the results were superb.

D However, a random change can also lead us into behaving in a way that we might not have imagined.

E The reason we haven't made them already is probably because we tend to stick with what is safe and familiar.

F Nonetheless, it is important to know when to stop.

G He asked people who were agonizing over a life decision to take part in an experiment he had set up.

4 Discuss the questions. Give examples.

1 Do you believe that people 'make their own luck' or that it is down to chance?

2 Do you try to plan your life or wait and see what happens?

3 Are you prepared to take risks to get what you want?

EXAM TIP

Make sure you read the whole text for gist before focusing on the missing sentences.

Big decision ahead? Just take a chance

The decision-making process is never easy. Emotions can cloud our judgement. The more information you have, the easier a decision should be but more choice frequently results in information overload, which can be overwhelming and have the opposite effect. In fact, at times, relying on chance or an outside intervention can actually help us to make better decisions.

The first reason for this is that by deciding to follow a random instruction, we can end up making decisions that we should have been making all along. [1] Tossing a coin and deciding that 'if the coin comes up heads, I'll propose or resign or have a baby' may be the only way that some of us can find the energy to make tough decisions.

A few years ago the economist Stephen Levitt found evidence for this theory. [2] They were required to log onto the website he had launched, answer some questions and then hand over responsibility to the flip of a digital coin.

As the months went past, Levitt followed up, asking the volunteers whether they had obeyed the coin or ignored it and how they were now feeling about the decision.

It's an odd experiment but what makes it powerful is that the toss of the coin randomly divided people into two groups, one pushed towards action and one pushed towards caution, depending on whether the coin came up 'heads' or 'tails'. In fact, people did tend to obey the coin, and the majority of those in the 'action' group reported being happier several months on. [3] The research also suggests that, if this is the case, we should probably get on with it, with the help of a coin if necessary.

Randomness, then, can prompt us into taking actions that we fear. [4] A simple example of this unpredictable behaviour emerged after an Underground strike in London. Three economists looked at data which identified regular commuters who had to find a different route to work during the strike. What was surprising was that one in 20 of these individuals stuck to their new routes after the strike was over. Even commuters, whom we would imagine had perfected the most efficient way to make their daily journey, can come up with a better route when forced to do so.

Many creative types have used this principle to their advantage. Perhaps the most famous example is the *Oblique Strategies*, a set of cards assembled by artist Peter Schmidt and musician Brian Eno. The cards are full of complicated instructions which were used while working with David Bowie on some of his celebrated albums, and also with the band Coldplay. Great guitarists would find themselves having to play the drums or jump randomly between chords that Eno was indicating on a blackboard. [5]

One can, of course, take the idea too far. It is true that randomness may well help us to think and behave more creatively. [6] Once we have found a life we love, we are probably better off staying with the status quo.

Vocabulary
chance

5 Look at these expressions and collocations with *chance*. Which one means *impossible, unlikely, possible, very likely*?

1 There's a good chance that we'll be able to catch that train.
2 There's a slight chance of rain.
3 There's no chance of him changing his mind at this stage.
4 There's a chance that I'll be able to pay you back soon.

6 Choose the correct word in italics.

1 I bumped into Matt *by/on* chance yesterday in the street.
2 I'm going to *make/take* a chance and employ him.
3 We are leaving the decision *at/to* chance.
4 I think, with your qualifications, you may be *in/on* with a chance of getting the job.
5 Are you hungry yet, *with/by* any chance?

opportunity, possibility

7 Replace the word *chance* with either *opportunity/opportunities* or *possibility*. Then complete the rules below.

1 I am grateful to have the chance to go and work in France.
2 There's no chance of me passing the exam this year.
3 I doubt there will be another chance for me to explain my side of things.
4 There is a slight chance that they could win the match.
5 There must be equal chances for everyone in education.
• .... is used for a situation in which it is possible to do something you want to do.
• .... is used for something that may or may not happen.

8 Complete these sentences about your own life (e.g. plans, jobs, marriage, family) and discuss them in pairs.

1 There's no chance …
2 At the earliest opportunity, I hope to …
3 I … by chance.
4 I'd like to have the opportunity …
5 There is a slight possibility …

Conditional forms

▶ **GRAMMAR** REFERENCE p.158

1 Read the extract. Is this the same in your country?

The world's favourite number

<u>When you ask</u> people around the world to pick an odd number between 1 and 10, more often than not <u>they choose</u> 7. <u>If you ask</u> them why, <u>they'll probably say</u> it's their favourite number. Known as 'lucky 7', there are seven days in the week, seven colours of the rainbow, seven seas and seven continents.

For most people, 13 is regarded as unlucky, although <u>if you're speaking</u> to an Italian <u>they'll probably choose</u> 13 as their lucky number and <u>may say</u> 17 is unlucky!

Of course <u>if you were playing</u> the lottery, <u>you might never</u> win even <u>if you chose</u> your lucky number every time. But <u>if you won, you would doubtless say</u> it was because it was a lucky number!

2 Which underlined verb patterns in Activity 1 are:

a) generally true?
b) possible/likely?
c) imaginary?

3 Write verb forms for:

a) zero conditional (if + ………… + …………).
b) first conditional (if + ………… + …………).
c) second conditional (if + ………… + …………).

4 Answer these questions about the form of conditionals and check in the Grammar Reference.

1 In the first conditional, which modals and verb forms can be used instead of *will*?

2 In the second conditional, which other modals can be used instead of *would*?

5 Complete the questions about imaginary situations with the correct form of the words in the box. Add pronouns where necessary.

drive/ring/answer   find/do   pay for/can   see/say
take/return   wear/not suit/tell

1 If you accidentally ………… something expensive from a shop, ………… it?

2 If you ………… a wallet with lots of money in the park, what ………… with it?

3 If you ………… and your mobile phone ………… , ………… it?

4 If a friend ………… something which ………… him/her, ………… him/her the truth?

5 ………… music if you ………… download it for free?

6 If you ………… a child bullying another child, ………… anything to him/her?

6 Ask a partner what he/she would do if he/she had the 'moral dilemmas' in Activity 5. Be honest!

Example: *1 Yes, I might be tempted to keep it, but I'd definitely take it back.*

7 Decide how likely these situations are, and use the words in brackets to make questions. Then work in pairs and ask each other the questions.

1 If (*you/become*) a famous film star, who (*you/want*) to be your co-star?

2 If (*you/meet*) anyone in the world, who (*you/want*) it to be?

3 If (*you/decide*) to learn another language, which one (*you/choose*) to learn?

4 If (*you/have*) the opportunity to go to any place in the world, where (*you/go*)?

5 If (*you/have*) the chance to do anything this evening, what (*you/love*) to do?

6 If (*the weather/be*) chilly this weekend, what (*you/do*)?

7 If (*you/get married*), what kind of ceremony (*you/have*)?

8 If (*someone/follow*) you down the street, how (*you/react*)?

8 Complete the sentences so they are true for you.

1 If I didn't live in ………… , I ………… .
2 If I could change one thing in the world, ………… .
3 If I ………… , I always ………… .
4 If it's possible, I ………… .
5 I'm going to ………… if ………… .
6 If I could live twenty-four hours in the life of anyone in history, ………… .

Example: *6: I'd be Neil Armstrong in 1969. I'd love to be able to walk on the moon.*

Vocabulary
word building

1 What are the factors that make someone a successful sportsperson?

2 Look at the sentences in Activity 3. What kind of word is missing (e.g. a noun, adjective, adverb)?

3 Use the word given in capitals to form a word that fits in the gap in the following pairs of sentences.

COMPETE

1 It is argued that encouraging children to be .... puts them under too much pressure.

2 The top football teams have now been knocked out of the ....

PERFECT

3 Many sportspeople are .... and insist on getting it right every single time.

4 A gymnast will hope for .... in every performance.

ATHLETE

5 The sport of .... includes running and jumping.

6 You need to be more .... to be a ballet dancer than a footballer.

4 Mark the main stress in the words you wrote and practise saying them.

Word formation (Part 3)

▶ **EXAM** FOCUS p.186

5 Read the text and decide which is the best summary. Don't worry about the gaps yet.

  A superstitious athletes are the most successful

  B reasons why athletes are superstitious

  C the most common superstitions among athletes

6 Use the word given in capitals at the end of some of the lines to form a word that fits in the gap in the same line. There is an example at the beginning (0).

> **EXAM TIP**
>
> Look carefully at the text around the gaps to see what part of speech the word should be.

Sport: Superstitious athletes

Athletes develop superstitions by associating particular behaviour with good **(0)** _performance_ . Typical examples **PERFORM** include insisting on wearing the same item of clothing, only eating certain food or always listening to the same song before a match or a race. These superstitions usually have no **(1)** .... with success **CONNECT** but many athletes believe that they bring them good luck. **(2)** .... sport at a **COMPETE** professional level is extremely difficult and athletes are under pressure to achieve as close to **(3)** .... as they can possibly **PERFECT** manage. Many athletes find this extremely **(4)** .... So anything that helps them **STRESS** to feel less **(5)** .... isn't necessarily a **COMFORT** bad thing and some athletes maintain their lucky charms give them more **(6)** .... However, these little **CONFIDENT** superstitions could also be potentially **(7)** .... for athletes' mental health **DANGER** because they can develop an unhealthy **(8)** .... on them. They should be **DEPEND** focusing on improving their athletic ability instead of worrying about superstitions.

7 Discuss what superstitions are common in your country. Which do you believe in?

Examples:

A lot of people think black cats are unlucky.

If you break a mirror, it's supposed to mean bad luck for seven years.

Some people think opening an umbrella in the house is unlucky.

Multiple choice (Part 4)

▶ **EXAM** FOCUS p.189

1 To what extent do you think success is about being in the right place at the right time?

2 You will hear an interview with a journalist called Max Wilson about success in sport. Look at question 1 in Activity 4 and think of paraphrases for the options (A–C).

Example: *'Good fortune' could be expressed as 'luck'.*

3 ▶ 29 Listen to the part which relates to question 1. What paraphrases did you hear?

4 ▶ 30 Listen to the whole interview and, for questions 1–7, choose the best answer, A, B or C.

1 Max says that top sportspeople usually believe their success is due to
   A good fortune.
   B hard work.
   C raw talent.

2 According to Max, sportspeople are achieving more these days because
   A people in general have become stronger and fitter.
   B standards are getting higher.
   C technology is responsible for improved performance.

3 What does Max say about very talented young children?
   A It's easy to tell which will be the top performers.
   B They will succeed without special training.
   C As they get older their development may be slower.

4 According to Max, in his book *Bounce,* Matthew Syed says he had a greater chance of success because of
   A his parents' love of table tennis.
   B his competitive brother.
   C his own ambition.

5 For Matthew, the advantage of joining the Omega Club was that
   A it was open all the time.
   B it had a lot of good players.
   C it had great facilities.

6 Matthew thinks the reason Omega Club members have been so successful is
   A hard to explain.
   B because they met famous players.
   C a happy accident.

7 Max says that a ten-year investigation has shown that lucky people
   A believe they will succeed.
   B look for good opportunities.
   C depend very little on talent.

EXAM TIP

Check your answers carefully the second time you listen.

5 Work in pairs and compare your answers and give reasons for your choices. Check your answers with the audio script on page 215.

6 Talk about a time in your life when you were lucky/unlucky.

Third conditional

▶ **GRAMMAR** REFERENCE p.159

1 **Which of these statements about Matthew Syed do you agree with?**

1 If he'd lived in a different street, he wouldn't have become a table tennis champion.

2 He might still have become a champion even if he hadn't practised so hard.

3 If his parents hadn't bought a table-tennis table, he couldn't have gone to the Omega Club.

2 **Look at the rules below and choose the correct option in italics.**

1 The third conditional is used to speculate about things in the *past/present*.

2 The 'if clause' *always comes first/can come either first or second*.

3 'If' can be followed by *the past perfect/would have*.

3 **Complete the text about Olympic cyclist Mark Cavendish using the third conditional form of the verbs in brackets.**

If Cavendish **(1)** .... (*not crash*) in the Tour of Britain he **(2)** .... (*not injure*) his shoulder. However, if he **(3)** .... (*not have to*) take eight weeks off training, he's convinced he **(4)** .... (*not/have*) the time to plan his strategy for the next season so in fact his enforced rest turned out to be useful.

He says that people didn't believe he could win at the age of thirty-one and that if he **(5)** .... (*not feel*) he had to prove people wrong, he **(6)** .... (*might not be*) so determined to train as hard as he did. He also believes he **(7)** .... (*not succeed*) if the entire team **(8)** .... (*not support*) him at all times.

4 **Complete the sentences below to express criticism. Use the third conditional and the cues in brackets.**

1 **A:** I was only just able to brake in time when a deer ran out in front of me. (*drive more slowly*)

   B: If you'd been *driving more slowly, you wouldn't have had to brake* so suddenly.

2 **A:** I hit my head on the windscreen when I stopped. (*wear a seatbelt*)

   B: You ....

3 **A:** We set off a bit late and got held up in the traffic. (*leave earlier*)

   B: If you .... in the traffic.

4 **A:** We got stuck on a mountain because a heavy fog suddenly came down. (*check weather forecast*)

   B: If .... on a mountain in the fog.

5 **A:** I went to get a coffee and lost all the work I was doing. (*save the document*)

   B: You ....

6 **A:** I was doing something else so I didn't hear what she said. (*pay attention*)

   B: If .... what she said.

5 **Work in pairs.**

1 Make a note of five regrets you have about the past. Then discuss what would or might have happened if you had/hadn't done what you did.

   Example: *I didn't audition for a dance school. If had, I might have become a famous dancer by now.*

2 Write down the names of three people who have been important in your life. Then discuss how life would have been different if you hadn't met them.

   Example: *If I hadn't admired my drama teacher so much, I probably wouldn't have become an actress.*

6 **Discuss your answers with the class. Did you learn anything new about your partner?**

1 Work in pairs. What do you think makes people good at sport?

2 ▶ 31 Listen to two students answering a similar question. Which of these factors do they mention?

ambition	confidence	determination	family support
fitness	money	personality	talent

3 How do the speakers express *confidence, talent* and *fitness* in other ways?

Example: *confidence = sure of your ability*

Compensation strategies

4 Match strategies A–C to examples 1–3. Then listen again and tick the language the students use.

A correcting yourself/explaining something in other words

B giving yourself time to think

C checking you understand

1 Do you mean …?
I'm sorry, did you say …?
So, what you're saying is …?

2 OK, let me see.
Well, it's difficult to say, of course, but …
As far as I know, …
Right, …

3 I mean …
What I meant was …
What I'm trying to say is …
… or rather, …

Discussion (Part 4)

▶ **EXAM** FOCUS p.190

5 Work in pairs. Take turns to ask and answer the questions. Use some of the expressions from Activity 4.

1 What sports do you most enjoy playing or watching?

2 Do you think anyone can become good at sport if they practise hard enough?

3 How important is sport for good health?

4 What are the advantages and disadvantages of team sports over individual sports?

5 Would you say you were a competitive person?

EXAM TIP

Try to keep talking. If you have no ideas, you could ask your partner what he/she thinks.

Examples:

Do you have a view on this?

Would you like to go first?

Have you got anything to say about … ?

Collocations

adjectives and nouns: success and failure

1 Cross out the word in italics which does NOT collocate in the following phrases.

1 *make/do/have* a success (of something)

2 be a *big/large/great* success (at something)

3 be *deeply/highly/extremely* successful (at something)

4 fail *at/with/in* (something)

5 be a(n) *complete/entire/total* failure (at something)

2 Think of an example of success and failure. Describe it to your partner.

verbs and nouns

3 Match the verbs in the box to the nouns 1–5. You can use more than one verb with some of the nouns.

achieve beat give up lose miss reach waste win

1 an opportunity

2 an ambition

3 a competition

4 an opponent

5 a target

4 Complete the sentences with the correct form of the verbs in Activity 3. There may be more than one possible answer.

1 Great players never .... an opportunity to score a goal.

2 We were disappointed that we were knocked out before we .... the second round.

3 Well done, everyone. You deserved to .... that match.

4 It's a pity she played so badly. She .... the opportunity to show everyone just how talented she is.

5 Only a lucky few ever .... their dream of becoming an Olympic medallist.

6 I don't mind .... to an opponent if I know he played better than me.

7 It was frustrating being .... so easily. I thought we had a good chance of winning.

8 She's the most competitive person I've ever met. She never .... even when she's losing badly.

5 Complete the quotes with the verbs in the box.

accomplish be come across cope fulfil have overcome set

To be successful, people need to **(1)** .... a strong competitive streak and **(2)** .... totally single-minded. They will often **(3)** .... problems which they need to **(4)** .... if they are to succeed.

Successful people often **(5)** .... themselves goals or deadlines so that they can **(6)** .... their potential. They have to learn to **(7)** .... with pressure in order to **(8)** .... what they set out to do.

6 Work in pairs and discuss the questions. Use some of the language from Activities 1, 3 and 5.

1 How well do you think you cope with success and failure?

2 Do you have a drive to succeed or are you more laid-back?

3 To what extent can a successful person also be a kind person?

4 Is it true that people learn from their mistakes?

7 Find out what ambitions your partner has achieved/given up on.

Essay (Part 1)
structuring a paragraph
▶ **WRITING** REFERENCE pp.166 and 167

1 Read the exam task. Then look at the student's introduction and say whether sentences A and B are true (T) or false (F).

You have been discussing in class how to be a successful person. Now, your teacher has asked you to write an essay, giving your opinion on the following statement.

Without failure there can be no success.
Do you agree?
Notes
Write about:

1 motivation
2 experience
3 problems of instant success
  (your own idea)

Without failure there can be no success.

It's often said that it's impossible to succeed the first time you do something, and that the most successful people in life have failures behind them.

A The introduction repeats the statement in the title but in different words.

B The writer states his/her opinion in the introduction.

2 Look at the student's second paragraph and put sentences A, B and C in the correct order.

A Perhaps they appreciate their success more if it hasn't come easily. **B** In sport, for example, if top athletes lose a race or fail to score a goal, this may be just the motivation they need to inspire them. **C** Sometimes failure can make people more determined.

3 Read the rest of the essay and decide whether you agree with the student's argument. What other examples could be used?

.... Many writers, for example, don't achieve success until they are quite old. This is because it takes a lot of time to learn how to write well. Making mistakes and learning from them is very important, whatever you do.
.... Young actors and singers often find it difficult to deal with instant success and the money and fame that comes with it. We all know many examples of people who have suffered because of this. It can have very tragic consequences.
To sum up, it is possible to have success without failure, but in my opinion, it may be better to fail first.

4 Which sentences best introduce the third and fourth paragraphs in Activity 3?

1 A lot of experience is required to become successful.

2 You need to work hard to get a lot of experience.

3 Too much success too young can bring unhappiness.

4 Sudden success is increasingly common among young people.

5 Read the exam task and write your own essay, using Activities 1–4 to help you.

EXAM TIP

It's important to give your opinion in the conclusion.

You have been discussing in class how to be a successful person. Now, your teacher has asked you to write an **essay**, giving your opinion on the following statement.

Sporting heroes should try to be good role models. Do you agree?
Notes
Write about:

1 teamwork

2 influence on young people

3 .... (your own idea)
You should write between **140** and **190** words.

1 **Choose the correct option (A, B, C or D) to complete the sentences.**

1 To be successful you often need to overcome ....
   A goals   **B** problems   **C** motivation
   D deadlines

2 It's important to try to .... your potential.
   A succeed   **B** aim   **C** fulfil   **D** commit

3 In order to achieve things, you need to .... yourself goals.
   A set   **B** find   **C** make   **D** expect

4 I was lucky enough to meet David Beckham once .... chance.
   A by   **B** with   **C** on   **D** at

5 To perform well in sports you need to be able to cope .... pressure.
   A in   **B** on   **C** for   **D** with

6 Successful people rarely .... opportunities they are given.
   A lose   **B** deny   **C** waste   **D** save

7 Because I was too tall, there was never any .... of me becoming a ballet dancer.
   A occasion   **B** possibility   **C** opportunity
   D potential

8 High achievers are unlikely to leave anything .... chance.
   A to   **B** with   **C** at   **D** for

2 **Correct the mistakes with the verb forms.**

1 If I met Usain Bolt, I take a photograph of him.

2 We can get tickets for the match if we would book them today.

3 If you will practise harder, you could be a good player.

4 If you helped me more, I didn't have so many problems.

5 He can become world champion if he'd had a different coach.

6 He might have decided to join another team if the club wouldn't have offered him so much money.

7 She didn't become a world champion if she hadn't taken her trainer's advice.

8 They would have travelled to South Africa to see the final if they could afford it.

3 **Complete the sentences with the correct form of the word in brackets.**

1 Mental imagery is a technique often used by an athlete to improve their .... (perform)

2 There is a strong .... that thinking positively makes you less nervous. (possible)

3 Most athletes show a huge amount of .... and focus. (determined)

4 The idea of .... is difficult for many to accept. (fail)

5 Many performers are extremely .... (superstition)

6 It is common for sportspeople to be .... (perfect)

7 .... is probably as important as ambition for athletes. (confident)

8 Too much pressure on athletes can lead to .... (happy)

PROGRESS TEST 3

Multiple-choice cloze (Part 1)

1 For questions 1–8, read the text below and decide which answer (A, B, C or D) best fits each gap. There is an example at the beginning.

Journey into space

When the first man landed on the moon, twelve-year-old Claudie Haigneré was on holiday on a French campsite. The first Frenchwoman in space recalls that day: 'My father, who was always **(0)** _A, curious_ about the world, **(1)** .... us that something really extraordinary was about to happen. It was a beautiful evening, so we sat under the stars and watched TV. To see the moon so **(2)** .... away in the sky and then to see a man climb down a ladder onto the **(3)** .... of it was just incredible.' After the moon landing, Haigneré read and watched whatever she could about space. But **(4)** .... into space herself seemed unimaginable. However, much later she heard that France's space centre was **(5)** .... for astronauts. It was an opportunity that Haigneré couldn't **(6)** .... Of 1,000 candidates, seven were chosen: six men and Haigneré. Haigneré eventually went into space twice. What was it like being completely **(7)** .... from life on Earth? 'I usually had no time to sit and watch the earth turn. However, once I decided to **(8)** .... some time to enjoy the spectacle; it was extraordinary.'

Open cloze (Part 2)

2 For questions 9–16, read the text below and think of the word that best fits each gap. Use only one word in each gap. There is an example at the beginning.

Success

I have **(0)** _never_ met anyone successful who didn't have a plan. I believe this is an essential key to success. Knowing what you want to **(9)** .... achieved in ten years' time, **(10)** .... if it doesn't seem a realistic goal for today, will give you the passion and drive needed to reach your ultimate goals. **(11)** .... you can answer the question 'What do I want to do?' clearly and confidently, then you have little chance **(12)** .... achieving anything significant. For young people it's very important to remember that you'll **(13)** .... spending the rest of your life working. You'll spend more time at work than you will with friends and family, so it's incredibly important to identify what it is you really want to aim **(14)** .... On the **(15)** .... hand, just because you're passionate about what you want to do, it doesn't necessarily mean you'll be any good at it. You need to recognise your capabilities and accept your limitations. There are certain skills you can learn but real talent is **(16)** .... that people are born with and it's impossible to learn this.

0	**A** curious	**B** surprised	**C** interested	**D** fascinated
1	**A** said	**B** told	**C** explained	**D** suggested
2	**A** far	**B** long	**C** remote	**D** outside
3	**A** top	**B** side	**C** level	**D** surface
4	**A** making	**B** finding	**C** reaching	**D** travelling
5	**A** asking	**B** looking	**C** offering	**D** requesting
6	**A** miss	**B** lose	**C** wait	**D** avoid
7	**A** put off	**B** cut off	**C** set out	**D** got away
8	**A** do	**B** get	**C** take	**D** spend

Word formation (Part 3)

3 For questions 17–24, read the text below. Use the word given in capitals at the end of some of the lines to form a word that fits in the gap in the same line. There is an example at the beginning.

Tired of waiting

Although Simon is going to university this autumn to study **(0)** journalism , **JOURNAL** he has been working as a waiter for six months to pay for a holiday. At first, he says, he was absolutely **(17)** .... **USE** at the job. It took him far longer than he'd expected to be able to do it **(18)** .... This was partly because **SUCCESS** he was given no formal **(19)** .... **TRAIN** at all. He says that the job would not have been his first **(20)** .... but it **CHOOSE** had been difficult to find any kind of temporary **(21)** .... at all, so he'd **EMPLOY** had to take what he could get. The salary is not good either, especially in view of the number of hours he works. Waiters can't rely on being given a share of the service charges because they aren't passed on by the **(22)** .... of some restaurants. So **MANAGE** he just has to hope for generous tips instead. He would never consider working in a restaurant again, mainly because of the rude and **(23)** .... **PLEASE** attitude of many chefs towards waiters. However, he admits there were very few **(24)** .... about **COMPLAIN** the food.

Key word transformation (Part 4)

4 For questions 25–30, complete the second sentence so that it has a similar meaning to the first sentence, using the word given. Do not change the word given. You must use between two and five words, including the word given. Here is an example.

Example:

We're going to camp whether or not it's raining.

EVEN

We're going to camp even if it's raining.

25 They are going to stay with my brother when they go to Madrid.

PUT

My brother is going to .... when they go to Madrid.

26 I am sure that Emilia hasn't remembered we have an appointment.

MUST

Emilia .... we have an appointment.

27 There were so many people at the station that I couldn't find my friend.

SUCH

There were .... people at the station that I couldn't find my friend.

28 It's a waste of time entering the competition because I won't win.

NO

There's .... the competition because I won't win.

29 Tim was annoyed because his son didn't pay his car tax.

PAID

If his son .... his car tax, Tim wouldn't have been annoyed.

30 'You shouldn't swim here,' the instructor told us.

WARNED

The instructor .... there.

10 Friends for life

1 **Work in pairs and discuss the questions.**

1 What qualities do you look for in a friend?

2 How easy is it to be a good friend?

2 **Do the quiz.**

What kind of friend are you?

1 How many close friends would you say you have?

A 1–3   B 4–8   C more than 8

2 Which of these things is the most damaging to friendship?

A disloyalty   B selfishness   C dishonesty

3 Do you think the best test of a close friend is

A always being there to have fun with?

B always being ready to do a favour?

C always being able to pick up where you left off last time?

4 Where would you place friendship in relation to career and family?

A more important than career and family

B more important than career, less important than family

C important, but less important than either career or family

5 Do you have someone you could call a best friend?

A I used to.

B Definitely.

C No – I have lots of friends.

6 When you haven't seen a close friend for a long time, do you

A not worry about it?

B contact them via social media?

C feel guilty?

7 Which do you most value in a friendship?

A loyalty   B generosity   C trust

8 The most important quality you need to be a good friend is to be

A self-aware.

B content with your own life.

C lively and outgoing.

3 Look at the results on page 138 and add up your score. Discuss in groups whether the results describe you accurately or not.

Vocabulary
compound adjectives: personality

4 Complete the sentences about people's characters with compound adjectives, using the words in the box.

---
even   kind   level   like   mild   quick   single   strong
---

1 We enjoy the same kind of things; we're very .... -minded.

2 My brother hardly ever argues but my sister's always been .... -tempered.

3 He's the kind of person who always has to get his own way; he's very .... -willed.

4 You can rely on Matt to make rational decisions, he's very ....-headed.

5 She doesn't get upset easily; she's always very .... -tempered.

6 Jessica always goes out of her way to help people. She's a very .... -hearted person.

7 My granddad was modest and .... -mannered – a contrast to my grandmother who was extremely loud and opinionated.

8 I think the reason Daniel is so successful is because he was always so ambitious and .... -minded.

5 Work in pairs. Put the adjectives in Activity 4 in order of preference for qualities you look for in a friend.

Multiple matching (Part 3)

▶ **EXAM** FOCUS p.189

6 You will hear five short extracts in which people are talking about their closest friend. Look at options A–H and say which are true about your relationship with your best friend(s).

7 ▶ 32 Listen and choose from the list (A–H) what each speaker says about their relationship with their closest friend. Use the letters only once. There are three extra letters which you do not need to use.

A We can rely on each other for support.

B Having an argument doesn't damage our relationship.

C Despite having very different personalities, we enjoy each other's company.

D We're very close, despite only knowing one another for a short time.

E Our first impressions of each other weren't positive.

F We contact each other frequently.

G We're unable to meet up as much as we did in the past.

H We've got closer as we've got older.

Speaker 1 ☐
Speaker 2 ☐
Speaker 3 ☐
Speaker 4 ☐
Speaker 5 ☐

8 Listen again and note down the matching paraphrases for options A–H.

9 Describe your closest friend(s). Say

1 how you met.
2 what you do together.
3 why you like him/her/them.
4 what kind of person she/he is/they are.

Conditionals
conditional linking words

▶ **GRAMMAR** REFERENCE p.160

1 **Look at the examples from the recording and answer the questions.**

Unless we're very organised, it can be hard to arrange to go out.

1 Do they need to be organised in order to see each other?

As long as we plan ahead, it's fine.

2 Is it essential for them to plan ahead?

Even if we haven't seen each other for a few months, we can catch up really easily.

3 Does it matter if they don't see each other often?

We never go to football matches together. Otherwise we end up arguing.

4 Do they argue if they go to a football match together?

2 **Do the following pairs of sentences have the same meaning?**

1 A Even if you phone him, he'll be upset.
   B Unless you phone him, he'll be upset.

2 A There should be time to eat before the film provided that you get there early.
   B As long as you get there early, there should be time to eat before the film.

3 A I can't decide whether to buy a ticket for the match.
   B I can't decide if I should buy a ticket for the match.

3 **Complete the sentences with the linking words/phrases in the box. More than one answer may be possible.**

as long as   even if   otherwise   unless
provided that   whether

1 .... you make an effort, it's too easy to lose touch with old friends.

2 I message my boyfriend every day. .... he gets upset.

3 I want to invite all my friends, ... they can't all come to the party.

4 .... I know some people who are going, I don't mind going to parties on my own.

5 I don't know .... or not to talk to him about the problem.

4 **Complete the sentences with information about your friends. Then compare with a partner.**

1 It's usually .... who decides whether or not we ....

2 My friends are always fun to be with unless ....

3 As long as I don't mention .... , I get on fine with ....

4 I would never tell .... about .... even if ....

5 **For questions 1–6, complete the second sentence so that it has a similar meaning to the first sentence, using the word given.**

1 I'll phone you tonight if it isn't too late when I get home.
   UNLESS
   I'll phone you tonight .... too late.

2 He'll get a ticket for the match whether he has enough money or not.
   EVEN
   He'll get a ticket for the match .... have enough money.

3 Unless it's raining, I'll wait for you outside the cinema.
   LONG
   As .... raining, I'll wait for you outside the cinema.

4 We couldn't go to the party because of the snow.
   HAVE
   If it hadn't been snowing, we .... to the party.

5 We should finish by four o'clock but it means we can't take a break for lunch.
   PROVIDED
   We should finish by four o'clock .... take a break for lunch.

6 Depending on the amount of traffic, I might be a bit late.
   WHETHER
   I might be a bit late .... much traffic or not.

Easily confused adjectives

1 Complete the sentences with the adjectives in the box. More than one answer may be possible.

---
actual   current   present
---

1 We have no more information at the .... time.

2 I know she's in her early twenties but I don't know her .... age.

3 He's very interested in .... affairs.

---
common   typical   usual
---

4 He's not as lively as ....

5 On a .... Saturday night we would stay up late and watch a movie.

6 It's very .... to meet your future husband or wife at work.

---
individual   particular   unique
---

7 She doesn't get much .... attention from the teacher on the art course she's doing.

8 We decided to drive to the coast for no .... reason.

9 It's a(n) .... opportunity to make new friends.

Multiple-choice cloze (Part 1)

▶ **EXAM** FOCUS p.186

2 For questions 1–8, decide which answer (A, B, C or D) best fits each gap. There is an example at the beginning (0).

Need a friend?

I **(0)** *B, arrange* to meet my friend Andy in a café. Over a coffee we chat about music, **(1)** .... affairs and the ups and downs of our working lives. We don't **(2)** .... a lot of time talking about our feelings or our relationship, or the past. It's just not that kind of friendship. I **(3)** .... it that way, and I know Andy doesn't mind because I'm paying him to be my friend for a few hours.

Not so long ago, a friend was one **(4)** .... that money couldn't buy. Friendships were special. But not anymore. You can hire someone to show you around town, hang out at the gym or **(5)** .... you company while you shop. My friend Andy is an actor. He has never been paid to be someone's friend before but he understands why someone might **(6)** .... buying companionship. When he first came to London from Scotland a year and a half ago, he **(7)** .... socialising difficult. But Andy thinks it could be the desire for undemanding companionship, rather than loneliness, that is driving the growth in friend-hire: 'The average person doesn't want to have loads of **(8)** .... friends because it makes life too complicated.'

0	**A** organise	**B** arrange	**C** book	**D** fix
1	**A** common	**B** usual	**C** current	**D** actual
2	**A** have	**B** take	**C** lose	**D** spend
3	**A** choose	**B** wish	**C** select	**D** prefer
4	**A** fact	**B** matter	**C** thing	**D** point
5	**A** stay	**B** keep	**C** give	**D** provide
6	**A** decide	**B** think	**C** consider	**D** encourage
7	**A** experienced	**B** realised	**C** discovered	**D** found
8	**A** real	**B** right	**C** present	**D** certain

3 Work in pairs. Do you agree with what Andy says about making friends?

4 Discuss where it is easiest to make friends and why. Use the ideas in the box to help you.

---
at college   at the gym   at a party   at work   in the park
---

1 **Work in groups and discuss the questions.**

1 Think of some happy couples you know. What makes their relationships successful?

2 Do you believe in love at first sight?

A match made in heaven

Is there anything wrong with wanting to find a 'soulmate' – that one special person who will make the perfect partner? Many of us believe that this is the only kind of true love there is because we've been brought up on a diet of romantic pop songs and films that idealise love. We cling to the idea, even though we suspect it's doomed to failure. After all, around 50 percent of marriages end in divorce in many western countries. So why is the soulmate myth so powerful? Maybe it's because we don't like thinking that life is messily random. Or we need a romantic way of describing intense physical attraction. Or maybe it's just shorthand for the kind of overwhelming emotion we don't quite understand.

Throughout history, many great works of literature such as Shakespeare's *Romeo and Juliet* have been based on the idea of romantic love, as have popular works of contemporary fiction such as *One Day* and *Twilight*. This isn't a preoccupation found only in Western cultures either. A Chinese story about lovers destined to be together, regardless of social class, background or geography, dates back to the ninth century. Many of these stories have tragic endings; *Romeo and Juliet* being a famous example.

The founding father of romance is often thought to be the ancient Greek philosopher, Plato. But it was actually the Romantic poet, Samuel Taylor Coleridge, who came up with the term 'soulmate', as we understand it today. 'To be happy in married life ... you must have a soulmate,' he said in a letter in 1822. This was an unconventional opinion, which probably seemed revolutionary at the time, but these days, searching for spiritual completion is the norm.

Not everyone subscribes to this view, however. A recent study on attitudes to long-term relationships found that couples who have been together a long time are more likely to refer to each other as 'best friends' rather than 'soulmates', and are unconvinced by the representation of romance in popular culture. They know these over-idealised romances don't bear any relation to reality – so they don't take them seriously.

A pragmatic approach to love would seem to give relationships a better chance of survival. Research carried out by a professor of social psychology at the University of Houston showed that people believing in romantic destiny tend to have relationships that are passionate but short-lived. Only perfection will do – if things go wrong, this can't be 'The One'. Research published by Prof. Spike Lee, of Toronto University, and Prof. Norbert Schwarz, of the University of Southern California, confirms these findings. 'People who implicitly think of relationships as perfect unity between soulmates have worse relationships than people who implicitly think of relationships as a journey of growing and working things out.'

Finding a partner can seem overwhelming if you're convinced you've got to search the entire world for just one person, so these days many of us have come round to the idea that fate may need a helping hand. This is why one in five UK relationships starts online. As Lori Laius, of Telegraph Dating, says, 'You're using today's technology to help you find someone special.' This suits men in particular, who typically have always been more hard-headed about the possibility of finding a match made in heaven. And although meeting online doesn't quite live up to the romantic ideal, it's now just as normal as meeting someone at a party or at work.

Line 27

Multiple choice (Part 5)

▶ **EXAM** FOCUS p.187

2 **Read the article about finding a soulmate. For questions 1–6, choose the answer (A, B, C or D) which you think fits best according to the text.**

1 What point is the writer making in the first paragraph?

   A Attitudes to love are changing.

   B People's lack of romance leads to divorce.

   C Accepted beliefs about love are hard to explain.

   D People should forget about trying to find a soulmate.

2 What does 'this' refer to in line 27?

   A *Romeo and Juliet*

   B a Chinese love story

   C the idea of romantic love

   D contemporary fiction

3 What does the writer say about the use of the word 'soulmate' in paragraph three?

   A It was used earlier than was previously thought.

   B It took a long time for it to be widely understood.

   C The meaning has changed very recently.

   D It was first used to describe an unusual and unfamiliar concept.

4 According to the study, how do people in long-term relationships react to the way romance is portrayed in popular culture?

   A They are able to separate fact from fiction.

   B They think it is a worrying problem.

   C They feel sorry for people who idealise love.

   D They are disappointed that reality is different.

5 What conclusion can be drawn from the university research?

   A It is unrealistic to expect love to last.

   B It is necessary to put some effort into a relationship.

   C It is impossible to give a definition of the perfect relationship.

   D It is better to have low expectations of love.

6 The writer says that online dating agencies are popular because they

   A mean people are less reliant on chance.

   B give people hope of finding the perfect soulmate.

   C are more reliable than traditional ways of meeting the right person.

   D give people a much wider choice of potential partners.

3 **Do you agree/disagree with the statements? Work in pairs and discuss.**

1 A best friend is better than a romantic partner.

2 Romance is dead.

Vocabulary

phrasal verbs with *come*

4 **Match the phrasal verbs in italics to the definitions A–H.**

1 I *came across* my future wife while we were both waiting for a bus.

2 The writer *came up with* the idea for the story after seeing an old photograph.

3 My parents have *come round to* the idea that I'll never get married.

4 They've got their 25th wedding anniversary *coming up* soon.

5 It's easy to *come across* as too keen when you meet someone you're really attracted to.

6 The news that the billionaire is getting married for the 6th time *came out* yesterday.

7 They decided to get married when Jack *came into* some money.

8 They *came through* a difficult period in their relationship and are now stronger than ever.

   A agree to something you're not sure of

   B find/meet by chance

   C be made public

   D survive

   E invent

   F inherit

   G give the impression/appear

   H happen

5 **Work in pairs. Ask and answer the questions.**

1 Do you think you come across as a different kind of person online?

2 What would you do if you came across a boyfriend/girlfriend's old love letters?

3 How would you feel if you came into a lot of money?

4 Have you got any important events coming up soon?

Participles (-*ing* and -*ed*)
participle clauses

▶ **GRAMMAR** REFERENCE p.160

1 **Match a participle clause to a main clause to make statements you agree with.**

A People marrying at a very young age
B People using online dating websites
C People going on blind dates

1 usually regret it.
2 shouldn't judge people on appearances.
3 need to have a lot of confidence.

2 **Look at the underlined participles in extracts from the text on page 106. Which participles have an active meaning? Which have a passive meaning?**

1 A Chinese story about lovers <u>destined</u> to be together, regardless of social class, background or geography, dates back to the ninth century.

2 Research <u>carried out</u> by a professor of social psychology at the University of Houston showed that people <u>believing</u> in romantic destiny tend to have relationships that are passionate but short-lived.

3 **Look at the extracts rewritten with relative pronouns. Which words are missed out in participle clauses? Which words change?**

A A Chinese story about lovers who are destined to be together …
B Research which was carried out by a professor at …
C People who believe in romantic destiny …

4 **Replace the underlined words to make participle clauses.**

Example:

The woman <u>who lives</u> next door is my best friend.
The woman <u>living</u> next door …

1 She is a kind-hearted woman, <u>who bursts</u> with energy.
2 Her sense of style, <u>which was developed</u> during her stay in France, is famous.
3 She recently twisted her ankle <u>while we were playing</u> tennis.
4 She has blonde hair, <u>which is cut</u> very short.
5 She gave me a fantastic picture, <u>which was painted</u> by her brother.
6 Anyone <u>who meets</u> her is impressed by her charm.
7 She has a job <u>in which she designs</u> clothes.

other uses of participles

5 **Match the sentences to other uses of participles A–D.**

1 People don't like admitting that they are lonely.
2 Disappointed by his behaviour, she broke up with him.
3 After chatting online, they arranged to meet for a coffee.
4 Deciding to get married is a very important step.

A after certain verbs
B after conjunctions
C as the subject of a sentence
D as an adjective

6 **Complete the text using the present or past participle form of the verbs in the box.**

age   escape   feel   fill   get   have   jump   plan   shock   travel

https://MyBlog/Travelling solo

Travelling solo

I went on my first solo trip **(1)** .... just 19. It felt like **(2)** .... off a cliff as I boarded the flight to Australia; **(3)** .... with a mixture of excitement and fear. I remember **(4)** .... sick with nerves as I walked into the hostel in Melbourne. But I needn't have worried – after ten minutes I'd already been introduced to a dozen people and been invited out to eat with a group of Canadians. **(5)** .... by yourself makes it so much easier to talk to strangers and make new friends. By **(6)** .... the trip alone, you've also got the added benefit of **(7)** .... total control over what you decide to do and when.

Since then I've insisted on **(8)** .... for a solo trip every year, even after **(9)** .... married. My husband totally gets it and goes off on fishing trips alone. We've become used to the **(10)** .... reaction we get when we explain to people that we are spending our holidays apart.

7 **Work in pairs and discuss the questions.**

1 What do you think are the advantages and disadvantages of travelling alone?
2 Do you think it's a good idea for couples to spend time apart?
3 Which activities do you prefer to do with friends and which do you prefer to do alone?

Collaborative task (Part 3)
turn taking

▶ **EXAM** FOCUS p.190

1 ▶ 33 Look at the diagram and listen to two students talking. Number the order in which they discuss the different stages.

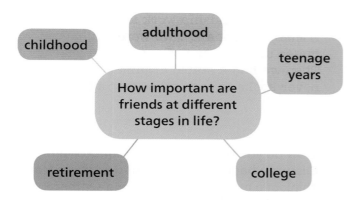

childhood — adulthood — teenage years

How important are friends at different stages in life?

retirement — college

2 Listen again and complete the extracts.

1 OK, ... we begin?
2 We .... start ....
3 .... you think?
4 .... , oh, sorry!
5 No, that's OK. ....
6 .... you said, it must be lonely …
7 .... men and women have a different kind of friendship?
8 As you .... , men like doing things together.

3 Which of the conversational strategies (A–D) do sentences 1–8 in Activity 2 fit into?

A starting a discussion
B interrupting someone when you want a turn
C encouraging the other person to say something
D developing your partner's ideas

emphasis

4 Complete the sentences with the adverbs in the box. You can use the adverbs more than once and there may be more than one answer. Compare your answers in pairs.

absolutely   extremely   incredibly   totally

1 I think that having a best friend at school is .... essential.
2 Staying at home with a baby must be .... lonely.
3 I used to .... love seeing my friends every day at college.
4 What I find .... difficult is keeping in touch with old friends.
5 I .... agree with you; the strongest friendships are formed when you're young.
6 I'm .... certain I will have the same friends when I'm fifty.

5 Work in pairs. Practise giving emphasis by saying the sentences in activity 4 with the stress on the adverb.

6 Complete the sentences so that they are true for you.

1 I honestly believe that a best friend …
2 Personally, I would be very upset if one of my friends …
3 I seriously think that it's impossible to be friends with …

7 Work in pairs. Take turns to say your sentences from Activity 6. Respond to your partner's statements with the following questions.

Do you really think so?/Are you absolutely certain about that?/What makes you so sure about that?

8 Work in pairs and do the task with the diagram in Activity 1. You have about two minutes to do this.

EXAM TIP

Take turns to speak and don't dominate. If you feel your partner is talking too much, interrupt politely by saying *Can I say something here?*

9 Work in pairs and decide at which two stages in life people might need friends the most. You have about a minute to do this.

Article (Part 2)
using a range of vocabulary
▶ **WRITING** REFERENCE p.171

1 Work in pairs. Discuss how your friends have influenced you.

2 Read the exam task and check you understand what you have to include in your article.

> You see this advertisement on an English language website.
>
> ### ARTICLES WANTED
>
> **My closest friend**
>
> Where did you meet him/her?
> How long have you known him/her?
> What influence has he/she had on your life?
>
> Write us an article answering these questions. We will publish the best articles on our website.
>
> Write your **article** in **140–190** words.

3 Discuss the questions in the advertisement about your closest friend with a partner.

4 Read the first two paragraphs of a model article opposite and answer the questions about the techniques the writer has used to engage the reader.

1 Look at the words/structures in italics. What is the effect of using these?

2 Underline the 'more colourful' verbs which are used to express the following: *saw, walking with difficulty, ran, took, a lot.*

3 Think of similar words or expressions for *immediately, attracted by, unusual, have an argument, stupid, spoke.*

My closest friend

From the moment I saw Lucie, I knew we would be friends. She was so cool! How could I resist her?

It was my very first day at university *when* I first set eyes on her. I was struggling up the stairs when she rushed out of her room and grabbed one of my cases. *Not only did* she insist on carrying it for me, *but* she helped me unpack too. I was immediately attracted by her unusual clothes, mass of dark curly hair, bright eyes and energy. But *what* really made the friendship work *was* her warm friendly personality. We were *really* good mates until the end of our second year. Then we had a stupid argument and never spoke to each other *ever* again!

5 How do you think the article might continue? Discuss what might be in a third paragraph and think of a memorable concluding sentence.

6 Plan and write your own article using the guidelines 1–4.

1 Think about who you are going to write about and plan what will be in each paragraph.

2 Think of how you will make your introduction and conclusion effective, using some of the techniques from Activity 4 to interest and engage the reader.

3 Include a range of vocabulary.

4 Check your article for spelling, punctuation and grammar mistakes.

7 Swap articles with a partner. Look at the verbs and adjectives. Are there more interesting words/expressions that could be used instead?

EXAM TIP

Instead of repeating the same words, use a near synonym or more extreme adjective to make your writing more interesting and demonstrate your range of vocabulary.

1 Choose the correct word/phrase in italics to complete the sentences.

1 *As long as/Even if* he doesn't turn up, we can still go to the cinema.

2 *Provided that/Unless* the train's on time, I'll meet you at six outside the restaurant.

3 I still think he should apologise *whether/if* it's his fault or not.

4 Let's agree to disagree, *otherwise/even if* we'll have a big argument.

5 *As long as/Unless* it doesn't rain, I'll invite everyone for a barbecue in the evening.

6 We would never have met *if/whether* you hadn't got lost on your first day at university.

2 Choose the correct option (A, B, C or D) to complete the sentences.

1 She's a very kind-............ person; she'd do anything for you.

  A tempered   **C** headed

  B minded   **D** hearted

2 Staying with my friend in China was a(n) .... opportunity to learn about the culture.

  A usual   **C** particular

  B common   **D** unique

3 We have a lot in common – we're very like-............ .

  A willed   **C** tempered

  B minded   **D** hearted

4 At the .... time there are nearly two billion users of Facebook worldwide.

  A actual   **C** current

  B present   **D** typical

5 Let's meet for a coffee at our .... place.

  A usual   **C** individual

  B typical   **D** unique

6 She's very level-............ and good at making decisions.

  A minded   **C** headed

  B willed   **D** hearted

3 Join these sentences using an *-ing* or an *-ed* participle.

Example:

My favourite possession is this book. It was signed by the author.

My favourite possession is this book, signed by the author.

1 That woman is waving to us. She's one of my work colleagues.

2 That's the path. It leads to the sea.

3 I saw your brother. He was waiting for a train.

4 I found the money. It was hidden under my bed.

5 I'm living in a flat. It's owned by an old friend.

6 Shall we book the flight to Rome? It leaves at 6p.m. from Heathrow.

4 Complete the sentences with the prepositions in the box. You will need to use some prepositions more than once.

across   into   out   through   up

1 She comes .... as being quite shy.

2 We came .... with the idea after a lot of consideration.

3 We've got a revision test coming .... soon.

4 When his grandfather died, Archie came .... a lot of money.

5 Her secret will come .... one of these days.

6 The film comes .... on Friday. Shall I book tickets?

7 They relied on their friends to help them come .... a very difficult period.

8 I'd never come .... this writer before – I think he's amazing.

5 Complete the sentences with the correct form of the word in brackets.

1 I could never be friends with someone who was .... (loyal)

2 Not everyone is ...., which is absolutely fine. (ambition)

3 Giving up her holiday to help her friend was a true act of .... (self)

4 Tell me what really happened. I can always tell when you're being .... (honest)

5 She's such fun to be with because she's so .... (live)

6 Some people are really sociable and have a natural talent for .... (friend)

Gapped text (Part 6)

▶ **EXAM** FOCUS p.187

1 **Look at the photo. How would you feel about doing a sky dive or a bungee jump?**

2 **Look at the text and read the title and first paragraph. Work with a partner and answer the questions.**

1 What do you think 'leaving your comfort zone' means?
2 Predict what kinds of challenges the article will mention.

3 **Read the rest of the text. Were your predictions correct? Were any of the challenges surprising?**

4 **Six sentences have been removed from the article. Choose from the sentences A–G the one which fits each gap (1–6). There is one extra sentence which you do not need to use.**

A Then find something else interesting and new to try.
B It gives us a feeling of security and stability.
C However, most people say it's the best decision they've ever made.
D Yoga for some people can be just as inspiring as skydiving.
E They lack the motivation needed to expand their interests and knowledge.
F What you don't want is for a justified sense of achievement to become routine and therefore dull.
G This will only confirm your belief that change is frightening and so is something to be avoided.

5 **Work in pairs and discuss the questions.**

1 Do you agree it's important to *expand your horizons*? Why/Why not?
2 Would you find yoga or scuba-diving more of a challenge? Why?
3 Why do you think some people try increasingly challenging activities?

Leaving your comfort zone

Anyone who's ever pushed themselves to achieve anything difficult knows that facing up to a challenge can lead to surprising results. What once seemed hugely challenging and threatening often turns out to be much easier than expected. What's more, forcing yourself to be brave can increase your confidence and inspire you to expand your horizons.

But trying new things takes courage. You have to be willing to break away from the routines and activities that make you feel secure, the state of mind known as your comfort zone. [1] It's a familiar place where we feel most relaxed.

The problem with being in our comfort zone is that it encourages us to minimise risk so it makes us lazy and stifles innovation. If people don't have the pressure of meeting targets or rising to new challenges, they have a tendency to do no more than the minimum expected of them. [2] But we need to make sure we grab every opportunity that comes our way; if we don't, we may live to regret it when we're older.

There are lots of ways to stretch your personal boundaries, both big and small. It's not limited to exciting and daring physical challenges. [3] Simple things, like trying a new filling in your favourite sandwich bar or changing your hairstyle, may well prove to be as revelatory as doing something more dramatic, like taking a scuba-diving lesson. The things you try may prove to be earth-shattering, a mixed blessing or mind-numbing, but that's not the point. What you are doing when you try something new is learning to break through the mental blocks that are holding you back.

Having said all that, if you push yourself too hard, it can end in tears. [4] What might inspire someone else could terrify you so don't be afraid to take one step at a time. You don't have to throw yourself in at the deep end right away. Work out what your fears are and deal with them gradually.

Obviously, it's not healthy to live constantly beyond your comfort zone. [5] This condition, which is known as *hedonistic adaptation*, is the constant desire for impressive new experiences that quickly become routine. A typical example would be someone who decides that completing an ordinary marathon is not satisfying enough and feels they need the extreme challenge of running in arctic conditions, or completing seven marathons in one week.

Being prepared to step out of your comfort zone is about being open to new experiences. Your objective isn't to be interested only in novelty or extreme situations but to test your boundaries and take time to reflect on your experiences so you can enjoy the benefits and apply them to your day-to-day activities. [6] Make it a habit if you can. So stop saying 'No' to things which make you feel uncomfortable and start saying 'Yes!'

6 Work in pairs. Complete the table with the highlighted words in the text and answer the questions.

Noun	Verb	Adjective
challenge		
		threatening

1 What are the verb/ noun/adjective forms of each word?

2 Which words have the same noun and verb form?

3 Which word has more than one noun form? What is the difference in meaning?

7 Look at the underlined idioms in the text. What do you think they mean?

8 With a partner think of:

- a situation which you think could end in tears/ended in tears for you.
- a time when you threw yourself in at the deep end.

Mixed conditionals

▶ **GRAMMAR** REFERENCE p.161

1 **Work in pairs and discuss the questions.**

1 What important decisions have you made about studies/work/relationships/travel?

2 What's the best decision you've ever made?

A decision that changed my life
By Sally Burns

I'd been working as a manager in a café for two years and life was becoming predictable and boring. Then at a party I met an old friend who'd just come back from volunteering in Kenya. I'd never considered doing anything like that, partly because I wasn't brave enough and partly because I didn't have any teaching or nursing skills but he told me this didn't matter. The next day I got in touch with the volunteering organisation and signed up for six months. It was the best decision I've ever made.

I was given lots of training and I ended up working as a carer in an orphanage and that experience changed my life. I realised how lucky I'd been to have a home and a family and a good education. I discovered that I loved working with children. I also met my husband Paul while I was there. He was working as a volunteer teacher in the orphanage.

When we returned home I retrained to become a teacher. Soon we hope to get a job working in Africa together.

2 **Read the text and look at these pairs of sentences. In each sentence, underline the verb forms in both the *if* clause and the conditional clause.**

1 **A** If Sally hadn't gone to Kenya, she wouldn't be married to Paul.

   B If Sally hadn't gone to Kenya, she wouldn't have married Paul.

2 **A** If Sally hadn't enjoyed working with children, she might not have become a teacher.

   B If Sally didn't enjoy working with children, she might not have become a teacher.

3 **A** Sally might still be working in a café if she hadn't met an old friend at a party.

   B Sally might have still been working at the café if she hadn't met an old friend at a party.

3 **Look at the sentences in Activity 2 again.**

1 Which sentence in each pair is a 'mixed' conditional, where one part refers to past time and one part refers to present time?

2 In which sentence is something which is true now caused by an event in the past?

4 **Complete the sentences using the correct form of the verbs in brackets. If there is more than one possibility, say why.**

1 If I'd left the party earlier, I .... (*not/feel*) so tired today.

2 I would have got that job if I .... (*speak*) fluent French.

3 If you'd let me drive, we .... (*not/be*) lost now.

4 I'd be much happier if I .... (*speak*) to Tom yesterday.

5 I .... (*might/earn*) more now if I'd gone to university.

5 **Change these sentences using mixed conditional forms.**

1 My car broke down because it's so old.
   If ....

2 I spent too much money in the sales, which is why I'm broke.
   If ....

3 He plays football all the time ever since I took him to that Liverpool match.
   If ....

4 The only reason I learnt Russian is because my aunt lives in Moscow.
   If ....

5 The reason I know so many people is that Paula introduced me to them.
   If ....

6 I went to live abroad because I couldn't get a job at home.
   If ....

6 **Work in pairs and discuss the questions. Give reasons for your answers.**

1 If you could have chosen your nationality, which country would you be living in now?

   Example: *I think I'd have chosen to be Norwegian because they're supposed to be the happiest people in the world. So I'd be living in Norway!*

2 If you had had the choice at birth, which famous person would you be now?

3 If a machine allowed you to go back in time, what would you have done differently?

4 If you were a different sex, how do you think it would have affected your life?

Vocabulary
prefixes that change meaning

1 Look at the words in the box and match the underlined prefixes to meanings 1–5.

<u>hyper</u>active <u>inter</u>war <u>pre</u>date
<u>mis</u>behave <u>super</u>natural

1 extreme/beyond
2 before
3 bad
4 too much/more than usual
5 between

2 How does adding the prefix *under/over* change the meaning of the following verbs? Write example sentences that are true about you using *under/over* with these verbs.

achieve charge cook
do estimate feed work

3 Look at the examples. What does the prefix *re-* mean?

1 We'll have to *review* the situation in a year's time.
2 After the fire, they had to *rebuild* the school.

Word formation (Part 3)
▶ **EXAM** FOCUS p.186

4 Read the text quickly. Then work in pairs and answer the questions.

1 How did Steven Osborne overcome stage fright?
2 Find examples in the text of words used with prefixes.

Befriending stage fright

Stage fright is a problem which is sometimes **(0)** <u>underestimated</u> by musicians. It is often accompanied by alarming physical symptoms such as a racing heart and trembling fingers. Classical performers are especially vulnerable because a superhuman level of **(1)** .... is required.   **ESTIMATE**   **ACCURATE**

Even the most experienced musicians can suffer from stage fright. It happened without warning to the Scottish pianist Steven Osborne. In the middle of a performance, he suddenly started worrying that he was about to forget the next note. This kept happening and soon he began to fear he was **(2)** .... of performing and even considered giving up. After trying **(3)** .... therapies, he decided that the only way to overcome this irrational fear was to treat his stage fright in the same way as he treated a piece of music – as an interesting challenge. He had to retrain himself to think in a different way and not to put so much pressure on himself. 'I realised that getting impatient and being very **(4)** .... of myself was counterproductive and I gave up aiming for **(5)** ....'   **CAPABLE**   **VARY**   **CRITIC**   **PERFECT**

And strangely enough, this seemed to be the **(6)** .... to the problem. Trying to eliminate **(7)** .... such as stage fright is not always the right approach. For Steven, accepting that his performances would contain some mistakes helped him to **(8)** .... his confidence so that he could trust himself to perform again.   **SOLVE**   **ANXIOUS**   **GAIN**

5 Use the word given in capitals at the end of some of the lines to form a word that fits in the gap in the same line. There is an example at the beginning (0).

EXAM TIP

Read the text again when you have finished to make sure your answers make sense and the words are spelt correctly.

6 Work in pairs and discuss the questions.

1 Why do you think so many people experience stage fright or other types of performance anxiety?
2 What do you think is the best way to overcome these fears or other fears and phobias?

1 **Look at the photos and discuss the questions.**

1 Which of these jobs/situations do you think is the most frightening?

2 Do you think bravery is something people can learn?

3 Which of these situations would make you feel nervous?

having a job interview   learning a new skill
starting a new job   talking to strangers at a party

2 **Which adjectives refer to the activity and which to the person who does them?**

adventurous brave breathtaking demanding
determined exciting exhausting irresponsible
skillful terrifying worthwhile

Short extracts (Part 1)

▶ **EXAM** FOCUS p.188

3 ▶ 34 **You will hear people talking in eight different situations. For each question, choose the best answer, A, B or C.**

EXAM TIP

Underline the key words in the question and make sure the option you choose answers this question.

1 On the radio, you hear a man talking about extreme sports.
   How does he feel about taking risks?
   A He is excited about the challenge.
   B He is unsure why he enjoys doing this.
   C He is worried about having an accident.

2 You hear a man and a woman talking at a party.
   Why isn't the woman enjoying the party?
   A None of her friends are there.
   B She finds talking to strangers difficult.
   C There is no-one to dance with.

3 You overhear two friends discussing learning Mandarin. What have they both found easier than expected?
   A writing
   B grammar
   C pronunciation

4 You hear a man talking to a student. What is the man's job?
   A a journalist
   B a charity worker
   C a careers advisor

5 You hear two friends talking about rugby. What do they agree about?
   A how dangerous the sport is
   B how interesting it is to watch
   C how enjoyable it is to play

6 You overhear a woman talking to a friend about her new job. What does she think of her new boss?
   A She is very demanding.
   B She is very inspiring.
   C She is very supportive.

7 You hear a man telling a friend about travelling alone. What disadvantage does he mention?
   A There is no support when things go wrong.
   B There are too many choices to be made
   C There is no one to share memories with.

8 You overhear a woman leaving a message for her son. Why is she phoning him?
   A to tell him about an appointment
   B to make a new arrangement
   C to explain where to meet

4 **Discuss the questions in pairs.**

1 Do you think it's better to be a risk-taker or risk-averse?

2 Which is the riskiest behaviour (A–D), and why?
   A not wearing a helmet when cycling or skiing
   B driving above the speed limit
   C walking home alone late at night
   D eating food that's past its sell-by date

Adjectives and verbs with prepositions

1 Cross out the adjective which does NOT fit in the sentence.

1 She's very *committed/involved/dedicated/devoted* to teaching young people about safety.

2 She was very *concerned/worried/timid/anxious* about taking part in the race.

3 He felt *sure/convinced/determined/confident* of his ability to win.

4 He's *thrilled/excited/enthusiastic/keen* about joining the skydiving team.

2 Use four of the adjectives to write sentences that are true for you. Then discuss your sentences with a partner.

3 Complete the sentences with the prepositions in the box. You can use them more than once.

about from in on to with

1 He complained .... the inaccurate map of the area.

2 She always insists .... the best diving equipment.

3 My father admitted .... feeling nervous.

4 He was involved .... a skiing accident.

5 He was prevented .... competing because of an injury.

6 She has to deal .... many dangerous situations.

7 You have to rely .... your partner when you're climbing.

8 He's determined .... enter the race.

9 My boss congratulated me .... my achievement.

10 He's very keen .... skydiving.

Phrasal verbs with *off*

4 Replace the phrasal verbs in italics with the correct form of the words in the box so that the meaning stays the same.

cancel delay explode get rid of go away
say goodbye separate shout at someone

1 They *put off* the start of the climb because of the storm.

2 I try to *work off* any negative feelings by exercising in the gym.

3 The trip was *called off* because the weather was too bad.

4 The guide *told us off* for breaking the safety rules.

5 A lot of people came to the port to *see us off* before we started the yacht race.

6 There was a loud bang and we realised one of the fireworks had *gone off* by accident.

7 When I hit my knee on the rock it hurt really badly but the pain gradually *wore off*.

8 The village was *cut off* from the outside world by the flood.

5 Find out if your partner has

1 ever been cut off by snow or flooding.

2 ever called off something important.

3 ever been told off by a neighbour.

4 put anything off recently.

5 ever seen anyone off at an airport.

6 experienced something painful that gradually wore off.

7 tried to work off anger or stress by exercising.

Hypothetical meaning

wish, if only, it's time

▶ **GRAMMAR** REFERENCE p.162

1 ▶ 35 **Listen to a man talking about giving up skateboarding and answer the questions.**

1 Why did he give up skateboarding?

A His wife wanted him to.

B He had too many accidents.

C He felt he was too old.

2 Do you think he should have given it up?

2 **Look at the examples and answer the questions.**

1 *Everyone kept saying 'It's time you stopped'.*

Did everyone think it was a good idea for him to stop skateboarding? Had he already stopped?

2 *If only I hadn't given up.*

Did he give up skateboarding? Is he sorry he gave up?

3 *If only I could start again!*

Would he like to start skateboarding again? Is this possible?

4 *I wish I was twenty years younger.*

Would he like to be younger? Is this possible?

5 *I wish my wife wouldn't tell me I need a new hobby all the time.*

Does his wife tell him he needs a new hobby? Does he mind?

3 **Look at the examples 2–5 in Activity 2 and match 1–4 below to A–D.**

1 We use *wish/if only/it's time* + past simple

2 We use *wish/if only* + could

3 We use *wish/if only* + would

4 We use *wish/if only* + past perfect

A to wish that something could have been different in the past.

B to wish that something could be different about other people in the present/future.

C to wish for a change in the present/future about ourselves.

D to wish that something could be different about ourselves now.

> **LANGUAGE TIP**
> - Use *if only* when your feelings of regret are strong.
> - *I wish/If only/It's time* can be followed by *was/were* in spoken English, but *were* is used in formal written English, e.g. *I wish I were able to help you.*

4 **Complete the sentences to make true wishes about yourself. Then say which of your partner's wishes are also true for you.**

1 I wish I could ....

2 I wish I didn't have ....

3 I wish my parents would ....

4 I wish I'd never ....

5 It's time I tried ....

other expressions with hypothetical meaning

5 **Choose the correct alternative in italics so that the second sentence means the same as the first.**

1 Suppose we didn't go to work tomorrow …

They *have decided not to go/are thinking about not going* to work tomorrow.

2 I met my friend Alison last night and it was as though we'd only seen each other the day before.

It felt like I *had/hadn't* seen my friend Alison very recently.

3 I'd rather you didn't go climbing this weekend.

I don't want you/You're not allowed to go climbing this weekend.

4 What if we just told him the truth?

They *have already told him the truth/are considering telling him the truth.*

6 **Complete the sentences with the correct form of the verbs in brackets.**

1 Suppose we .... (*go*) there next week instead of tomorrow?

2 I felt as if someone .... (*gave*) me a million dollars!

3 I'd rather you .... (*not take*) so many risks.

4 What if we .... (*stay*) at home instead of going to the party?

7 **Work in pairs.**

Student A, turn to page 138 and follow the instructions.

Student B, turn to page 139 and follow the instructions.

Long turn (Part 2)
responding to your partner's photographs

▶ **EXAM** FOCUS p.190

1 Look at the two photographs above. Which of the sports would you least like to do?

2 ▶ **36** Listen to a student called Layla doing the task below and answer the questions.

> These photographs show people taking risks in different situations. I'd like you to compare the two photographs and say which person you think is taking the most risks.

1 Does Layla cover both parts of the task adequately?

2 Do you agree with her opinion? Why/Why not?

3 Match the expressions Layla uses to the reasons for using them A–D.

1	Both photos show …	**A**	giving an opinion
2	I'd imagine …	**B**	talking about differences
3	I'd say …	**C**	talking about similarities
4	In a way, … whereas …	**D**	speculating

4 Listen again. What other expressions does Layla use for categories A–D?

5 Work in pairs and think of at least two other useful expressions for each category.

6 ▶ **37** After your partner has finished speaking, the examiner will ask you a question. Listen and say whether you agree with Leo.

EXAM TIP

When you answer the follow-up question, you only have to give a short response. Try not to repeat what your partner has said.

7 Work in pairs. Student A, look at the photos on page 135 and do the exam task in Activity 2. Student B, which of these activities would you prefer to do?

8 Student B, look at the photos on page 137 and do the exam task in Activity 2. Student A, would you enjoy doing dangerous activities like these?

Review (Part 2)
expressing personal opinions
▶ **WRITING** REFERENCE p.172

1 **Work in pairs and discuss the questions.**

1 What makes you decide to go and see a film at the cinema?

2 How reliable do you think film reviews are?

2 **Read the exam task. What kind of information do people want to know when they read a film review?**

You see this announcement in an English language newspaper.

> ## FILM REVIEWS WANTED
> **Have you seen a really exciting film recently, at the cinema or on TV?**
> Write a review, describing it and saying why you would recommend it to other people of your age.

Write your **review** in **140–190** words.

3 **Read the model review and match each paragraph with a topic A–D.**

A summary of plot and comment on the acting

B factual details about the film

C overall opinion/recommendation

D details of the film-making

127 Hours

127 Hours is a survival drama film, based on a true story and set in an isolated part of Utah in the USA. It is co-written and directed by the Oscar-winning director, Danny Boyle.

The film stars James Franco, who is totally convincing as the real-life mountaineer, Aron Ralston, trapped for five days when his arm got jammed under a huge rock. As food and water begin to run out, he has to make a terrible decision if he isn't going to die. Then he walks for seven miles before he is eventually rescued.

With his unique creative and visual style, Boyle lets the camera do a lot of the talking with the fascinating shots of the Canyon and each and every expression of the unfortunate Aron. The rhythmic music is every bit as wonderful, and should have won the award it was nominated for.

Personally, I haven't been so gripped by anything for a long time. I hadn't expected to find it so totally inspirational. It may well put you off extreme sports for life, but afterwards you'll start wondering 'What would I have done in that situation?'

4 **Read the review again and tick the things that are mentioned.**

cast   director   producer

costumes location   script

cinematography music   story

5 **Match the words in the box to the headings 1–5. Some words may match more than one heading.**

complicated confusing convincing
disappointing entertaining exciting
fast-paced frightening impressive
outstanding stunning witty

1 Performances

2 Cast

3 Special effects

4 Plot

5 Script

6 **Read the exam task and brainstorm ideas. Think about how to organise your review and what kind of language to include. Then write the review.**

EXAM TIP

Make it clear at the end of the review what your overall opinion is and whether or not you would recommend the film/product/experience to someone else.

You see this announcement in an English language magazine.

> ## WANTED
> **Where do you shop in our area?**
> We'd like to know your opinion of a shop in the area. Include the types of thing sold, value for money, quality, the staff and service.
> We will publish the best reviews every week.

Write your **review** in **140–190** words.

7 **Read your review and check you have answered the question and included all the relevant information. Make sure you have used a range of language and organised your ideas.**

1 **Complete the second sentence so that it has a similar meaning to the first sentence, using the word given. Use between two and five words, including the word given.**

1 Ella is sorry she didn't learn to snowboard when she was younger.

   WISHES

   Ella .... how to snowboard when she was younger.

2 I would prefer you to wear a helmet when you ride your bike.

   RATHER

   I .... a helmet when you ride your bike.

3 I think you should go home now.

   TIME

   I think .... home.

4 It felt as if my legs were made of jelly.

   THOUGH

   My legs .... were made of jelly.

5 I took the bus because the train is so expensive.

   BEEN

   If the .... so expensive, I wouldn't have taken the bus.

6 I didn't get up in time and now I'm late for work.

   WOULD

   I .... late for work if I'd got up in time.

2 **Complete the sentences with the correct form of the word in brackets.**

1 Living in China for two years .... my horizons. (broad)

2 The race had a very .... finish. (drama)

3 Meeting my hero was very .... (inspire)

4 People were very .... of his decision to climb the mountain in such bad weather. (critic)

5 In order to work .... , it's important to take frequent breaks. (produce)

6 Many people find that yoga reduces their .... (anxious)

7 This meat is really tough. It's completely .... (cook)

8 It's taken far longer than I expected – I .... how long this project would take me to do. (estimate)

9 The road was destroyed in the storm and had to be .... (build)

10 It was very................. to go surfing alone in such a strong wind. (responsible)

3 **Complete the text with the correct prepositions.**

TEENAGER COMPLETES WORLD SAILING TRIP

Returning **(1)** .... her 200-day solo trip around the world, sixteen-year-old Jessica Watson said: 'I'm just a girl who believed **(2)** .... her dream. You don't have to be someone special to succeed **(3)** .... achieving something big.' She was congratulated **(4)** .... her success by the Australian Premier. Critics questioned whether she was experienced enough to take **(5)** .... the treacherous journey and whether her parents should have called it **(6)** .... , but she said: 'The one thing I won't accept is when someone calls this reckless. We spent years preparing **(7)** .... this trip.' The first few months of the trip went well, although the lack **(8)** .... human contact inevitably had an impact **(9)** .... her state of mind at times. Jessica admitted **(10)** .... being 'pretty moody and a little homesick' and in April wrote on her blog: 'I think I am ready to come home now.' But harder times were to come. In the final stages of her trip Jessica had to deal **(11)** .... waves as large as a four-storey building, towering 'like liquid mountains'. She had to strap herself into her bunk and put on a crash helmet to prevent herself **(12)** .... being injured in the wild seas.

12 Crime scene

1 Work in pairs and discuss the questions.

1 What would you expect being in prison to be like? Think about the accommodation, food, staff, clothing, rules, etc.

2 How would you feel about staying in a hotel which used to be a prison?

Sentence completion (Part 2)

▶ **EXAM** FOCUS p.188

2 You will hear a journalist called Nick talking about a new type of hotel for paying guests. Read the gapped summary first and predict what the answers might be.

3 ▶ 38 Listen and complete the sentences 1–10 with a word or short phrase.

PRISON HOTELS

The growth in (1) .... has encouraged owners of former prisons to turn them into hotels. The majority of guests at Karosta prison are on (2) .... visits. Each guest's (3) .... is inserted in a prison document. Only (4) .... is available to drink at dinner. When they are in their cells, guests must remain (5) .... , unless given permission to do otherwise. The journalist says the advertisement's description of the (6) .... at the prison is accurate. One tour around Latvia offers accommodation at Karosta prison for a period of just (7) .... The journalist does not recommend the (8) .... in cell rooms at the Alcatraz Hotel. In the Alcatraz Hotel, the (9) .... are very different from those in a real prison. A small double room at the Alcatraz Hotel costs (10) .... euros.

4 Why do you think that people might want to stay in an ex-prison?

5 What is the purpose of a prison? Put these reasons in order of importance, then compare with a partner.

- to protect the public
- to discourage other people from committing crimes
- to punish criminals
- to rehabilitate criminals into society

6 Discuss what alternatives there are to prison for these crimes. Look at the examples in the box.

- dangerous driving
- burglary
- shop-lifting
- fraud
- domestic violence

---
acquit   ban   community service   a fine
put on probation   suspended sentence

Example: *If it were a first crime, a dangerous driver could be fined and banned from driving.*

Obligation, prohibition and necessity

must, have to, need, allowed to

▶ **GRAMMAR** REFERENCE p.163

1 What would it be like to work as a prison officer? What kind of person would you need to be?

2 Read the statements and decide who said each one: a) a police officer, b) a prison officer or c) a prisoner.

1 We have to inspect all mail sent to prisoners.

2 We mustn't talk to journalists about cases we are investigating.

3 We don't have to work or go to classes if we don't want to.

4 We are not allowed to have more than three visitors at a time.

5 I must try and stay positive until I'm freed.

6 I needn't have spent so long preparing for the trial because in the end the defendant pleaded guilty.

3 Which of the statements in Activity 2 refer to

A an obligation the speaker feels is necessary?

B an obligation someone else says is necessary?

C things that aren't permitted?

D a lack of necessity/obligation?

E something that was done but wasn't necessary?

LANGUAGE TIP

Must is only used in the present. To talk about obligation in the past or future, use *have to*.

*We **had to** wear a school uniform until we were sixteen; I **will have to** save more if I want to buy a car.*

4 Choose the correct option in italics.

1 When you are arrested you *don't have to/are not allowed to* answer all the police's questions.

2 Witnesses *mustn't/don't have to* tell lies in court.

3 We *must/had to* stay in our prison cells for up to twenty-three hours per day. It was awful.

4 Don't forget. You *must/need* remember to carry your identity cards with you at all times.

5 I *didn't need to wait/needn't have waited* so long this time to go into the visitors' room.

6 I wasn't sure if I would *have to/be allowed to* give him the present I'd brought with me.

5 Complete the second sentence so that it has a similar meaning to the first sentence, using the word given. You must use between two and five words, including the word given.

1 It was good to see you but it wasn't necessary for you to visit me in prison.
   NEED
   You .... visited me in prison but it was good to see you.

2 You mustn't open the door to strangers.
   ALLOWED
   You .... the door to strangers.

3 Members of the jury are prohibited from talking to the press.
   MUST
   Members of the jury .... to the press.

4 It isn't necessary for suspects to answer police questions.
   HAVE
   Suspects .... answer police questions.

5 His job involves collecting evidence at the scene of a crime.
   HAS
   He .... evidence at the scene of a crime.

6 Was getting advice from a lawyer really necessary?
   NEED
   Did he really .... advice from a lawyer?

6 Discuss what people in court (e.g. the judge, lawyers, witnesses, defendants, jury, police officers)

1 have to do.

2 mustn't do/aren't allowed to do.

3 are allowed to do.

4 needn't do/don't have to do.

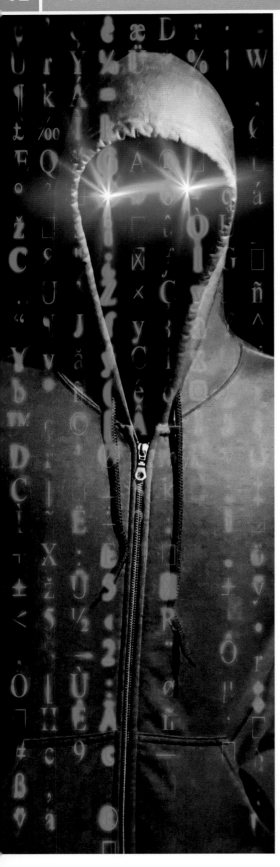

Cybercrime

1 **Work in pairs and discuss the questions.**

1   In what ways do you think the internet can be a dangerous place?
2   What can people do to protect themselves and others against cybercrime?
3   What could the government do to cut down on cybercrime?

2 **What do you think of people who**

1   download music/films/books illegally?
2   post a picture of someone without their consent on social media?
3   hack into people's accounts?
4   bully, stalk or 'troll' people online?
5   threaten national security?
6   steal other people's identity?

3 **What could the possible consequences of doing these things be? Think about**

1   the individuals.
2   society.
3   the industries involved.

Discussion (Part 4)

▶ **EXAM** FOCUS p.190

4 **In pairs, look at the examiner's questions 1–4 and make notes on what you will say.**

1   Which technological device is the most important to you?
2   Do you think people are too dependent on technology?
3   How would you feel if you couldn't access the internet for a month?
4   To what extent do you think social media contributes towards people's wellbeing?

5 **Join another pair. Each pair will take turns to answer the questions. The other pair of students must listen carefully and note down whether the students speaking**

A   only gave very short answers.
B   tried to include each other in the discussion and make follow-up comments.
C   used a wide variety of language.
D   asked for something to be repeated if necessary.
E   dominated the discussion.

   Then swap roles.

> **EXAM TIP**
>
> You can expand your ideas by giving specific examples (e.g. examples of people you know who rely too much on technology).

6 **Work in groups and discuss your feedback.**

Shopping online
verb/noun collocations

1 What are the advantages and risks of shopping online?

2 Match the first part of the safety advice 1–6 to the second part A–F.

1 In order to access
2 You need to install/download
3 Ensure that you take
4 Safeguarding
5 There are important steps to follow before making
6 You have to register/update/check

A the appropriate software.
B your personal details each time you use your credit card.
C security precautions/measures to protect your data.
D your privacy online from potential fraudsters is essential.
E the internet, you will have to set up an account with a service provider.
F an online transaction/payment/purchase.

3 Use the verb/noun collocations in Activity 2 to talk about yourself.

> **Example:** *It can take me ages to make an online purchase because I keep forgetting my passwords.*

adjective/noun and noun collocations

4 Match the adjectives/nouns 1–6 to the nouns A–F to make a phrase connected to computers and online shopping.

1 credit card   A case
2 browser   B retailers
3 strong   C scams
4 in upper/lower   D password
5 security   E measures
6 established   F window

5 Read the text and complete it with the correct form of collocations from Activities 2 and 4. There may be more than one possible answer.

Top tips on how to stay secure online

Online shopping is big business these days. However, great care should be taken when making any online **(1)** .... , whether they are for clothes or services. Unfortunately, cybercriminals are all too ready to exploit consumers benefitting from the <u>convenience</u>, affordability and choice which the internet offers so it is crucial to **(2)** .... your <u>privacy</u>.

- Sometimes it is difficult to differentiate between the genuine and fraudulent. Even seemingly professional-looking websites can be fake so stick with **(3)** .... retailers where possible as they will have good <u>security</u> **(4)** .... in place.

- <u>Ensure</u> the website is reputable by looking out for a small padlock symbol in the **(5)** .... window when you attempt to log in or **(6)** .... your personal details. The web address should begin with https:// – the 's' stands for 'secure'.

- Make it a priority to **(7)** .... effective and updated antivirus/antispyware before you go online.

- Be suspicious of tempting offers – there are plenty of scams around and if it seems too good to be true, it probably is! It could indicate that a site is selling illegal items or trying to infect your device.

- Before you **(8)** .... a <u>payment</u>, make sure you have a **(9)** .... password – ideally a <u>combination</u> of letters in upper and lower **(10)** .... , numbers and symbols.

- Use your mobile phone network rather than public wifi connections when using a card to pay, as many hotspots are insecure.

word formation

6 Complete the sentences with the correct form of the verb in brackets.

1 Most people these days appreciate the .... (*convenient*) of shopping online.
2 For .... (*secure*) reasons, people are advised to change their passwords frequently.
3 These days it is increasingly difficult to .... (*sure*) a person's .... (*private*) online.
4 A .... (*combine*) of factors may be the reason for the growth in cybercrime.
5 It is sometimes better to make a .... (*pay*) with a credit, rather than a debit, card.

7 Discuss the questions. Use words from Activities 2 and 4.

1 Which goods or services do you buy online? What is your experience of this?
2 Have you ever been 'scammed'? If so, what happened?

Multiple choice (Part 5)

▶ **EXAM** FOCUS p.187

1 **Discuss the questions.**

1 Why do you think crime fiction is one of the best-selling genres in many countries?

2 Which crime novels, films or TV programmes are popular in your country?

2 **You are going to read an extract from a crime novel. First skim the extract to get an idea of what and who it is about.**

3 **For questions 1–6, choose the answer (A, B, C or D) which you think fits best according to the text.**

> **EXAM TIP**
>
> Make sure you read all the options carefully before making your decision.

1 The writer mentions Martin's unwillingness to kill flies to show that he
   A has a lot of patience.
   B wishes he was braver.
   C avoids being aggressive.
   D is fond of small creatures.

2 The people in the queue didn't try to stop the incident because they
   A were afraid of getting involved in it.
   B realised it was none of their business.
   C wanted to know what would happen next.
   D didn't want to lose their place in the queue.

3 Martin threw his bag at the Honda driver
   A to protect himself from being hit by the bat.
   B because the Honda driver was damaging the victim's car.
   C because he had decided it was the only sensible solution.
   D to distract the Honda driver from killing the Peugeot driver.

4 A *missile* in line 53 refers to
   A a heavy bag.
   B a type of laptop.
   C an object intended to hurt someone.
   D a weapon which can cause an explosion.

5 *that* in line 56 refers to
   A using magic.
   B closing his eyes.
   C trying to hide from people.
   D making himself anonymous.

6 Martin was astonished that
   A his bag had missed the Honda driver.
   B the Honda driver had decided to leave.
   C the Honda driver was unable to find him.
   D the crowd were supporting the Honda driver.

Kate Atkinson

Martin had never done anything like that in his life before. He didn't even kill flies in the house, instead he patiently <u>stalked</u> them, trapping them with a glass and a plate before letting them free. The meek shall inherit the earth. He was fifty and had never knowingly committed an act of violence against another living creature, although sometimes he thought that might be more to do with cowardice than pacifism.

He had stood in the queue, waiting for someone else to <u>intervene</u> in the scene unfolding before them, but the crowd were in audience mode, like promenaders at a particularly brutal piece of theatre, and they had no intention of spoiling the entertainment. Even Martin had wondered at first if it was another show – a faux-impromptu piece intended either to shock or to reveal our immunity to being shocked because we lived in a global media community where we had become passive voyeurs of violence (and so on). That was the line of thought running through the detached, intellectual part of his brain. His primitive brain, on the other hand, was thinking, Oh, this is horrible, really horrible, please make the bad man go away. He wasn't surprised to hear his father's voice in his head (*Pull yourself together, Martin*). His father had been dead for many years but Martin often still heard the bellow and yell of his parade-ground tones.

When the Honda driver finished breaking the windows of the silver Peugeot and walked towards the driver, <u>brandishing</u> his weapon and preparing himself for a final victory blow, Martin realised that the man on the ground was probably going to die, was probably going to be *killed* by the crazed man with the bat right there in front of them unless someone did something and, instinctively, without thinking about it at all – because if he'd thought about it he might not have done it – he slipped his bag off his shoulder and swung it, hammer-throw fashion, at the head of the insane Honda driver.

Vocabulary
verbs

4 **Match the underlined verbs in the text to their meanings 1–8.**

1 do what is necessary to complete something
2 turn around quickly
3 follow something quietly in order to catch it
4 hold something or someone tightly
5 become involved in a difficult situation
6 hurt or frighten someone who is less powerful than you
7 wave something in a threatening way
8 move someone or something away

KATE ATKINSON

Author of *Case Histories*

One Good Turn

'That rarest of things – a good literary novel and a cracking read' *Observer*

One Good Turn

He missed the man's head, which didn't surprise him – he'd never been able to aim or catch, he was the kind of person who ducked when a ball was thrown in his direction – but his laptop was in the bag and the hard weighty edge of it caught the Honda driver on the shoulder and sent him <u>spinning</u>.

The nearest Martin had been to a real crime scene previously had been on a Society of Authors' trip around St Leonard's police station. Apart from Martin, the group consisted entirely of women. 'You're our token man,' one of them said to him, and he sensed a certain disappointment in the polite laughter of the others, as if the least he could have done as their token man was to be a little less like a woman.

Martin expected the Honda driver to pick himself up off the ground and search the crowd to find the culprit who had thrown a missile at him. Martin tried to make *line 53* himself an anonymous figure in the queue, tried to pretend he didn't exist. He closed his eyes. He had done that at school when he was <u>bullied</u>, <u>clinging to</u> an ancient, *line 56* desperate magic – they wouldn't hit him if he couldn't see them. He imagined the Honda driver walking towards him, the baseball bat raised high, the arc of annihilation waiting to happen.

To his amazement, when he opened his eyes, the Honda driver was climbing back into his car. As he drove away a few people in the crowd gave him a slow hand-clap. Martin wasn't sure if they were expressing disapproval of the Honda driver's behaviour or disappointment at his failure to <u>follow through</u>. Whichever, they were a hard crowd to please.

Martin knelt on the ground and said, 'Are you OK?' to the Peugeot driver, but then he was politely but firmly <u>set aside</u> by the two policewomen who arrived and took control of everything.

5 **Work in pairs. Choose three verbs from Activity 4 and use them to make two true sentences and one false sentence about your life. Take turns to read your sentences out. Can your partner guess which one is false?**

6 **Discuss these questions about the text.**

1 What kind of person is Martin?
2 What do we learn about Martin's background?
3 Do you think that Martin was right to get involved? What would you have done?
4 What examples of road rage have you experienced or witnessed?

Open cloze (Part 2)

▶ **EXAM** FOCUS p.186

1 Read the text quickly. In what way has tourism been affected by crime novels?

2 Read the text again and think of the word which best fits each gap. Use only one word in each gap. There is an example at the beginning (0).

EXAM TIP

Read the text again when you have finished to make sure your answers make sense and the words are spelt correctly.

In the footsteps of the fictional detective

Detective novels have been extremely popular ever (0) *since* Sherlock Holmes first caught the public's imagination over a hundred years ago. However, nowadays this particular genre of novel seems to (1) .... selling even more than ever. Novels (2) .... *The Da Vinci Code*, for example, have sold millions of copies all (3) .... the world and have been made into blockbuster films. In fact, *The Da Vinci Code* has become (4).............. popular that walking tours are available in Paris in order (5) .... people to be able to see the places which were mentioned in the novel.

One of the (6) .... popular fictional detectives these days is Wallander, the main character in a series of novels written (7) .... the Swedish author, Henning Mankell. For millions of people worldwide, Ystad, a small town in Sweden, has now established (8) .... as being synonymous with murders and the man who solves them. People flock there in huge numbers to visit, which proves that crime is a tourist attraction.

3 Have you ever been on, or would you consider going on, a tour of a place where a book, film or TV show was set? Why/Why not?

Reflexive pronouns

▶ **GRAMMAR** REFERENCE p.163

4 Read the Language Tip and say why the answer to question 8 in Activity 2 is a reflexive pronoun.

LANGUAGE TIP

- Use reflexive pronouns with transitive verbs (verbs that take a direct object) when the subject and object are the same person/thing.

Martin expected (the Honda driver) to pick **himself** *(NOT him) up off the ground.*

Martin tried to make **himself** *(NOT him) an anonymous figure in the crowd.*

- Intransitive verbs (verbs which do not take a direct object), e.g. *remember, relax, feel*, do not take a reflexive pronoun.
- Some verbs can be reflexive or not reflexive.

I always **enjoy myself** *at your parties. I really* **enjoyed** *the party.*

- Notice the difference between *each other/one another* and reflexive pronouns.

They think about **themselves** *a lot. They think about* **each other** *a lot.*

5 What's the difference in meaning between the following sentences?

1 **A** Florence reminded herself to record the new crime series on TV.

B Florence reminded her husband to record the new crime series on TV.

2 **A** Suzy and Sam blamed themselves for not reporting the crime straightaway.

B Suzy and Sam blamed each other for not reporting the crime straightaway.

3 **A** I went to the police station myself.

B I went to the police station by myself.

6 Complete the sentences with a pronoun (e.g. *me*), a reflexive pronoun (e.g. *myself*) or (–) where no pronoun is needed.

1 We enjoyed .... a lot at the prison hotel.

2 My husband finds it hard to relax .... at work functions in case he forgets someone's name.

3 I wish you'd stop pulling her hair. You're hurting ....

4 They both really enjoyed .... the wonderful meal.

5 My brother was so good at the piano that my parents always compared .... to Mozart.

6 A man I didn't know recognised me from work and introduced .... to me.

7 In pairs, give each other advice on how to remember important information, using the words in the box. Decide whether to use a reflexive pronoun or not.

relax   remember   remind
send   write   test   tell

Example: Ask one of your family to remind you about important dates.

have/get something done

▶ **GRAMMAR** REFERENCE p.164

1 **Read the dialogue. Which of the phrases in italics refer to**

1 something over which people had no control?

2 something which happened as a result of an arrangement?

Zara: I heard there was a break-in at your office the other night. Did they take anything?

Dan: Luckily, not much. We *had some computers stolen* but that was about it.

Zara: What did the police do about it?

Dan: The usual. They *got the rooms fingerprinted* but I don't expect they'll catch anyone.

2 **Complete the rule to show how causative *have/get* is formed.**

have or .... + object + ... of the verb

3 **Look at the list of some things victims have to do after a crime has been committed and follow the instructions 1–4.**

- report the crime to the police
- change their locks
- repair broken windows
- buy a guard dog
- stop their credit cards
- clean the house
- find their insurance policy
- install an alarm

1 Put a tick (✔) next to the things people often do themselves.

2 Put a cross (✗) next to the things people would probably have done for them/get somebody to do for them.

3 Add anything else you can think of to the list.

4 Discuss your lists in groups. Have you ever had to do any of these things?

4 **Read the dialogues 1–6 and complete the responses using the correct forms of the words in brackets.**

1 **A** This room looks different?

   B Yes, we .... (*have/just/paint*).

2 **A** This tooth has been aching for ages now.

   B Why don't you go to the dentist's and .... (*get/look at*)?

3 **A** My hair is so long it takes ages to wash and dry.

   B Why don't you .... (*have/cut*)?

4 **A** I think I must be getting a bit short-sighted!

   B Go to the optician's and .... (*get/test*).

5 **A** Did you put that shed up yourself?

   B No, I .... last year (*get/a friend/put it up*).

6 **A** What a beautiful family photograph!

   B Yes, we .... by a professional (*have/take*).

LANGUAGE TIP

Have/Get + noun phrase + *-ed* (sometimes called the causative) is a form of the passive. It is often (but not always) used to say that somebody causes something to be done by someone else.

*I **had/got** my hair cut.*

It is commonly used in spoken language. *Got* is more informal, and not generally used to describe unpleasant experiences.

*I **had** (not got) my car stolen.*

Report (Part 2)
making recommendations
▶ **WRITING** REFERENCE p.170

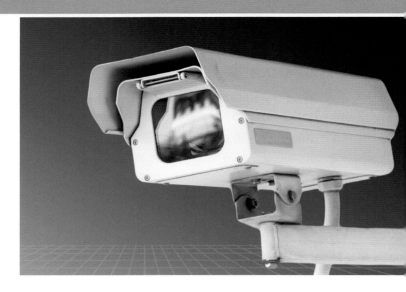

1 Read the exam task and a student's report. Then answer the questions.

1 Is all the necessary information included?
2 Is there any irrelevant information?
3 Is the report written in an appropriate style?

> The college where you study has been given some money to spend on improving security, either by installing lockers for students to keep valuables in or security cameras inside the building. Now the director of the college has asked you to write a report describing the benefits of both ideas and saying which one the money should be spent on and why.
>
> Write your **report** in **140–190** words.

Introduction
The purpose of this report is to recommend how the money provided for improving security at the college should be spent. It has been suggested that either lockers for students' valuables or security cameras should be installed.

Benefits of installing lockers
Currently there is nowhere for students to keep valuable possessions such as laptops or sports equipment. If lockers were installed, students would no longer have to carry valuables around with them, thereby reducing the risk of theft. It would also mean less likelihood of accidents. I dropped and broke my laptop last year.

Benefits of installing security cameras
• would reduce the number of valuables stolen each year
• would discourage people from stealing
• would make it easier to identify thieves

Recommendations
Although both ideas would be popular with students, I think security cameras would be more successful at improving security and reducing crime. In any case, there isn't space in the college for enough lockers to be installed. I would therefore either recommend spending the money on putting security cameras inside the building or simply discouraging students from bringing valuable items to college.

2 Complete the sentences with the correct form of *spend*. Sometimes more than one answer is possible.

1 I would therefore recommend .spending. the money on security cameras.
2 My recommendation would be .... more money on security cameras.
3 I recommend the college .... more money on security cameras.
4 It is recommended that the money .... on security cameras.

3 Which verbs/nouns could be used to replace *recommend/recommendation* in each sentence in Activity 2?

4 Work in pairs. Read the exam task and make notes under the headings *Advantages*, *Disadvantages* and *Recommendations*.

> A large number of mobile phones has been stolen from your college recently. The director of the college wants to avoid this problem by banning mobile phone use in college and has asked you to write a report about this. You should explain what the advantages and disadvantages of this idea would be and make recommendations.
>
> Write your **report** in **140–190** words.

5 Write your report. Remember to check your work using the writing checklist on page 165.

EXAM TIP

You should finish your report by giving one or two recommendations. It doesn't matter what solutions you suggest as long as your ideas are expressed appropriately.

1 Choose the correct option (A, B, C or D) to complete the sentences.

1 It is important to .... security precautions before going online.

   A take   **B** do   **C** have   **D** make

2 Before paying online, you need to register your personal ....

   A facts   **B** details   **C** factors   **D** points

3 Could you help me to .... this software?

   A place   **B** establish   **C** install   **D** position

4 My daughter helped me to set .... my account online.

   A down   **B** off   **C** out   **D** up

5 Before .... a payment online, you have to give personal information.

   A doing   **B** getting   **C** making   **D** performing

6 Do everything you can to .... your privacy on social media.

   A safeguard   **B** hold   **C** save   **D** watch over

2 Complete the second sentence so that it has a similar meaning to the first sentence, using the word given. You must use between two and five words.

1 We went to the lesson but it wasn't necessary because it was cancelled.

   NEED

   We .... to the lesson because it was cancelled.

2 The police officer didn't give us permission to go into the courtroom.

   ALLOWED

   We .... go into the courtroom.

3 During the lesson, you aren't allowed to speak unless you raise your hand.

   MUSTN'T

   During the lesson, you .... raising your hand.

4 Why don't you talk Harry into checking your brakes for you?

   GET

   Why don't you .... your brakes for you?

5 I hope you have a good time at the party.

   ENJOY

   I hope you .... at the party.

6 I'm going to ask a friend of mine to make my wedding dress.

   HAVE

   I'm going to .... by a friend of mine.

3 Complete the text using the correct form of the words in capitals.

What happens when you report a crime?

A woman went into the police station to report a theft and was able to give a full **(1)** .... of the man who stole her purse. Another witness had also reported the same man as acting **(2)** .... , so it wasn't very long before the police were able to find enough **(3)** .... to go to the **(4)** .... firm where he worked and arrest him.

DESCRIBE

SUSPECT

EVIDENT
SECURE

At the station, a request was made for a **(5)** .... to be present while the interviews were taking place. In the meantime, the police discovered that the man had been responsible for another **(6)** .... offence several years earlier, involving **(7)** .... behaviour. In court, the man was eventually found **(8)** .... and sentenced to six months' community service.

LAW

CRIME
THREAT

GUILT

PROGRESS TEST 4

Multiple-choice cloze (Part 1)

1 For questions 1–8, read the text below and decide which answer (A, B, C or D) best fits each gap. There is an example at the beginning.

Watch your (body) language

Most research now shows that as much as 70 to 80 percent of human interaction may be non-verbal. This kind of communication has been **(0)** *C, widely* studied since ancient times in an **(1)** .... to understand people's characters, and experts have endlessly **(2)** .... the significance of the way we move and position our bodies. **(3)** .... many feel that the study of body language can be over-simplistic, there is some evidence to show that some postures and movements indicate our emotional state of mind. The **(4)** .... people shake hands, for example, can be a good indicator of the power balance between them. Pulling the person towards you or grabbing hold of someone's elbow can show you want to **(5)** .... control. Personal space is another interesting area. The vast **(6)** .... of westerners feel uncomfortable if a friend stands closer than 45 centimetres away from them, although this will **(7)** .... from country to country.

And finally, it is likely that, if someone is **(8)** .... to you, they will copy the way you stand or move. If you're trying to make somebody relax, it can also help to 'mirror' their movements in this way.

Open cloze (Part 2)

2 For questions 9–16, read the text below and think of the word that best fits each gap. Use only one word in each gap. There is an example at the beginning.

The benefits of TV crime dramas

It can be irresistible to sit down and watch TV **(0)** *rather* than going for a run or cleaning the house. So **(9)** .... is good news for all those people who feel guilty about wasting time in this way. It seems that watching certain dramas is good for the brain.

According to recent scientific research, crime dramas exercise the brain more than any other kind of TV programme **(10)** .... of their complexity. For example, in order to work **(11)** .... the identity of the murderer, you have to remember who is who as well as their relationship to **(12)** .... other. Over a period of several weeks, you also need to recall what **(13)** .... already happened in previous episodes.

We are all aware that the human brain needs to **(14)** .... kept active. A good way of doing **(15)** .... is to be required to pay close attention to complicated stories. The more you challenge your brain, the more stimulation it receives, **(16)** .... will help to keep it healthy.

	A	B	C	D
0	highly	deeply	widely	strongly
1	act	action	attempt	approach
2	talked	argued	disagreed	discussed
3	But	Although	However	Nevertheless
4	way	style	custom	manner
5	be	take	bring	stay
6	number	quantity	majority	amount
7	vary	alter	compare	contrast
8	attracted	appealed	approved	fascinated

Word formation (Part 3)

3 For questions 17–24, read the text below. Use the word given in capitals at the end of some of the lines to form a word that fits in the gap in the same line. There is an example at the beginning.

Memory Champions

Do you have what it takes to become a memory champion? You would need the **(0)** _ability_ to remember up to 1,000 numbers in a sequence in under an hour plus several other seemingly **(17)** .... challenges. — **ABLE** / **POSSIBILITY**

The 'mind sport' of Memory was created in 1991. Today there are **(18)** .... from thirty countries participating in the sport with the aim of becoming the next World Memory Champion. — **COMPETITION**

None of even the most **(19)** .... memory champions would claim to be **(20)** .... gifted at memorising things. So how do they do it? Well, apparently the brain is better at remembering **(21)** .... images so memory champions spend a lot of time training their brains to translate abstract symbols into pictures. It's important to have a good **(22)** .... in order to create memorable images which the brain can store and then instantly recall at a later date. — **SUCCESS** / **SPECIAL** / **VISION** / **IMAGINE**

Training your brain in this way can be very **(23)** .... for anyone who needs to learn a lot of information in a short time. Some people also believe that this kind of training can be an **(24)** .... way of preventing memory loss as people get older. — **HELP** / **EFFECT**

Key word transformation (Part 4)

4 For questions 25–30, complete the second sentence so that it has a similar meaning to the first sentence, using the word given. Do not change the word given. You must use between two and five words, including the word given. Here is an example.

Example:

I'd strongly advise you not to get a dog just yet.

IF

I wouldn't get a dog just yet _if I were you_.

25 You mustn't cycle without wearing a helmet.

ALLOWED

You .... cycle without wearing a helmet.

26 Someone had already called the police so it wasn't necessary for you to call them.

NEED

Someone had already called the police so you .... them.

27 My parents would prefer me not to travel alone.

RATHER

My parents .... travel alone.

28 My grandfather would love to do extreme sports but he's too old.

WISHES

My grandfather .... extreme sports but he's too old.

29 'Don't forget to text me when you arrive,' Jake's mother said.

REMINDED

Jake's mother .... when he arrived.

30 He'll be able to finish the marathon provided he doesn't run too fast.

UNLESS

He'll be able to finish the marathon .... too fast.

Visuals for Speaking

Unit 3, Speaking focus, Activity 7
Student A

Your photos show people receiving gifts. Compare the photos and say what makes people happy about giving or receiving gifts.

> **What makes people happy about giving or receiving gifts?**

Unit 5, Speaking focus, Activity 6
Task 1

Student A: Look at the photos, which show people shopping for food. Compare the photos and say what the advantages and disadvantages are of shopping in these different places.

Student B: Do you prefer to go shopping in town or shopping online?

> **What are the advantages and disadvantages of shopping in these different places?**

Unit 7, Speaking focus, Activity 5
Task 1

Student A: Look at the photos, which show unusual places to live. Compare the photos and say why you think people might choose to live in these places.

Student B: Which of these places would you prefer to live in?

| Why do you think people might choose to live in these places? |

Unit 11, Speaking focus, Activity 7

| Which person is taking the most risks? |

Unit 3, Speaking focus, Activity 7
Student B

Your photos show people who love horses. Compare the photos and say what might make these people feel so strongly about their horses.

What might make these people feel so strongly about their horses?

Unit 5, Speaking focus, Activity 6
Task 2

Student A: Look at the photos, which show people having dinner. Compare the photos and say what the people enjoy about eating in these different ways.

Student B: Do you prefer to eat in front of the TV or to sit at the table with other people?

What might the people enjoy about eating in these different ways?

Unit 7, Speaking focus, Activity 5
Task 2

Student A: Look at the photos, which show unusual places to work. Compare the photos and say how difficult you think it would be to work in these places.

Student B: Which of these places would you prefer to work in?

| How difficult do you think it would be to work in these places? |

Unit 11, Speaking focus, Activity 8

| Which person is taking the most risks? |

Communication activities

Unit 2, Use of English focus, Activity 3

Score	24–30 points	13-23 points	6-12 points
Very likely = 5 points Quite likely = 4 points Neither likely nor unlikely = 3 points Quite unlikely = 2 points Very unlikely = 1 point	You are an extrovert. You are extremely sociable and confident. You much prefer being out with other people to staying at home. You're fun to be with but because you prefer to be the centre of attention, you're not always the best listener. You often have very strong opinions.	You are an ambivert, which means you have some introverted and extroverted qualities. You need to have a balance between having an exciting time out with friends and quiet times at home alone or with your family. You're happy to give your opinions when asked but also prepared to change your mind.	You are an introvert. You enjoy spending time alone and you tend to have just a few close friends. People trust you to keep a secret. People often think you are shy. You tend to think carefully before you speak and you're cautious when making decisions. You always see both sides of an argument.

Unit 10, Listening focus, Activity 3

Results: Add up your score.

	1	2	3	4	5	6	7	8
3 points	A	C	C	A	B	C	C	A
2 points	B	A	B	C	A	A	B	B
1 point	C	B	A	B	C	B	A	C

Circle friendships
Score: 12 or less

You have, or want, a wide circle of friends, and people might say you have a gift for friendship. You seek to know people in many walks of life, with different lifestyles and characters. You like nothing more than being with them all but you may also worry that different friends of yours won't get on. This shows that you have many parts to your character, and different friends appeal to different parts. The risk of your friendship type is that you may not actually get to know any of your friends very well. They are drawn to your extrovert character, though that can act as a barrier to intimacy.

Ladder friendships
Score: 13-18

You view life as a journey of change, evolution and progress. You therefore value friends who share your journey, or who are experiencing the same things as you. You like to encourage and help your friends get on in life and value it when they encourage and help you. You're very self-confident and enjoy meeting new people and make friends easily. But sometimes old friends will feel you've left them behind, though they will admit that you are an inspiring person to be with, someone who both challenges and excites them.

Soulmate friendships
Score 19-24

You value a small number of close friends, perhaps just one, and regard other people in your life as acquaintances. The benefit of soulmate friendship is the chance of knowing someone well and allowing them to know you. You are loyal and completely trustworthy. The risk you face is of disappointment with friends, since it's quite hard to meet someone you connect with so strongly. In fact, you may well have had a close friend in the past, and now feel that you don't. You value friendship so much because you know the treasure it offers.

Unit 11, Grammar focus, Activity 7
Student A

Think of what you might say in the following situations. Use *I wish/If only* and other expressions with hypothetical meaning. Then role-play the situations with your partner.

1 You are at a theme park with Student B. You want to go on a new roller-coaster ride.

2 You are lost in the mountains and Student B is reading the map. You know that you are better at reading maps than Student B. You are angry with yourself for getting into this situation.

Unit 2, Writing focus, Activity 7

Read the exam task. Brainstorm ideas and decide whether you agree/partly agree/disagree with the question. Look at the notes and decide which points to include in each paragraph. Then write your essay.

In your English class you have been talking about family relationships. Now, your teacher has asked you to write an essay.

Write an essay using all the points and give reasons for your point of view.
Write **140–190** words.

Is it better to have older or younger parents?

Notes

Write about:

1 things in common

2 experience

3 .... (your own idea)

Unit 4, Listening focus, Activity 1

1B   **2**A   **3**C   **4**A   **5**C

Unit 7, Writing focus, Activity 5

Read the exam task. Brainstorm ideas and plan how you will organise your answer. Then write the essay.

In your English class you have been talking about different kinds of holidays. Now, your teacher has asked you to write an essay.

Write an **essay** using all the points and give reasons for your point of view.
Write **140–190** words.

Is it better to have a holiday abroad or stay in your own country?

Notes

Write about:

1 cost

2 environmental issues

3 .... (your own idea)

Unit II, Grammar focus, Activity 7
Student B

Think of what you might say in the following situations. Use *I wish/ If only* and other expressions with hypothetical meaning. Then role-play the situations with your partner.

1 You are at a theme park with Student A. Student A wants to go on a new roller-coaster ride at the theme park. You are afraid of heights and don't want to go on the ride. Try to persuade Student A to choose a different activity.

2 You are on a walking trip in the mountains with Student A. You are reading the map but you think you are lost. Suggest what action you should take.

Grammar reference

Unit 1

1 Adverbs of frequency

1.1 Meaning

These adverbs are used to talk about how often we do things. We can put them in order from most often to least often like this:

always	most often
almost always	
generally/normally/regularly/usually/	
frequently/often	
sometimes/occasionally	
rarely/seldom/almost never/hardly ever	
never/not … ever	least often

1.2 Position

In statements, these adverbs usually come

- after *be* when it is the only verb in the sentence.
  I'm always a bit depressed in winter.

- before the main verb when there is only one verb.
  We sometimes watch a video on Friday evenings.

- after the first auxiliary verb when there is more than one verb.

  I have often been told that.

In questions, these adverbs usually come after the subject.

  Don't you usually work with Jenny?

In negative sentences, *not* comes before *always, generally, normally, often, regularly* and *usually*.

  We don't often see him nowadays.

With imperatives, *always* and *never* come at the beginning of the sentence.

  Always look on the bright side of life.
  Never refuse an opportunity.

Adverbials consisting of several words, such as *every day, on Friday evenings* or *every few years* usually come at the end of the sentence, but can also come at the beginning.

  I'm always a bit depressed in winter.
  I phone my brother every few days.
  On Friday evenings we sometimes watch a film.

Exercise 1

Add the adverb in brackets to the correct place in each sentence.

1 Does she come by car? (generally)
2 Take care when using this machinery. (always)
3 They're a little nervous at the beginning. (sometimes)
4 I don't go to the gym on Fridays. (usually)
5 They've been told that. (often)

2 Present time

2.1 Present simple

Use	Examples
For routine or regular repeated actions and habits (often with adverbs or adverbial phrases of frequency like *always, usually, never, every Saturday morning, twice a week*).	*We **go** for a **run every** evening.* *She **doesn't do** any work **at weekends**.* *I **never get** home before eight o'clock.*
When we are talking about permanent situations, and a particular time reference is not important.	*She **comes from** South America.* *They **live** in London.*
With stative verbs. These usually relate to states, thoughts, emotions and senses, e.g. *be, have, depend, know, think, understand, disagree, like, want, hear, love, see, smell, taste.*	*They **don't have** a car.* ***Does** she **understand?*** *I'm sorry, but I **disagree** completely.* *That perfume **smells** too strong.*
With scientific facts, to say something is always or generally true.	*Water **freezes** at 0°C.*

Watch out! When using stative verbs to describe things we sense (sights, sounds, smells, etc.) we often use the modal verb *can*.

*I **can see** you.*
*I **can't hear** the music.*
***Can** you **feel** the heat?*

2.2 Present continuous

We can use the present continuous with dynamic verbs (verbs that describe actions or things that happen) in the following ways:

Use	Examples
for actions happening at this moment	He's *watching* TV in his bedroom.
for changing/developing situations	I'm *getting* better at French.
for temporary situations	I'm *staying* at this hotel for two weeks.
with *always* for habits which we may find annoying	She's *always* losing her keys.

We can also use the present continuous with some stative verbs such as *be, have, take, think, depend, appear*, but this usually changes the meaning.

- *She's overconfident.* (stative – it's a permanent state)
  She's being overconfident. (dynamic – it's a temporary feeling)
- *I have my own apartment.* (stative – I possess it)
  I'm having a great time here. (dynamic – I'm experiencing it)
- *I think it's a good book.* (stative – it's my opinion)
  I'm thinking about changing my job. (dynamic – I'm considering it.)
- *She depends on her parents for money.* (stative – it's a long-term state)
  I'm depending on you to help me. (dynamic – it's a temporary situation)

Occasionally, as with the verb 'feel', there may be little or no difference in meaning.

> *I feel great!*
> *I'm feeling great!*

2.3 be used to/get used to

Be used to + *-ing* describes habits and states that we have become accustomed to.

> *She's used to sleeping in a tent because she often goes camping.*
>
> *She isn't used to sleeping in a tent as she's never been camping.*
>
> *Is she used to sleeping in a tent?*

Get used to + *-ing* describes habits and states that we are becoming accustomed to.

> *He's getting used to living in London but he still misses the countryside.*
>
> *Is he getting used to living in London?*

For the negative, **can't** is usually added.

> *He can't get used to living in London.*

Exercise 2

Complete the sentences with the correct present form of the verb in brackets.

1 I usually .... to the gym on Sundays. (*go*)
2 The children .... very quickly. (*grow up*)
3 I think she .... a bit unfair – he didn't mean to upset her. (*be*)
4 She .... any better at maths even though she has a private tutor. (*not get*)
5 Sally .... to be enjoying the course. (*appear*)
6 Even when I have a bad headache I .... painkillers. (*not take*)
7 Colin .... used to walking to school – he's always done it. (*be*)
8 It seemed very cold at first but now we .... used to the weather. (*get*)

3 Habit in the past

3.1 *used to* + bare infinitive

Used to + bare infinitive refers to past habits and states that do not occur now or no longer exist.

- *People **used to buy** CDs, but now they pay to download music.*
- *What **did** people **use to do** before electricity was invented?*
- *I **didn't use** to be good at English but I am now.*

> **Watch out!** In the negative and question form we use *use to* + bare infinitive.

3.2 *would*

Would is used to talk about past habits and repeated actions but NOT about past states, thoughts, emotions, etc.

- *When I was little, I **would/used to play** with my brother's toys. (habit)*
  NOT *We ~~would live~~ in a small village. (state)*

3.3 Past simple

If it's clear from the context that a habit or state is being referred to, the past simple can be used instead of *used to* or *would*.

- *When I **was** a child, I **walked** to school every day.*

Exercise 3

Decide if one or both verbs are possible.

1 When I was six years old, my best friend *was/would be* Billy Street.
2 Billy and I *used to sit/sat* next to each other in class.
3 Our families *didn't/wouldn't* have much money at that time.
4 Every evening Billy and I *played/would play* in the park.
5 We *didn't use to/wouldn't* go home until it was dark.

Exercise 4

Put the words into the correct order to make sentences. The first word is given.

1 school years my many used take sister to For I to little (For …)

2 during were What use to do a when the did holidays you child you ? (What …)

3 tickets me often parents concert give would My for money (My …)

4 photos I to my stick musicians on walls my bedroom used of favourite (I …)

5 very I often use out when go I to was didn't younger (I …)

6 see Every grandparents my weekend we to went (Every …)

Unit 2

1 Adverbs and adjectives

1.1 Form

1 Many adverbs are formed by adding -ly to the adjective form of the word, e.g. clear → clearly.

For adjectives ending in -y, drop the y and add -ily, e.g. happy → happily.
For adjectives ending in -le, drop the e and add -y, e.g. gentle → gently.
For adjectives ending in -ic, add -ally, e.g. automatic → automatically.

2 Some words ending in -ly are adjectives only, not adverbs, e.g. cowardly, friendly, lonely, silly. If an adverb is needed, a phrase must be used:
- They greeted us **in a friendly way/manner**.

3 Some words ending in -ly can be used both as adjectives and adverbs, e.g. hourly, daily, nightly.
Take the medicine twice **daily** (adv).
There is a **daily** (adj) flight to the island.

4 Some adverbs have the same form as adjectives, e.g. **early, fast, hard, still, straight, better, best, worse, worst**.
He's got a **fast** (adj) car and he drives it **fast** (adv).
She has **straight** (adj) hair. He looked **straight** (adv) at me.

5 Some adverbs have two forms, one like the adjective and the other form ending in -ly, e.g. **clear, close, direct, free, hard, high, late, wrong**. There is usually a difference in meaning.
Stand **clear** of the doors. (keep away)
Try to speak more **clearly**. (so we can understand)
He works very **hard**. (He makes a lot of effort.)
He had **hardly** any petrol left. (almost none)
The balloon was **high** up in the sky. (a long way up)
They think very **highly** of you. (have a good opinion)

Children under twelve travel **free**. (don't have to pay)
You can walk **freely** in the hotel grounds. (without restrictions)
The train arrived **late**. (after the time it was expected)
He's not been very well **lately**. (recently)

> **Watch out!** Wrongly and wrong have the same meaning but wrongly is used before the main verb (but after the auxiliary, if present), while wrong is used after the verb (and object, if present).

She **wrongly** advised me to accept the money.
His name was **wrongly** spelt.
He went **wrong** at the turning.
He got the answer **wrong**.

2 Extreme adjectives, modifiers and intensifiers

We can use adverbs to make adjectives, other adverbs and verbs stronger (intensifiers) or weaker (modifiers).

1 Some intensifiers and modifiers can only be used before gradable adjectives (adjectives that can be used in the comparative form, e.g. big, fast, good). These include:
- very, extremely, really, particularly, terribly (emphatic)
- quite, pretty, fairly, rather (weaker than very)
- a bit
I felt **terribly upset** when I heard the news.
He drives **rather fast**.
I thought the story was **a bit silly**.

2 Some intensifiers can only be used before non-gradable adjectives (extreme or absolute adjectives that cannot be used in the comparative form, e.g. amazing, boiling, disastrous, fantastic, freezing, impossible, marvellous, superb, wonderful). These include:
- absolutely, really, completely
The special effects were **absolutely amazing**.
I've just read a **really superb** new book about Egypt.

> **Watch out!** quite has two meanings.

The picture was **quite** good. (modifier with gradable adjective, meaning good but not very good)
Her cooking was **quite** wonderful. (intensifier with non-gradable adjective, meaning very, very good)

3 We can use some adverbs to emphasise both adjectives and verbs.
- just, completely, totally (= in every way)
You look **just fantastic**.
It's **completely impossible** to finish in time.
I **totally** forgot about your birthday.

Exercise 1

Complete the sentences with the adverbs in the box.

hard hardly high highly late lately wrong wrongly

1 Paul's parents were surprised his teacher thought so .... of his work.

2 Susie used to get on well with her brother, but they've been arguing a lot ....

3 I was sure I knew the answer to that question, but I got it ....

4 There's .... anyone in our class who knows the answer.

5 I got home .... and my dad was furious with me.

6 Oliver tries .... but he never gets very good marks.

7 You might see eagles flying .... overhead.

8 The student was .... accused of cheating.

Exercise 2

Match 1–5 to A–E to make sentences.

1 It's not just bad

2 It's not all that simple

3 I thought she'd be surprised

4 I thought I might be a bit tired

5 He'd expected his results to be bad

A but actually I was completely exhausted.

B it's absolutely awful.

C but they were absolutely disastrous.

D in fact it's a bit difficult.

E but she was really amazed!

3 Verb patterns: *-ing* or infinitive

3.1 Verbs followed by *-ing* or infinitive

Form	Common verbs	Examples
verb + *-ing*	admit, appreciate, consider, delay, deny, detest, dislike, enjoy, escape, feel like, finish, give up, imagine, involve, mention, mind, miss, postpone, practise, put off, recommend, resent, risk, suggest	I've **considered giving** up coffee. I don't **recommend going** to that restaurant. Has Peter **finished putting up** the tent?
verb + *to* infinitive	afford, agree, appear, arrange, ask, attempt, begin, choose, consent, decide, expect, fail, happen, hate, help, hesitate, hope, intend, learn, like, love, manage, offer, prefer, prepare, pretend, promise, refuse, seem, swear, try, want, wish	I **happened to see** Susie in the market. I can't **afford to eat** in that restaurant. Did Carl **expect to see** us here?
verb + object + *to* infinitive	advise, allow, ask, cause, encourage, expect, forbid, force, get, help, instruct, intend, invite, leave, like, mean, need, order, persuade, prefer, remind, request, teach, tell, tempt, want, warn	He **asked me to phone** him. I'd **prefer him to go** now.
verb + object + bare infinitive	let, make, hear, help, see	He **made me repeat** the exercise. Her parents **won't let her stay** out late.

Watch out! *Help* can be used with or without *to*. There is no difference in meaning.

*Can you **help me (to)** fix the bike?*

3.2 Verbs/Expressions followed by both *-ing* or infinitive with a difference in meaning

1 *can't bear/stand, hate, like, love, prefer*

When these verbs are used with the infinitive, they tend to refer to more specific situations. When they are used with *-ing*, they often refer to more general situations. However, the difference in meaning is very slight. (The infinitive is more commonly used with these verbs by speakers of American English.)
*We sometimes **like to go out** for a meal on Fridays.*
*We **like going out** for a meal on Fridays.*

2 *remember, forget, regret, stop, try*

The meanings of these verbs change according to whether they are followed by *-ing* or the infinitive. When used with *-ing* the meaning tends to be related to something in the past.

• *remember/forget + -ing* refers to an action that happened before the moment of remembering or forgetting.
*I **remember seeing** you somewhere before.*
(= that I have seen you)
*She had completely **forgotten telling** him about her cat.*

When used with the infinitive, the meaning tends to be related to something in the present or future, or to purpose.

- *remember/forget* + *to* infinitive refers to an action after the moment of remembering or forgetting.
  *Did you **remember to lock** the door?*
  *I **forgot to give** Sally the book.*
- stop + *-ing* means stop something you were doing, e.g. a habit.
  *I've **stopped drinking** coffee: it kept me awake at night.*
- stop + *to* infinitive means stop what you are doing in order to do something else.
  *We **stopped to have** a coffee on the way home.*
- regret + *-ing* means be sorry about an action that happened in the past.
  *I **regret not telling** him about it earlier.*
- regret + *to* infinitive means be sorry about a present action.
  *I **regret to tell** you that your car has been stolen.* (= formal)
- *try* + *-ing* means do an experiment. (= doing the action may not be successful)
  *Try **studying** in the morning – it might suit you better.*
- *try* + *to* infinitive means make an effort. (= the action may be difficult or impossible to do)
  *Try **to study** at regular times.*

Exercise 3

Choose the correct verb pattern in italics.

1 You have to learn *putting up with/to put up with* certain things in a big family.
2 My parents can't afford *buying/to buy* me a lot of new clothes.
3 I tried *doing/to do* a weekend job in a shop but I didn't enjoy it.
4 The manager wanted me *starting/to start* at 6.30a.m. but that was too early.
5 Most of the time we enjoy *helping/to help* with the housework.
6 If we forget *doing/to do* our jobs at home, we get into trouble.
7 There's always someone who will agree *helping/to help* me if I have a problem.
8 I've never resented *being/to be* part of a big family.

Unit 3

1 Using modifiers for comparison

1.1 Types of comparison

There are three types of comparison.

1 to a higher degree (comparative form + *than*)
  *Mountain climbing is **more dangerous than** windsurfing.*
  *The Andes mountains are **higher than** the Alps.*
2 to the same degree (*as … as*)
  *Hiring a car would cost **just as much as** getting a taxi.*
  *I don't enjoy swimming **as much as** I used to.*
3 to a lower degree (with *less* + *than* and *the least*)
  *I am **less keen** on taking risks **than** I used to be.*
  *Antarctica is **the least** densely populated continent.*

1.2 Using modifiers for comparison

Modifiers	Comparative/ Superlative	
(very) much far a lot rather slightly a bit/little no not any	more/less expensive cheaper more/less time more/less difficult	than …
just almost/nearly not quite not nearly	as cheap/expensive as much time as/so unusual as/so difficult	as …
(by) far	the most/least expensive the cheapest the most time	

Exercise 1

Choose the correct option in italics.

1 Paris *isn't any/isn't quite* cheaper than Milan – in fact it's more expensive.
2 It's *a lot/by far* the most beautiful city I've ever visited.
3 Renting an apartment can be *rather/not quite* cheaper than a hotel.
4 I was feeling *slightly/just* better so I decided to go for a walk.
5 This car is *not quite/a little* more expensive than the other one.

2 Present perfect and past simple

	Use	Examples
Present perfect simple	To talk about states, or single or repeated actions, over a period of time up to and including the present (often with *ever, never, often, always, for, since, this week/month/year*).	*I've always wanted to be an actor.* *I've never entered a surfing competition.* *Have you ever been to Australia?* *She's read that book at least ten times.* *That's the first time I've ever eaten octopus.* *It's the worst concert I've ever been to.* *We haven't had a holiday this year.*
	To talk about completed single actions, with some relevance to the present (often with *just, already, yet*).	*I've already seen that film, let's go to another one.* *Our friends have just arrived.* *Have you had breakfast yet?* *I haven't finished writing yet.*
Present perfect continuous	To talk about a recent completed activity when the effects of that activity are still relevant.	**A:** *Why are you out of breath?* **B:** *I've been running.*
	To talk about an action that's been going on for a long time, or that's been repeated many times. The action may or may not be finished.	*I've been replying to emails all morning.* *Has he been training ever since last year?* *He hasn't been singing at all for the past few years.*
	To suggest that an activity is temporary.	*I've been living here for five years but I'm going to move soon.*
	To suggest that an action is not complete.	*I've been reading his biography, but I haven't finished it yet.*
Past simple (See also Grammar Reference Unit 4 for more uses of the past simple)	To talk about a finished event that happened at a specific time in the past.	*I saw Paul last night.* *I went to Brazil five years ago.* *I didn't phone him yesterday.*
	To talk about a habit in the past.	*Did your parents read to you when you were a child?*
	To talk about a state in the past.	*The house belonged to my father for many years.*

Watch out! We don't use verbs that refer to a state (e.g. *be, know, love*) in the continuous form.

Exercise 2

Match the phrases in bold in sentences 1–9 to the tenses and uses A–I.

1 You can see she**'s been swimming** – her hair's still wet.
2 I **knew** almost everyone at the party.
3 Carol**'s been working** here for the last few weeks while Chloe's away having a baby.
4 I**'ve only worn** that shirt three times since I bought it.
5 I**'ve been having** driving lessons for months but I'm not getting any better.
6 All my friends at school **played** football, not rugby.
7 I**'ve just seen** Carrie, she sent you her best wishes.
8 Harry's birthday party **didn't end** until three in the morning.
9 They**'ve been building** that house for ages and it's still only half-finished.

A Present perfect continuous: to emphasise that an action has been going on for a long time
B Past simple: for a state in the past
C Present perfect continuous: to suggest that an activity is not complete
D Present perfect: for an action repeated up to the present time
E Past simple: for a finished event that happened at a specific time in the past
F Present perfect continuous: to suggest that an activity is temporary
G Present perfect: for a completed single action, with some relevance to the present
H Past simple: for a habit in the past
I Present perfect continuous: for a recent completed activity when the effects are still relevant

3 as and like

3.1 like

1 *like* can be a preposition, meaning 'similar to' or 'in the same way as'.
*Do you look **like** your sister?*
***Like** John, I hate cooking.*

2 *like* can mean 'such as/for example'.
*Let's buy her something nice, **like** a bunch of flowers.*

3 We use the question *What … like?* when we are asking for a description of a person, place or thing.
*'**What's** the restaurant **like**?' 'Oh, really good.'*

4 *feel like* + object/-*ing* is used to talk about something that we want or want to do.
*I **feel like** (eating) some crisps.*

5 *seem/sound/look like* + object is used to introduce an idea we may not be completely sure about.
*It **seems like** a good idea.*

6 *like* is not used before an adjective on its own.
They seem ~~like~~ happy.

3.2 as

1 *as* can be a preposition, coming before the name of a role or job, or it can be used to describe the purpose of something.
*She works **as** a sales manager.*
*We use the loft **as** a play room for the kids.*
*I think of her **as** my best friend.*

2 *as* can be a conjunction, followed by subject + verb, to describe manner.
*You should do **as** your parents say.*
*I'll do **as** we agreed earlier.*

> **Watch out!** In colloquial English *like* is also used as a conjunction in this way, but this is regarded as incorrect by some people and is not used in formal writing.

***Like** I said, he's a really nice guy.* (colloquial)
*I want you to do **like** I tell you.* (colloquial)

3.3 as if/as though

As if/As though are conjunctions followed by subject + verb.

- They are followed by the present or present perfect when referring to something likely.
*He looks **as if** he's crying.*
*It looks **as if** it's stopped raining.*

- To show that something is imaginary or unlikely, they can be followed by the past tense.
*He behaves **as if** he **knew** more than us.*
*He looked **as if** he **had seen** a ghost.*

> **Watch out!** In colloquial English *like* is also used instead of *as if/as though*.

*You look **like** you're worried.* (colloquial)
*It looks **like** we're going to win.* (colloquial)

Exercise 3

Match 1–8 to A–H to make sentences.

1 I have long dark hair,
2 He's always losing things,
3 I suggested going shopping,
4 She says she doesn't feel like
5 Buying a new printer looks
6 I've always thought of you
7 It's probably best to do
8 Conor acts

A doing anything tonight.
B as your father suggests.
C like his phone and his keys.
D as if he was in charge of us all.
E like my sister.
F as someone I could depend on.
G like the best solution to the problem.
H but she didn't feel like it.

Unit 4

1 Articles

1.1 The definite article: the

Use	Examples
when the person or thing referred to is unique	*The sun came out and soon we were dry.*
	The president is giving a speech tonight.
	He won a medal at the Olympic Games.
when the rest of the sentence makes it clear what we are referring to	*The head of my old school was called Mr Jones.*
	The woman who stopped me was wearing a badge.
when the surrounding context makes it clear what we are referring to	*Your shoes are in the cupboard.*
	Your dinner's in the fridge.
to talk about previously mentioned things or people	*A man and a woman walked past. The man was wearing sunglasses.*
with superlatives	*He's the bravest person in the team.*
to talk about a generic class of things (often on topics related to science or technology)	*The bicycle was invented about 200 years ago.*
	The panda is in danger of becoming extinct.

The definite article continued

Use	Examples
with some social and national groups, when making generalisations (followed by a plural verb)	*The unemployed need more support.* *Some of the English are descended from Danish invaders.*
with areas such as *north, centre,* etc.	*Most of the population live in the north.*
with oceans, seas, rivers and deserts	*He's sailed across the Atlantic.* *We went by canoe up the Orinoco.* *She said she'd driven across the Sahara.*
with plural mountain ranges and island groups	*Are the Andes as high as the Himalayas?* *The British Isles include the Isle of Wight and the Isle of Man.*
with countries whose name includes a common noun such as *republic, isles, islands, states*	*He's from the Czech Republic, but he's living in the United States.*

1.2 The indefinite article: *a/an*

Use	Examples
with singular countable nouns (mentioned for the first time or when it doesn't matter which one)	*I'd like a sandwich and a glass of water.* *What you need is a rest.* *A man has come to see you.*
to talk about (singular) jobs and interests	*She's a lawyer.* *I'm a big football fan.*
with these numbers: 100, 1,000, 1,000,000	*There were over a hundred people at the wedding.* *He made a million pounds in one year.*
in exclamations about singular countable nouns	*What an amazing view!*

1.3 Zero article (no article)

Use	Examples
for uncountable, plural and abstract nouns used in their general sense	*We had awful weather on holiday.* *Happiness isn't the only thing in life.*
for continents, countries, mountains and lakes	*They're going to visit Africa.* *Have you been to Nepal?* *He's climbed Mount Everest.* *Is Lake Titicaca in Peru?*
for villages, towns and cities	*Wellington is the capital of New Zealand.*
for streets and roads	*There are some nice houses on School Road.*
for some illnesses	*I've got flu and Sue's got indigestion.*

> **Watch out!** *I've got a headache and I think I'm getting a cold.*

There are no articles in the following expressions:

to/at/from school/university/college
at home
go home
in/to class
to/in/into/from church
to/in/into/out of prison/hospital/bed
to/at/from work
for/at/to breakfast/lunch/dinner
by car/bus/bicycle/plane/train/tube/boat
on foot
by accident/chance

Exercise 1

Complete the sentences with the definite article (*the*), indefinite article (*a/an*) or zero article (–).

1 .... future often brings surprises.
2 He's .... very keen cyclist.
3 You'd better get out of .... bed – it's late.
4 The climate is best in .... south-east of the country.
5 The doctor said she was suffering from .... depression.
6 Wait a minute – I'll just get my bag out of .... locker.
7 I think you ought to have .... holiday.
8 There'll be a special bus available for .... elderly.
9 .... nurse who I saw first said that nothing was wrong.
10 I'm hoping to study .... business at university.

2 Narrative forms

2.1 Past simple

Use	Examples
to talk about a finished event that happened at a specific time in the past (See Grammar Reference Unit 3)	I *saw* Paul *last night*. I *went* to Brazil five years *ago*.
to talk about a habit in the past (See Grammar Reference Units 1 and 3)	*Did* your parents *read* to you when you were a child?
to talk about a state in the past (See Grammar Reference Unit 3)	The house *belonged* to my father for many years.
to describe a sequence of finished events in chronological order	I *took out* my key, *opened* the door and *walked* in.
in reported speech	She said she *didn't want* to join us.

2.2 Past continuous

Use	Examples
to describe an action in progress in the past, often to set the scene for a particular event	I *was sitting* in the garden, reading a book.
to talk about temporary situations in the past	Rodolfo *was living* in South America at the time.
to talk about an event that was in progress in the past and was interrupted	I *was going* out of the house when I heard a noise.
to talk about multiple actions in progress at the same time in the past	While I *was painting*, he *was watching* TV.
to talk about anticipated events that did not happen	We *were going* to Rome for a holiday, but then I broke my leg.

2.3 Past perfect

Use	Examples
to refer to a time earlier than another point in the past, when this is needed to make the order of events clear	When the police arrived, the criminal *had disappeared*.
in reported speech	They said they *had never met* before.

Watch out! Be careful not to overuse the past perfect. Once we have established the time sequence, we can revert to the past simple.

*When I got home I realised that I **had lost** my phone. I'd definitely **had** it when I left work, because I **used** it to check when the next train was due, and I **called** my wife to tell her when I'd be home.*

The past perfect is not necessary with *before/after*, which make the sequence of events clear on their own, although it is not incorrect.

*Peter arrived after I **(had) finished** writing the letter.*

Exercise 2

Change each sentence to the form given in brackets.

1 He saw Annie at the concert. (question)
2 She enjoyed the long drive to work. (negative)
3 Brian was working at the hospital in 2015. (negative)
4 He was expecting the children to help. (question)
5 The whole family had gone on the expedition. (question)
6 The volunteers had had the chance to meet the public. (negative)
7 The car belonged to his older brother. (question + negative)
8 They had expected to meet you at the airport. (question + negative)
9 The books were being sold at reduced prices. (question + negative)
10 All the students had been on a trip to Paris. (question + negative)

Exercise 3

Decide if one or both verbs are possible.

1 I *had learnt/learnt* to ski before I went to Switzerland.
2 When he *had spent/spent* some years working in Southeast Asia he decided to return to England.
3 I started to work as a journalist after I *had married/married* Stefan.
4 The animals *had all disappeared/all disappeared* by the time we got to the water hole.
5 I *had first met/first met* Frances when I was working in a bank in London, but then we lost touch.

Unit 5

1 Expressions of quantity

1.1 Countable nouns

These have both a singular and a plural form, and can be used with *a/an*. For example: *table, house, child*.

1.2 Uncountable nouns

These have no plural and cannot be used with *a/an*. For example: *accommodation, advice, behaviour, furniture, health, information, knowledge, luggage, news, progress, research, rice* (and all other grains), *salt, scenery, spaghetti, traffic, transport, travel, trouble, water* (and all other liquids), *weather, work*.

> **Watch out!** Use *a slice* and *a piece* with uncountable nouns for food.
>
> *I'll just have a small slice of cake.*
> *Would you like another piece of toast?*

1.3 Some nouns can be countable or uncountable

These include

- nouns we can think of as a substance or as a single thing, e.g. *chicken, cake, chocolate, egg, hair, iron, paper, stone*.
  You've got chocolate on your T-shirt.
  There are only two chocolates left in the box.
  Green vegetables are rich in iron.
  We'll have to buy a new iron.
  I need to go and buy some paper for the printer.
  Have you read today's paper?
- nouns which are used to refer to particular varieties, e.g. wine, cheese.
  Would you like some wine?
  This is a very good wine.
- words for some drinks, e.g. *coffee, beer*. The countable noun means *a glass of, a cup of, a bottle of*, etc.
  Coffee is produced in Africa and South America.
  Shall we have a coffee and a piece of cake?
- time, space, room.
  There's no time to talk – we have to rush!
  I didn't have a very good time at the party.

There's no space left. You'll have to get another bag.
Fill in the spaces with the correct preposition.
There's room for seven people in this car.
This house has seven rooms.

Exercise 1

Choose the correct option in italics.

1 I don't eat *many/much* fresh fruit.
2 There aren't *a lot of/hardly any* green vegetables for sale.
3 I drink *very few/very little* water.
4 We eat *hardly any/very few* meat at home.
5 I only eat *a little/a few* eggs each week.
6 I'd like to have *some/a few* rice with my curry.
7 I drink *a lot of/many* orange juice.
8 There isn't *no/any* chocolate left.

2 Subject/Verb agreement

When a noun is preceded by a quantifier, the following verb is not affected – it still agrees with the noun that is the subject of the sentence.

*A lot of **people are** coming to the party.*

*Hardly any of the **students** in my class **like** maths.*

With sentences beginning *There is/are* the verb depends on the following noun.

*There **is** a lot of **cheese** left in the fridge.*

*There **are** quite a few **people** coming to the party.*

Exercise 2

Complete the sentences with *is* or *are*.

1 The first few weeks .... the most difficult.
2 Hardly any of the roses in the garden .... blooming.
3 Only a bit of the orange juice I bought for the children .... left.
4 There .... hardly any chocolates left in the box.
5 Very few of the players in that team .... any good.
6 There .... not much useful information in any of those books.

Expressions of quantity used with countable/uncountable nouns

	much	many	a lot of/ lots of	some	a few/very few	hardly any	a little/a bit of/very little	any	no
with countable nouns		•	•	•	•	•		•	•
with uncountable nouns	•		•				•	•	
in positive sentences		•	•	•	•	•		•	•
in negative sentences	•		•	•		•	•	•	•

3 Passive forms

3.1 Form

To form the passive, use the appropriate tense of *be* + past participle.

present simple	*Most phone calls **are made** on mobile phones.*
present continuous	*Calls **are being made** every day.*
past simple	*The first email **was sent** in 1971.*
past continuous	*I thought I **was being asked** to help.*
present perfect	*Millions of text messages **have been sent**.*
past perfect	*Once personal computers **had been invented**, they spread quickly.*
future *will*	*She'**ll be given** her own room.*
future perfect	*The arrangements **will have been made** by the end of the week.*
going to	*The event **is going to be organised** by the manager.*
modals	*The machine **must have been** left switched on.* *Messages **may not be delivered** immediately.*
-ing	*Our dog doesn't like **being left** on his own.*
present infinitive	*They hope **to be chosen** to take part.*
perfect infinitive	*I was happy **to have been selected** for the team.*

> **Watch out!**
>
> **1** If two verbs in a sentence both have the same subject and passive auxiliary, the second auxiliary can be omitted.
> *The fruit **is washed** and **peeled**.*
>
> **2** Verbs that do not take an object (e.g. *ache, arrive, sit down*) do not have passive forms. It is not possible to say *I was ached*.
>
> **3** For verbs with two objects, one of them a person, the passive sentence usually begins with the person.
> *Someone gave Mary a present.* → *Mary was given a present.* (NOT *A present was given to Mary.*)
>
> **4** The verbs *make, hear, see, help* are followed by the infinitive without *to* in active sentences, but the infinitive with *to* in passive sentences.
> *They made him go home.* → *He was made to go home.*
>
> **5** *Let* does not have a passive form. We use *be allowed to* in the passive.
> *They don't let us talk in class.* → *We are not allowed to talk in class.*

3.2 Use

The passive is used

- to talk about actions, events and processes when the action, event or process is seen as more important than the agent. This is often the case in formal or scientific writing.
  *The equipment **was checked** carefully.*
  *Rats **have been trained** to open boxes.*

- to link with a preceding sentence, and/or put new information, or a long phrase, later in the sentence. If the agent is mentioned, we use the preposition *by*.
  *In May the markets of Morocco are full of roses. **Many of these are grown by** the inhabitants of a remote valley high in the mountains.*

3.3 Passive reporting verbs

We often use reporting verbs such as *believe, claim, report, say, think* in impersonal passive structures when we don't know or don't wish to specify the subject.

- *it* + *be* + verb + *that*
  *It **is thought** that the criminal is a local man.*
  (= present)
  *It **was claimed** that the minister had been involved.*
  (= past)
- subject + *be* + reporting verb + infinitive
  *The criminal **is thought** to be a local man.*
  (= present)
  *The minister **was claimed** to have been involved.*
  (= past)

Exercise 3

Complete the passage with the correct auxiliary verbs.

The first pineapple **(1)** .... brought to Europe by Christopher Columbus in 1500 and presented to the King of Spain. Later, special heated glasshouses **(2)** .... built by wealthy landowners so that tropical pineapple plants could **(3)** .... made to produce fruit.

Now fresh pineapples which **(4)** .... been flown in from other countries can **(5)** .... bought relatively cheaply.

Exercise 4

Rewrite the sentences using passive reporting verbs.

1 People reported that there were gunshots.
It ....
2 People claim that the money was stolen.
It ....
3 People think that the suspect has left the country.
The suspect ....
4 People say that the police made a lot of mistakes.
The police ....
5 People believe that the criminal had a false passport.
It ....

Unit 6

1 Future forms

1.1 shall, will + infinitive without to

Use	Examples
for predicting something based on the speaker's belief or their knowledge as an expert	This medicine **will make** you feel sleepy. You'**ll feel** better when you've had a good night's rest. The train **will leave** from platform 10.
for future actions decided at the time of speaking	I think I'**ll take** the day off. I'**ll wear** my black dress.
for promises, threats, offers and requests	If you tell anyone, I'**ll kill** you! I promise I'**ll pay** the money back. I'**ll meet** you at the station if you want. **Shall** I **meet** you at the station? **Will** you **do** the washing-up for me?

Watch out!

1 We can also use *going to* in many of these cases, especially in spoken English, without much change in meaning.

This medicine'**s going to** make you feel a bit sleepy.
I think I'**m going to** take the day off.
I promise I'**m going to** pay the money back.

2 We can also use other modals instead of *will* to refer to the future, e.g. *might, could, should, would*. These generally suggest some uncertainty about what is being predicted. They may be a part of conditional structures.

I suppose **he might win** the race, but it seems unlikely.
The weather **could be** better tomorrow.
We **should be** able to afford it if we save up.
They **would** probably **agree** if you asked them.

1.2 going to

Use	Examples
to suggest that things are certain to happen because there is present evidence	Look out – you're **going to fall**! I've got no sense of direction – I know I'm **going to get lost**.
to talk about personal intentions	I'm **going to tell** him the truth. They're both **going to apply** for the job. She's decided she's **going to lose** ten kilos. They're **going to have** a party sometime soon. Where **are** you **going to have** the wedding reception?

1.3 Present continuous

Use	Examples
to talk about things that have already been decided or planned, often for a definite time in the future	We're all **meeting** at six o'clock. I'm **having** my hair cut tomorrow. They're **getting** the six o'clock train. We're **moving** to a new apartment next week.

Watch out! It's also possible to use *going to* in cases like this. With *going to* the intention is stressed more, but the difference in meaning between the two forms may be very small.

1.4 Present simple

Use	Examples
to talk about fixed arrangements for the future, for example, as expressed in timetables, regulations and programmes	The plane **leaves** at 8.45a.m. The new term **starts** in September.
in time clauses and conditional clauses with a future meaning, e.g. *after, as soon as, before, if, unless, until, when*	I'll see her **when/as soon as** she's free. Give this to Susie **if** you **see** her. Tom can't apply for the job **until** he **gets** the right qualifications.

Watch out! It's also possible to use *will* when talking about fixed arrangements, since these are predictions based on expert knowledge, but we cannot use *will* in time clauses or in conditional clauses.

Exercise 1

Complete the sentences with the correct future form of the verb in brackets.

1 The school year in Britain always .... in July. (*end*)

2 She assures me that she .... there on time. (*get*)

3 She .... to drama college, whatever her parents say. (*apply*)

4 They're rehearsing so hard – I'm sure the performance .... a great success. (*be*)

5 You know, I think I .... Steve to the party after all. (*invite*)

6 .... I .... you a secret? (*tell*)

7 I think you .... that it's actually quite simple if you follow my instructions. (*find*)

8 They .... a music festival in our town in July. (*hold*)

9 He'll open the door as soon as he .... us. (*see*)

Exercise 2

Match the uses of future forms 1–8 to the examples A–H.

1 *will* (a promise)

2 *will* (an expert opinion)

3 *will* (a decision made at the moment of speaking)

4 *going to* (an opinion based on present evidence)

5 *going to* (a personal intention)

6 present continuous (a planned event)

7 present simple (a timetabled event)

8 present simple (a time clause with a future meaning)

A The road will be closed.

B The conference is in the first week of April.

C She's gone very pale – she's going to faint.

D They're getting married sometime next year.

E I'll call Graham now, shall I?

F When you arrive at the airport, phone me.

G I won't tell anyone.

H I'm going to apply to university next year.

2 Future perfect and continuous

2.1 Future perfect (*will/shall/may/might/could + have + past participle*)

Use	Examples
with an expression of time to describe something that will be completed before a definite time in the future	*By the end of June I'll have been at this school for a year.* *By the time you get home, we'll have tidied everything up.* *Will you have finished your essay by this evening?*

2.2 Future continuous (*will/shall/may/might/ could + be + -ing*)

Use	Examples
to say that an action will be in progress at a definite time in the future (with an expression of time or frequency)	*I'll be living a normal life by this time next year.* *After we've sold the house, we'll be renting a flat for a while.* *We'd better not go at eight o'clock – they'll be having dinner then.*
to talk about things you expect to happen, often because some sort of arrangement has been made (with an expression of time or frequency)	*She'll be appearing in a performance of Romeo and Juliet next week.* *I'll be using my parents' car while they're away.* *We'll be moving to London soon.* *Will you be going to Spain this summer?*

Exercise 3

Read the passage and complete the gaps using the future continuous or the future perfect with *will*.

A bright future for our town

In five years' time our town will be completely different. More people **(1)** .... (travel) by bicycle as the council **(2)** .... (construct) more bike lanes. They **(3)** .... (pedestrianise) the city centre and people **(4)** .... (stroll) round the traffic-free streets. The council **(5)** .... (renovated) the old buildings such as the Town Hall and **(6)** .... (build) new facilities such as a gym and a concert hall.

The river authorities **(7)** .... (clean up) the river bank and people **(8)** .... (canoe) on the water. Of course, all these changes will cost money, but we're sure it will be worth it.

Unit 7

1 Modal verbs

1.1 possibility

Modal	Use	Examples
can or could	theoretical possibility	*Can there be life on Mars?* *The weather could be better tomorrow.* (= it's possible)
may, might, could + bare infinitive	likelihood in the present or future	*He may be in a meeting.* *She might/could be here already.*
could/may/ might + have + past participle (perfect infinitive)	the possibility that past events happened	*His face is familiar. We may have met somewhere before.* *He's not in the office. He might have finished work early.* *She could have been at the party, but I didn't see her.*

1.2 certainty (deduction)

Modal	Use	Examples
must	to say that we are sure about something in the present or past	*You must be pleased with your exam results.* (= present) *He must have touched up the photograph.* (= past)
can't or couldn't	in negative sentences, to say we are sure something isn't/ wasn't true	*That can't be the right answer.* (= present) *They can't have got lost – they had a map.* (= past) *Tom couldn't have been the thief.* (= past)

Watch out! We do not use *mustn't* in negative sentences expressing certainty. Instead we use *can't*.
She ~~mustn't~~ be pleased with her results.
She can't be pleased with her results.

1.3 ability

Modal	Use	Examples
can/could	to express general ability and typical behaviour of people or things	*Temperatures can rise to over 30°C in the summer.* *Employers can be unwilling to employ people over fifty.* *My father could be very generous.* (= past)
can/be able to	for present and future ability	*I can understand French but I can't speak it very well.* *Will your parents be able to help you?* *I like being able to cook my own meals.*
can	for the future, where there is a sense of opportunity	*I can come tomorrow if you like.* *You can practise your French when you go to Paris.*
could/couldn't and was able to	to talk about general ability in the past	*I could swim before I could walk.* *I was able to talk when I was eighteen months old.* *At that time I couldn't drive.*
was/wasn't able to	to talk about ability in a specific situation in the past	*Fortunately, he was able to swim to the shore.*
could/couldn't + perfect infinitive	to talk about unfulfilled ability in the past	*I could have gone to university, but I decided not to.* *I couldn't have been a ballet dancer. I was too tall.*

Other expressions for ability:

Do you know how to type?
He succeeded in becoming a professional footballer at eighteen.
We managed to find our way home. (suggests difficulty)

Exercise 1

Choose the best reply for each question.

1 Could Hannah have been at the party?
2 That must be Paula standing over there.
3 Will Frances be able to help tomorrow?
4 Couldn't Rosie have taken charge?
5 Could Lily ride a bike at that time?
6 Can't Emily make the coffee?

A It might be possible, if she's around then.
B No she couldn't, she didn't learn until much later.
C She might have been – I'm not sure.
D No, she couldn't have done anything to help – she was ill at the time.
E She probably could, but not just now.
F It can't be – she's too tall.

2 Relative clauses

2.1 Relative pronouns

The most common relative pronouns are:

who (= subject) and *whom* (= object) to refer to people.
which to refer to things.
that to refer to either people or things.
whose the possessive of *who* and *which*.
when used after nouns referring to time.
where used after nouns referring to place.
why used to refer to reasons.

> **Watch out!**
>
> The relative pronoun **replaces** the subject or the object.
>
> *People **who** (~~they~~) live in glass houses shouldn't throw stones.*
> *The vase, **which** I bought (~~it~~) years ago, is very valuable.*
> *What is not a relative pronoun.*
> *The car **that** ~~what~~ I bought was red.*

2.2 Defining relative clauses

In defining relative clauses

1 the relative clause defines or identifies the person, thing, time, place or reason.
*Chris is the son of a woman **who works in television**.*
*That's the man **whose son is an actor**.*
*Winter was the time **when people tended to get insufficient fresh food**.*
*I know the place **where the play is set**.*
*I can't imagine the reason **why he would want to leave you**.*

2 *that* can be used instead of *who* or *which*.
*The girl **that (who)** lives next door rides a motorbike.*
*The sports centre **that (which) is opening soon will offer great new facilities**.*

3 The relative pronoun can be left out if it is the object of the verb in the relative clause.
*The person **(who/that)** I spoke to yesterday said it was free.*
*Sue bought the watch **(which/that)** she'd seen.*

4 No commas are used before and after the relative clause.

2.3 Non-defining relative clauses

Non-defining relative clauses give extra information which **can** be omitted. Commas are used before and after the relative clause. It's also possible for brackets to be used instead of commas.

The pronoun *that* **cannot** be used instead of *who* or *which*.

*Entrance to the museum, **where you can see Roman pottery**, is free.*

*The witness **(who refused to be named)** said the police had acted unwisely.*

2.4 Prepositions in relative clauses

Prepositions can come before the relative pronoun or at the end of the relative clause, depending on whether the sentence is formal or informal.

*The person **to whom I spoke** told me the hotel was fully booked.* (formal)

*John, **who I bought my car from**, has gone abroad.* (informal)

Exercise 2

Complete the sentences with the words in the box. You can use the words more than once.

when	where	whom	whose	why

1 The letter is in the file .... I keep my bills.
2 It wasn't clear .... the children had stayed at home.
3 The lawyer from .... we had received the advice was well known.
4 Please give Luke this message at any point .... it is convenient.
5 The old men directed us to a small hotel, ... we spent the night.
6 Can you name the person from .... you received this information?
7 The car, ... owner was not insured, was involved in a crash.

3 so, such, too, enough, very

3.1 so and such

Use: *so* and *such* are used to introduce a clause of result, or for emphasis.

so + adjective/ adverb/ determiner (+ noun) (+ *that* clause)	My bag was **so heavy that** I couldn't carry it.
	He has travelled **so widely that** he's forgotten what home is like.
	They had **so much money that** they couldn't spend it all.
	It was **so hot!** (= emphatic)
such + (adjective) + noun (+ *that* clause)	The taxi took **such a long time** to come **that I decided to walk instead.**
	We had **such a good time!** (= emphatic)

3.2 too

Use: *too* has a negative meaning – the speaker is not happy about the situation.

too + adjective/ adverb/ determiner (+ noun) (+ *to* infinitive)	It was **too hot** to sleep.
	You're speaking **too quickly** – I can't understand you, I'm afraid.
	That's **too much (money)**. I can't afford it.

3.3 enough

Use: *enough* has a positive meaning – the speaker regards the situation as possible.

adjective/ adverb + *enough* (+ *to* infinitive)	He's **rich enough to buy up** the whole town.
	You're not doing that work **carefully enough**.
enough + noun (+ *to* infinitive/+ *for* + noun)	There's **enough time for a coffee**.
	Have you got **enough money to get a taxi?**

3.4 very

Use: *very* is used for emphasis in either a positive or negative statement. It is sometimes used when we wish to avoid using a negative word.

very + adjective/ adverb/ determiner (+ noun)	It's **very difficult** but I think I can do it.
	He's working **very hard** – he's bound to pass.
	Very few people agree with her.

Exercise 3

Complete the sentences with *so, such, too, enough* or *very*.

1 It wasn't a .... good party.
2 It had just .... space to hold everything.
3 It was .... cheap I just had to buy it!
4 It was .... cloudy to see the stars.
5 It was .... a good book that I read it twice.
6 It was warm .... to have dinner outside.

4 it is, there is

1 We use *there is/there are* to begin a sentence about something existing or not existing.

   There is a little house at the foot of the hill.
   There are some trees growing along the side of the road.

2 *There's no reason to worry about it.*
   We use *it is/was*, etc. to begin a sentence giving information about time, weather and distance.

   It is a bright, sunny day.
   It was half past six in the morning.
   It's just over ten kilometres to the nearest town.

3 We use *it is* as the subject of a sentence to refer forwards to a later clause with *that*, an infinitive or an *-ing* form.

   It is a pity that no one can help.
   It's good to see you again.
   It's no use crying over spilt milk.

Exercise 4

Put the words into the correct order to make sentences. Begin with the word shown.

1 it's I complaining useless think
   I ....
2 there no-one says She there's
   She ....
3 a perfect It's afternoon picnic a for
   It's ....
4 the best I if it's problem wonder solution to the
   I ....
5 that There was attractive town wasn't about much the
   There ....
6 didn't could anything do They think they was there
   They ....

Unit 8

1 Reporting verbs

Structure	Verbs	Examples
verb + infinitive	agree, decide, offer, promise, refuse, threaten	*We **agreed to go** to the meeting.*
verb + object + infinitive	advise, beg, encourage, invite, persuade, remind, tell, warn	*She **advised me to go** to the police.*
verb (+ *that*) + clause	accept, admit, claim, explain, recommend, say, suggest	*She **says (that) we should pay** for his ticket.*
verb + object (+ *that*) + clause	promise, remind, tell, warn	*He **told us (that) he would be on time**.*
verb + -*ing*	admit, deny, recommend, suggest	*He **admitted taking** the money.*
verb + preposition + -*ing*	apologise for, insist on	*She **apologised for being** late.*
verb + object + preposition + -*ing*	accuse (of), blame (for), congratulate (on), discourage (from)	*She **discouraged me from going** in for the competition.*
verb + *wh*- word + infinitive	describe, explain, know, wonder	*She **explained what to do**.*
verb + object + *wh*- word + infinitive	ask, remind, tell	*They **told us who to see**.*

> **Watch out!** Some verbs can be used with more than one structure.
> *She recommended **visiting** the castle.*
> *She recommended **that we should visit** the castle.*

Exercise 1

Rewrite each sentence beginning with the words given.

1 'I won't go to school,' he said.
   He refused ....

2 'Who's in charge?' he asked us.
   He asked us who ....

3 'How about going to a new restaurant?' he said.
   He suggested that we ....

4 'You must let me pay for the tickets,' she said.
   She insisted on ....

5 'It wasn't your fault that you got lost,' she said.
   She didn't blame me for ....

6 'Who can I ask?' she wondered.
   She wondered who ....

7 'It would be best for you to reserve a place,' she said.
   She recommended that I ....

8 'It won't be easy' she told me.
   She warned ....

9 'Don't forget that it's Carlotta's birthday soon,' he said.
   He reminded me that ....

2 Reported statements

2.1 Form

Reported statements are formed from a reporting verb (+ *that*) + a clause containing the statement.
'He works in television,' she said.
*She **said (that) he worked** in television.*
'I took the money,' she admitted.
*She **admitted (that) she had taken** the money.*

2.2 Changes to verb forms and pronouns

If the situation or event being reported happened in the past, the verb forms and pronouns generally change as follows:

Direct speech		Reported speech	
present simple/ continuous	'I like your shoes, Kate,' said Jack. 'I'm enjoying the party,' said Tom.	past simple/ continuous	Jack said (that) he liked Kate's shoes. Tom said (that) he was enjoying the party.
past simple/ continuous	'I saw that car advertised on TV,' said Susie. 'I was hoping to win the prize,' Tom told me.	past perfect simple/ continuous	Kate said (that) she had seen that car advertised on TV. Tom told me (that) he had been hoping to win the prize.
present perfect simple/ continuous	'I've bought a hat,' Helen told me. 'I've been working in Geneva,' said Chris.	past perfect simple/ continuous	Helen told me (that) she had bought a hat. Chris said (that) he'd been working in Geneva.
will	'I'll take you there if you want,' Luke said.	would	Luke said (that) he would take me there if I wanted.
must (obligation)	'You must buy a ticket,' he said.	had to	He said (that) we had to buy a ticket.
can	'I can speak Spanish,' said Mel.	could	Mel said (that) he could speak Spanish.

2.3 When the verb doesn't change

The verb form doesn't need to change (although it can do) when

- the situation being reported is unchanged.

  'Bananas **are** a good source of energy,' said the doctor.
  The doctor told us that bananas **are** a good source of energy.
  'The castle **is** 800 years old,' said the guide.
  The guide told us that the castle **is** 800 years old.

- the sentence being reported contains the modals would, could, might, ought to and should or must for logical deduction.

  'I **ought to** buy a new car,' she said.
  She said she **ought to** buy a new car.
  'I think he **must** be coming,' she said.
  She said she thought he **must** be coming.

- the sentence being reported contains the past perfect.
  'He **had already been given** a prize,' she said.
  She said he **had already been given** a prize.

2.4 Time expressions may also change in reported speech as follows:

Direct speech	Reported speech
tomorrow	the next day, the day after, the following day
yesterday	the day before, the previous day
last week	the week before
here	there
this morning	that morning
today	that day
next Friday	the following Friday
ago	before

3 Reported questions and imperatives

3.1 Reported questions

1 Reported yes/no questions

When there is no question word in the direct speech question, we use if/whether. Word order is the same as in the statement. The verb tense and other changes are the same as for other types of reported speech.
'Could I borrow your bike?' she asked.
She asked **if/whether** she could borrow my bike.

2 Reported wh- questions

The wh- word is followed by statement word order (subject followed by verb). All tense and other changes are the same as for other types of reported speech.
' Why did you leave that job?' she asked him.
She asked him **why he had left that job**.
' Where is the swimming pool?' he asked her.
He asked her **where the swimming pool was**.

3.2 Reported imperatives

verb + object + infinitive with to

'Please open your suitcase,' said the customs official.
The customs official **asked me to open** my suitcase.
'Don't walk on the grass!' said the official.
The official **told them not to walk** on the grass.

Exercise 2

Match the underlined examples with the verb forms 1–8. Some verb forms have more than one example.

Interviewer: Lauren, how (a) <u>did you hear</u> about the job?

Lauren: Well, I (b) <u>spotted</u> the advert while I was on the internet and I (c) <u>think</u> it's something I (d) <u>'d be</u> good at.

Interviewer: Being an entertainment coordinator (e) <u>will involve</u> looking after very small children. (f) <u>Have you had</u> much experience of doing this?

Lauren: Well, I (g) <u>look after</u> my niece and nephew every month and I (h) <u>'m taking</u> them on a cycling holiday tomorrow.

Interviewer: Well, you (i) <u>might be</u> unlucky, I'm afraid, because I've heard that it (j) <u>'s going to</u> rain … Anyway, thanks for coming. We (k) <u>'ll write</u> soon, but don't worry if you (l) <u>don't hear</u> anything for a few days.

1	present simple	**5**	*going to*
2	present continuous	**6**	*will*
3	present perfect	**7**	*would*
4	past simple	**8**	*might*

Exercise 3

Rewrite the sentences using direct speech.

1 She asked me how I felt about winning the prize.

' .... ' she asked me.

2 I told her I'd expected to see her at the station that morning.

' .... ,' I told her.

3 He said that he wasn't planning to apply for the job that day.

He said, ' ....'

4 She asked me if I'd got enough to drink.

' .... ' she asked me.

5 He enquired whether we'd be driving to work that morning.

' .... ' he enquired.

6 They said that they'd been waiting there for an hour.

They said, ' .... '

Unit 9

1 Conditional forms

1.1 Zero conditional

Form	Use	Examples
if + present simple + main clause with present simple, present continuous or present perfect	to refer to a general truth	*If the birds **find** a suitable place, they **make** their nest.* *If anyone **drives** a car without a licence, **they are committing** a crime.* *If you **get** to the finish line first, you've **won** the game.*

> **Watch out!**
>
> It's also possible to use 'will' in the main clause without changing the meaning.
> *If the birds **find** a suitable place, they'**ll make** their nest.*
> *If anyone **drives** a car without a licence, they'**ll be committing** a crime.*
> *If you **get** to the finish line first, you'**ll have won** the game.*

Exercise 1

Match 1–6 to A–F to make sentences.

1 Liquids freeze

2 Chocolates melt

3 Fish die

4 People have fewer diseases

5 Laws do not work

6 Plums are sour

A if they are not ripe.

B if they are cooled to a low temperature.

C if they eat healthy food.

D if they are not enforced.

E if they are kept in a warm place.

F if they are taken out of water.

1.2 First conditional

Use: to describe what is possible or likely in the present or future

Form	Examples
if + present simple + main clause with a modal verb (*will/should/must/might/ need to/ought to/can*), *going to* or imperative	*If we **lose** the match, I'**ll be** disappointed.* *If we **lose** the match, he **might be** upset.* *If we **lose** the match, I'**m going to be** disappointed.* *If you **feel** thirsty, **have a drink**.*
if + present continuous + main clause with a modal verb (*will/should/must/ might/need to/ought to/ can*), *going to* or imperative	*If Rose **is applying** for the job, I **won't have** a chance!* *If you're **feeling** ill, **call a doctor**.*
if + present perfect + main clause with a modal verb (*will/should/must/might/ need to/ought to/can*), *going to* or imperative	*If they'**ve got** our message, they'**ll be** in the restaurant already.* *If you'**ve finished** the exercise, **check your answers**.*

> **Watch out!**
>
> *When* can be used instead of *if* to suggest that the activity is expected to happen.
> *When my plane **lands**, I'**ll phone** you.*

Exercise 2

Decide if one or both options are possible.

1 If children are encouraged, they *will learn/would learn* quickly.

2 I'll let you know when *I've arrived/I arrive*.

3 You need to book now if *you're flying/you will fly* next week.

4 If you want to go, *let her know/you should let her know* straightaway.

5 When *you're feeling/you could feel* better, we'll go for a walk.

6 I'll send him the photo if you think he *would/might* like it.

1.3 Second conditional

Form	Use	Examples
if + past simple/ continuous + main clause with *would/ could/should/ might* + bare infinitive	to talk about something that is contrary to the present facts	*If I **was/were** twenty years younger, I'**d emigrate**.* *If I **was/were** prime minister, I'**d make** all health care free.*
	to suggest something is hypothetical, or unlikely to happen in the present or future	*If I **had** enough money, I **might go** on a cruise round the world.* *If she **was/were** working for the airline, she **could get** free air travel.*
	to give advice	*If I **were** you, I'**d stay** at home.* *If I **was/were** applying for that job, I'**d check out** the company first.*

> **Watch out!** *Was/Were* can both be used in the main clause. *Were* is more formal and often used in writing, while *was* is more common in spoken English. However, *was* is not possible in the fixed phrase *if I were you*.

Exercise 3

Correct the mistakes in the underlined clauses.

1 <u>If I would have the right qualifications</u>, I'd apply for that job.

2 <u>I will go to university</u> if I could find a course I liked.

3 Life would be easier <u>if we're living in the country</u>.

4 <u>If I was you</u>, I'd make a formal complaint.

5 We might be more successful <u>if we wouldn't have to employ so many staff</u>.

1.4 Third conditional

Form	Use	Examples
if + past perfect + main clause with *would/could/ might* + *have* + past participle	to describe something in the past that could have happened but didn't, or that shouldn't have happened but did	*If she **hadn't missed** the bus, she **could have got** there on time.* *If I'**d known** she'd spend the money on sweets, I **wouldn't have given** it to her.*

Exercise 4

Choose the correct answer to each question.

1 If Ruby had known the child needed help, she'd have done something.

   a) Did Ruby know the child needed help? Yes/No

   b) Did Ruby do anything? Yes/No

2 If the police had heard the alarm, the thief wouldn't have got away.

   a) Did the police hear the alarm? Yes/No

   b) Did the thief get away? Yes/No

3 She could have become a great painter if her parents had allowed her to study art.

   a) Did her parents allow her to study art? Yes/No

   b) Did she become a great painter? Yes/No

4 I might never have become a writer if I hadn't done that creative writing course.

   a) Did I do the creative writing course? Yes/No

   b) Did I become a writer? Yes/No

Unit 10

1 Conditionals

1.1 Conditional linking words

- Common conditional linking words used in a similar way to 'if' are: *as/so long as, even if, on condition that, providing, provided (that), unless, whether.*

  *Mum says I can have a dog **as/so long as** I agree to look after it.*
  *I won't go **unless you come with me**. (= if you don't come with me)*
  *We're going on the walk **even if it rains**.*
  *I'll help you **provided (that) you don't tell**.*
  *They'll be pleased to see us **whether they're expecting us or not**.*

- *in case* is used to describe things we do as precautions against what might happen.

  *I'll take my phone **in case** I need to get in touch with you.*

- *otherwise* is used to describe what would happen if we didn't do something, or did things differently. It can link two clauses, or begin a new sentence.

  *I'll pay you now, **otherwise** (= if I don't) I'll forget.*
  *I must leave by 3.30. **Otherwise** I'll get stuck in traffic.*

Watch out! When the conditional clause begins the sentence, there is usually a comma between the conditional clause and the main clause. When the main clause begins the sentence, there is no comma before the conditional clause.

<u>If they offer me the job</u>, I'll accept it.
I'll accept the job <u>if they offer me it</u>.
(*Otherwise* is an exception to this rule – see examples above.)

Exercise 1

Rewrite each pair of sentences as one sentence using the linking word in brackets and making any other necessary changes. Check your punctuation.

1 I'd love to buy that sofa. But are you sure we can afford it? (as long as)

   I'd love ....

2 We may end up living in different countries. However, I'll always be friends with you. (even if)

   I'll always ....

3 They're allowed to go canoeing, but they have to wear life-jackets. (on condition that)

   They're allowed ....

4 It shouldn't be too difficult. Just follow the instructions carefully. (providing)

   It shouldn't ....

5 I might go to the party or I might not. I haven't decided yet. (whether)

   I haven't ....

6 Belinda may not have been invited to the party. In that case I won't go. (unless)

   Unless ....

7 You might get thirsty. You should take some water with you. (in case)

   You should ....

8 You'd better tell Sarah straightaway. If you don't, she'll be upset. (otherwise)

   You'd better ....

2 Participles (*-ing* and *-ed*)

2.1 Participle clauses

We can use participle clauses to make writing more economical.

1 Present participles (*-ing*) have an active meaning. They can replace relative clauses which have an active verb.

   *People **using** online dating sites give mixed opinions about them. (= who use)*

   *There was a huge lamp **hanging** from the ceiling. (= which hung)*

2 Past participles (*-ed*) have a passive meaning. They can replace relative clauses which have a passive verb.

   *The film, **made** by a fifteen-year-old on her smartphone, was seen all over the world. (= which was made)*

2.2 Other uses of participles

Participle	Use	Examples
Present participle	after certain verbs (see Unit 2)	*I enjoy **running**.*
	after conjunctions	***Before going out**, I locked the door.*
	after prepositions	*She's really good **at swimming**.*
	as the subject of a sentence	***Eating** too much is bad for you.*
	to describe activities occurring immediately after one another	***Picking up** her bag, she started to walk away.*
Present or past participle	as an adjective	*The film was very **interesting**.*
		*The fans were **disappointed** by the result.*

Exercise 2

Complete the sentences using the present or past participle of the verbs in brackets.

1 *Jane Eyre* is a romantic story .... by Charlotte Bronte. (write)
2 The hotel .... the harbour has a swimming pool on the roof. (overlook)
3 We spent our honeymoon on an island .... by a coral reef. (surround)
4 A group of women, all .... brightly coloured clothes, could be seen in the distance. (wear)
5 The house had a large garden .... down to the river. (stretch)
6 .... the book, she turned over and went to sleep. (close)

Exercise 3

Complete the sentences with the words in the box. Then match each sentence to one of the uses of participles in the table above.

annoying doing entering joining opening walking

1 .... a club can be a good way to make new friends.
2 I've finished .... my homework.
3 .... the book, she began to read.
4 She finds the loud music quite ....
5 A locked gate prevented us from .... the garden.
6 While .... down the road, I bumped into Mrs Kent.

Unit 11

1 Mixed conditionals

Not all conditional sentences follow the patterns described in Unit 9 (zero, 1st, 2nd and 3rd conditionals). For example, it's possible to have:

- an *if* clause referring to the past with a main clause referring to the present or future.

  *If I **had invested** in that company ten years ago (past), I **would be** rich now (present).*
  *If we **hadn't been given** all that homework (past), we **could go** swimming. (future)*

- an *if* clause referring to the present or future with a main clause referring to the past.

  *If you **don't like** sweet things (present), you **shouldn't have ordered** that dessert (past).*
  *If you're **going to take** the exam tomorrow (future), you **ought to have started** revising by now (past).*

Exercise 1

What time (past, present or future) is referred to in each clause in the sentences below?

1 If <u>you're not playing</u> in the match this Saturday, you <u>shouldn't have told us</u> you were.

   If + ... *+* ....
2 If <u>they'd given me</u> the right instructions, I <u>wouldn't be having</u> all these problems.

   If + ... *+* ....
3 If <u>they're</u> so short of money, why <u>did they buy</u> that big house?

   If + ... *+* ....
4 If I <u>hadn't already made</u> other plans for tonight, <u>I'd go</u> to the party.

   If + ... *+* ....
5 She <u>would already be</u> there if she <u>hadn't missed</u> the bus.

   .... *+ if +* ....
6 I <u>won't tell</u> you the ending if you <u>haven't seen</u> the film.

   .... *+ if +* ....

2 Hypothetical meaning

2.1 *wish*

We use this structure when we want our situation (or the situation of the person who is doing the wishing) to be different.

- We use the past simple to express a wish that has not come true in the present.

  I wish Eleanor liked me.
  Don't you wish you had a big car?
  I wish she was/were going out with me.
  Henry wishes he had a job.

- We use *would/could* to talk about wishes we have for other people or things.

  I wish my sister would stop smoking.
  I wish he wouldn't chew gum all the time.
  I wish the sun would shine.

- We use *could* to talk about wishes we have for ourself.

  I wish they could come with us.
  I wish I could be in the basketball team.
  I wish I could stop smoking.

- We use the past perfect to refer to things we are sorry about in the past.

  I wish I had been invited to the party.

  She wishes she hadn't told him about Carlo.

2.2 *if only*

If only is used with the same verb forms as *wish*, and is used when your feelings are stronger. It is often written with an exclamation mark (!). It is often used with *would/wouldn't* to criticise someone else's behaviour.

If only I could find the answer!
If only they would stop talking!
If only I had never met him!

2.3 *it's time*

It's time is used with the past simple to talk about the present or future. We mean that the action should have been done before. For emphasis, we can also say *It's about time* and *It's high time*.

It's (about) time you started revising for the exam.
It's (high) time we set off. The train leaves in half an hour.

2.4 other expressions with hypothetical meaning

suppose/what if?

Form	Use	Examples
+ present simple	to describe something that may possibly happen	*Suppose someone sees her with us.* *What if someone hears you coming in?*

Form	Use	Examples
+ past simple	to talk about something in the present or future that is just imagination or that is unlikely to happen	*What if you could go anywhere in the world? Where would you go?* *Suppose you won the prize. How would you feel?*
+ past perfect	to talk about something that could have happened in the past but didn't	*Suppose we hadn't told her. Would she have found out?* *What if you had married Carlos? Would you have been happy together?*

as if/as though/like

These can be used to introduce imaginary situations, or situations that do not exist but are possible.
He behaves as if he knew more than us.
He looked as if he had seen a ghost.
I feel as if I'm getting a cold. (possible)
I feel as if I was/were in a dream. (imaginary)
It was as though we'd never met before.

Watch out! 'As though' is much less common than 'as if'.
'Like' is only used in informal writing or speech.
He looks like he's seen a ghost!
→ See also Grammar Reference Unit 3 Section 3.3

I'd rather …

We use this to describe preferences for the present or future.
I'd rather they went on their own, not with Daniel.
I'd rather they didn't go with Daniel.
Would you rather they went on their own?

Exercise 2

Complete the sentences with the verbs in the box. There are three extra verbs you don't need to use.

could   had   hadn't   have   heard   didn't   lent   might   need   were   would

1 He behaves as if he .... in charge of the whole class.
2 Do you wish she .... just give up the idea?
3 It's time we .... from Diana – I wonder what she's doing?
4 Would you rather I .... take the car?
5 Suppose I .... you the money – could you repay it?
6 What if the ladder .... been there – how would you have got down?
7 I wish I .... go skiing in the mountains with you.
8 If only they .... told us that in the first place!

Unit 12

1 Obligation, prohibition and necessity

Form	Use	Examples
must/mustn't (not) allowed to	for present and future obligations or prohibitions imposed by the speaker, often on him/herself	*Payment **must** be made in cash.* *I **must** get some new shoes.* *You **must** read that book, it's excellent!* (= recommendation) ***Must** I really go now?* (= appeal) *You **mustn't** park here.* (= prohibition) *You **mustn't** eat so much.* (= strong advice) *You **aren't allowed** to wear trainers to school.*
have to have got to (more common in British English)	for present and future obligations that are imposed by someone other than the speaker	*I **have (got) to** take my holiday in February.* *They **haven't got to/don't have to** wear uniform, do they?* ***Have** we **got to/Do** we **have to** pay to go in?*
had to had got to	for past and reported obligations of all kinds	*They told us we**'d got to** leave our bags in the cloakroom.* *I knew I **had to** make a decision.*
need to	for obligation and necessity	*You **need to** book tickets in advance.* *Do we **need to** type our work?*
needn't don't need to don't have to	for lack of obligation in the present or future	*You **don't need to/needn't** meet me at the station.* *We **don't have to wait**. We can go straight in.*
needn't + have + past participle	to say that somebody did something, but that it was unnecessary	*You **needn't have gone** to all that trouble.*
didn't need to + infinitive	to say that something wasn't necessary, without saying whether the person did it or not.	*He **didn't need to** bring any extra money.* *She **didn't need to** cook dinner for us.*

Exercise 1

Choose the correct option in italics.

1 We *mustn't/don't have to* have a visa, do we?

2 Shoes *have not/must not* be worn in the temple.

3 You *must/had to* go to the museum tomorrow – it's fascinating.

4 Visitors *are not allowed to/don't need to* feed the animals – it's forbidden.

5 He *didn't need to take/needn't have taken* a jacket as he already knew it was going to be hot.

6 Do the children *have/got* to pay too?

7 I *had to/needn't leave* early because the traffic was very heavy.

8 You *don't need to invite/needn't have invited* Becky, but I'm glad you did!

2 Reflexive pronouns

Reflexive pronouns (*myself, yourself, him/her/itself, ourselves, yourselves, themselves*) are used

• when the subject and object of a transitive verb are the same.

*He stopped **himself** from saying something.*
*I hurt **myself** when I fell over.*

• with *enjoy, behave*, etc. when there is no object.
*Enjoy **yourself**!*
*Behave **yourselves**!*

• to mean 'without the help of others'.
*I cleaned the car **myself**.*
*We booked the holiday **ourselves**.*

• with *by* to mean 'alone/on your own'.
*Are you going to town **by yourself**?*

• to add emphasis to the subject or object.
*The president **himself** spoke to me.*
*The actors were good but the film **itself** was boring.*

> **Watch out!** *Bob and Mary are in their nineties but they look after **themselves**.* (= they do it as a couple)
>
> *Bob and Mary look after **one another**.* (= Bob looks after Mary and Mary looks after Bob)

Exercise 2

Complete the sentences with reflexive pronouns.

1 I blame .... for not checking more carefully.

2 We were invited to meet the president ....

3 Miranda says she's sure we'll enjoy .... in Spain.

4 You all need to fill in this form .... then give it to your parents.

5 They're not going on holiday by .... , are they?

3 have/get something done

This is a form of the passive.

Form	Use	Examples
have + object + past participle (the most common form) *get* + object + past participle (also possible when people are speaking informally)	to say that someone else did something for you because you wanted them to, or as a result of an arrangement	*He **had his hair cut** specially for the interview.* *His feet are so big that he **has to have shoes** specially **made**.* *He's **having the invitations printed**.* *Where can I **get these papers photocopied**?* *He decided to **get the photograph enlarged**.*
have + infinitive + object + past participle *have* + object + past participle	to say that someone else did something to you (often when this was something unpleasant)	*He **had to have a kidney removed**.* *She said she'd **had her car stolen**.*
get somebody to do *make somebody do something*	when we want to persuade or force somebody to do something for us	*I **got my friend to drive me** to the shops.* *The police **made the man hand over** his car keys.*

Exercise 3

Complete the sentences using words from the table above.

1 I .... my brother to help me with my homework.

2 They're .... the house painted.

3 We'd better .... the children stay indoors as it's raining.

4 I'm afraid you'll .... to have that tooth filled.

5 She's .... her hair cut very short – it looks great!

6 I think I'll .... my teacher to check this for me.

Writing reference

Contents

Checklist of key points for writing

Checklist

Doing the writing tasks

Have you

- answered all parts of the question and included all the necessary information?
- written the required number of words?
- organised your ideas appropriately, using paragraphs where necessary?
- written clearly so that it is easy to read?

Accuracy

Have you checked for mistakes with

- grammar, such as agreement, verb tenses?
- vocabulary, such as incorrect word or wrong word formation?
- spelling or punctuation?

Range

Have you used a variety of grammatical structures, interesting vocabulary and linking words?

Style and layout

Have you

- used a layout appropriate for the type of writing?
- included an appropriate introduction and conclusion?
- used language appropriate for the type of writing?
- made your answer interesting for the reader? Would it have a positive effect?

1 Model answers with hints and useful phrases

1.1 Essay

(Part 1)

For work on essays, see pages 24, 46, 78 and 98.

TASK

In your English class, you have been talking about technology. Now, your English teacher has asked you to write an essay.

Write an essay using **all** the notes and give reasons for your point of view.

> Do people depend too much on technology nowadays?
>
> **Notes**
>
> Write about:
>
> 1 communicating
>
> 2 education
>
> 3 .... (your own idea)

Write your **essay**. (You should write **140–190** words.)

Model answer

DON'T start by saying *I agree with this* – your **essay** should present your own argument.

DO state the topic in your first sentence, but use your own words.

DO include supporting detail for the points in each paragraph.

DON'T forget to express your opinion in the conclusion.

Nowadays nearly every aspect of life is affected by technology. Computers are used for communication, teaching and entertainment; but do we depend on them too much?

Some people are afraid that if people spend all their time talking to others on their computers, they become unable to make real relationships. They live through computers or mobile phones, and feel uncomfortable if they are not online. Such people are clearly too dependent on technology, although easy communication has advantages in the business world.

Education has benefited from technology as students can find all the information they need in seconds without needing to spend time going through books. However, if students lose the ability to think for themselves, this is not a good thing.

It is very easy to find entertainment through technology, and it is also used in film-making. We all expect to see special effects in films nowadays and these are produced by technology. Are these films really better than the films of the past, though?

In my opinion, we have to accept the need for technology nowadays, but we should be aware of the dangers of becoming too dependent on it.

DO use rhetorical questions to engage the reader with the topic.

DO use linking expressions to introduce points in an essay.

TASK

In your English class, you have been talking about the importance of advertising. Now, your English teacher has asked you to write an essay.

Write an essay using **all** the notes and give reasons for your point of view.

> Nowadays there is a great deal of advertising everywhere. Do you think it should be restricted?
>
> **Notes**
>
> Write about:
>
> 1 health
>
> 2 information
>
> 3 .... (your own idea)

Write your **essay**. (You should write **140–190** words.)

USEFUL LANGUAGE

- **Some people claim that** your teenage years are the best years of your life.
- **It is often said that** TV is a bad influence on young people.
- **However, in my view/opinion, …**
- **However, on balance , …**
- **Firstly, it is clear that** money cannot buy happiness.
- **There is a strong argument for …**
- **While it is true/Although it may be said that** computer games are stimulating, they may not be good for you in the long run.
- **To clarify the point,** there is more advertising on TV than ever before …
- **From my point of view/In my view,** job satisfaction is more important than a large salary.
- **It seems clear to me that …**
- **Finally, it is important to remember/must be remembered that …**
- **Lastly, I feel that …**
- **To sum up/In conclusion, it seems to me that …**

Model answer

DO state the topic in your first sentence in general terms.

Advertising is everywhere, in shops, on posters, on television, in magazines – it is impossible to escape. Is it too much, and should it be restricted?

DO use rhetorical questions to engage the reader with the topic.

There is a strong argument for restricting advertising of unhealthy things like sweets on television, because these advertisements can influence children who want to try the products in the advertisements, and this can be bad for their health. Children can't tell the difference between an advertisement and a programme, and they have no choice about seeing the advertisement if they are watching the programme.

DO use linking expressions to introduce new points in a new paragraph.

On the other hand, advertisements in magazines give people the chance to see what is available and decide whether to buy a particular product or not. This information is useful, and allows freedom of choice.

DO remember to include your own idea.

Some people think that advertisements encourage people to buy things they can't afford and this is clearly bad. This seems to support the idea of restricting advertising or at least regulating advertisements well.

DON'T forget that your conclusion should follow your argument clearly.

Some advertisements can be helpful. However, on balance I feel that although advertising has a place in our lives, it should be restricted but only on television.

DO show that you appreciate the other point of view, even if you don't agree with it.

1.2 Informal letter/email
(Part 2)

For work on informal letters and emails, see page 14.

TASK

You have received this email from your English-speaking friend Carole.

> When you visit me next month, what would you like to do? You said something about visiting historic places, but I know you like sports as well. I've just passed my driving test, so we can get around easily. Have you got any questions for me about your visit?

Write your **email**. (You should write **140–190** words.)

USEFUL LANGUAGE

- **Beginning the letter or email**

Many thanks for your letter/email – it was great to hear from you again.
I thought I'd better write and tell you more about …
It's been such a long time since we contacted each other.
How are things with you?
How was your holiday?
Hope all's well with you.

- **Introducing the topic**

I know you're keen to hear all about my holiday.
You remember that I told you I was going to …

- **Ending the letter or email**

Give my love/regards to your family.
Write soon!
I'm really looking forward to meeting up again soon.
Take care!

Model answer

Hi Carole,

Thanks for your email – it was great to hear from you. I'm sorry I haven't written for a while, but I've been really busy preparing for my exams. It's good news that you've passed your driving test. Congratulations!

I'm really looking forward to my visit – thank you again for inviting me. I know you have a wonderful beach near your house, and I'd really enjoy spending some time there. I expect the weather will be hot, so I hope we can go swimming. As you know I'm also interested in history, so it'd be great if you could drive to the castle in the next town – you told me about it before.

I have a couple of questions. What sort of clothes should I pack? Casual or formal? Would you like me to bring anything for you? I'd like to bring something special for you and your family from my country.

I'd better stop now and get on with my studying. I hope you're enjoying driving your car, and I can't wait to meet up very soon!

All the best,

Irene

Annotations:

DO use your friend's name, and greet your friend in an informal way. Don't write *Dear friend*.

DO think of some specific details to include in each paragraph – this will make your **letter or email** more interesting.

DO think of some interesting questions to ask.

DO mention a **letter or email** you have received from the person you are writing to, or refer to a shared experience.

DO say what you've been doing recently, and give some interesting details.

DO mention the next time that you will see the person you are writing to.

DO use an appropriate phrase to end your **letter or email**, e.g. *Love, All the best, Best wishes*. DON'T finish your **informal letter or email** with *Yours sincerely/faithfully*.

1.3 Semi-formal letter/email
(Part 2)

For work on semi-formal letters, see page 88.

TASK

You see this advertisement in a local English language newspaper

Would you like some part-time work?

We need students of English to spend two mornings a week helping in the local tourist office.

Good pay and conditions for the right applicants.

Write to us, giving information about your level of English, and explaining why you would be suitable for the job.

Write your **letter**. Do not write any postal addresses. (You should write **140–190** words.)

USEFUL LANGUAGE

- **I have always been interested in** *using English in my work.*
- **One of the main reasons I am applying for this job is that** *I want to work in England.*
- **I have a lot of experience of** *dealing with the public.*
- **I am available to start work** *at any time/from the end of the month.*
- **Thank you for considering my application.**
- **I would be grateful if you would** *send me further details of the job.*
- **I can be contacted** *on 0849 58 48 43* **at any time**.
- **I look forward to hearing from you soon.**

Model answer

DO say which job you are applying for and where and when you saw it advertised. You can invent a newspaper and date if you need to.

DON'T make mistakes with time expressions and tenses.

DO say when and how you can be contacted.

DO organise your **application** so that you mention each of the areas in the advertisement.

DON'T forget to mention why you think you are suitable for the job.

DO begin and end your letter as you would other formal letters.

Dear Sir/Madam,

I am writing to apply for one of the positions helping in the local tourist office which were advertised in Kent Weekly on August 23rd.

I am 19 years old and come from Switzerland. German is my mother tongue and I have been learning English and French for five years at a comprehensive school. At the moment I'm a student at English International, studying for the Cambridge First Exam.

I have always been interested in working with people. As I have already spent three months in England, I know the local tourist attractions quite well. I would also say that I have a good knowledge of history and old places, because I have read a lot about the subject recently. In the near future, I would like to continue studying English, and so the job in your tourist office would be a great opportunity for me to improve my speaking.

I am available for interview at any time. I can be contacted on 0795 51 32 41 after 6p.m. every evening.
Thank you for considering my application. I look forward to hearing from you.

Yours faithfully,

Gabriella Daniels
Gabriella Daniels

1.4 Report
(Part 2)

For work on reports, see pages 66 and 130.

TASK

The school where you study English has decided to spend some money on **either** buying more computers **or** improving the library. You have been asked to write a report for the school director describing the benefits to the school of both these options, and recommending which one the school should spend money on.

Write your **report**. (You should write **140–190** words.)

USEFUL LANGUAGE

Introduction
- *The aim of this report is to …*
- *This report is intended to …*

Reporting results
- *Most people seem to feel that …*
- *Several people said/told me/suggested/thought that …*

Presenting a list
- *They gave/suggested the following reasons:*
- *They made the following points:*

1 …

2 …

Making recommendations
- *I would therefore recommend that we* expand the library/ install a new coffee machine.
- *It would seem that* banning mobile phones is the best idea.

Model answer

DO state the aim of the report at the beginning.

DO use headings because this makes it easier for the reader to find the main information.

DO include two or three points under each heading. DO use numbering or bullet points to highlight main points, but try to use a range of language.

DON'T include irrelevant details or description.

DO use formal language in your report.

DON'T begin and end your report with *Dear Sir/Madam*, like a letter.

DO say how you collected the information.

DO use a range of specific vocabulary or set phrases, e.g. *Some thought this was a good idea …/ other students said they preferred …,* **but DON'T use lots of adjectives and dramatic language as you do in a story. A report gives factual information.**

DO express opinions impersonally. DON'T express recommendations or opinions until the conclusion.

Use of money for school improvements

Introduction

The aim of this report is to compare the advantages of buying additional computers and of improving the library, and to suggest which would be best. I asked students for their views.

Buying more computers

Some students thought that this was a good idea, saying computers were useful for:
- practising writing.
- using the internet.
- playing games.

Others said that they preferred to use their own computers at home or use their phone.

Improving the library

The majority of students preferred this suggestion, for the following reasons:

1. Many do not have a quiet place to work at home. The library could be a good place for private study, but at present there are not enough tables and chairs for everyone.
2. More up-to-date reference books are needed, even though most students use electronic dictionaries.
3. They want to be able to read books written for young people, without having to buy them.

Recommendations

It was felt by most students that improving the library would be more useful and that adding to the workspace and buying more reference books would benefit the majority of students.

I would therefore recommend spending money in this way.

1.5 Article
(Part 2)

For work on articles, see pages 34 and 110.

TASK

You see this advertisement in a local English language magazine.

ARTICLES WANTED!

The most important celebration in your country.

What is the most important celebration in your country? Why is it so important? What do people do?

Write us an article answering these questions.

We will publish the best articles in the magazine.

Write your **article**. (You should write **140–190** words.)

USEFUL LANGUAGE

Involving the reader
- **Are you thinking of** *getting married in the near future?*
- **I'm sure you'll agree** *it was a great idea.*

Developing your points
- **Let's start with** *why it is so important to take plenty of exercise.*
- **Another advantage** *of using a computer is that …*
- **On top of that,** *…*

Giving your own opinion
- **I think that/In my opinion** *traditional celebrations are very important.*
- **It seems to me that** *people are much more aware of the importance of a good diet nowadays.*

Model answer

DO think of an interesting title. Use the title given in the task. If there isn't a title given, write one of your own.

Olinda's carnival – something for everyone

When most people think of Carnival, they think of Rio de Janeiro. But Rio isn't the only city in Brazil that knows how to have parties. I live in Olinda, a lovely city in the north-east of Brazil. What can we say about the carnival in Olinda? Just that it's the best in the world!

DO try to involve your reader directly, e.g. by using a question.

Carnival has its origins in ancient Egyptian and Roman festivals. It was introduced to Brazil by the Portuguese, and was influenced by African rhythms and Indian costumes. Now it's a big national celebration and everyone is involved, which makes it important.

Do make sure you answer all the questions in the task.

DO add some interesting information for the reader.

Once Carnival starts, the whole town goes crazy! Everyone's singing and dancing. Parades of people wearing costumes, typical of our north-eastern folklore, dance through the streets. I love the giant street dolls, both the traditional ones such as 'the man of midnight' and the new ones that appear each year.

DO use informal language to involve the reader.

DON'T forget to express your opinion or feelings.

The best thing about our carnival is that no one has to pay and there are no big stars. Everyone takes part, rich and poor, old and young, residents and tourists. If you come, I promise you'll never forget it!

DO finish your article by summarising your main point and giving your opinion or expressing your feelings.

1.6 Review
(Part 2)

For work on reviews, see pages 56 and 120.

TASK

You see this announcement in a local English language magazine.

> **Film reviews wanted**
>
> We want your views on popular films today! Write us a review of the last film you saw. Tell us about the story, characters and any special features of the film, and whether you would recommend the film to other people. The best review will be published in the magazine.

Write your **review**. (You should write **140–190** words.)

USEFUL LANGUAGE

Introduction
- *The film I would like to review is …*
- *The last film I saw/book I read was …*

Summarising the story
- *It's set in …*
- *The story is based on* a book …
- *It's about …*
- *There are many memorable characters including …*
- *The main theme of the* film is …
- *What the* film is saying is …
- *The key moments are …*

Recommending the film
- *I would recommend this* film *to anyone.*
- *Although I enjoyed it, I would not recommend it for …*
- *It's one of the best* shows *I've ever seen.*
- *Although I am not normally keen on* musicals, *I'm glad that I decided to go.*
- *The* film *lifts you out of your everyday life.*
- *The* film *makes you feel good.*

Model answer

DO say what the film is about, but not in too much detail.

DO try to use a range of interesting vocabulary, to bring the film to life for the reader.

DO remember to give your recommendation clearly, as this is the purpose of a review, but not until the end.

The last film I saw was not new; in fact it was *The Lord of the Rings*.

It is based on the well-known book, and tells the story of a creature called a hobbit who takes a dangerous magic ring back to the place where it was made in order to destroy it. There are many memorable characters apart from the hobbit and his friends, including a wizard called Gandalf and a suspicious creature called Gollum.

This is a film about friendship and loyalty. However, it is the special effects that make it truly magical. There are vivid battle scenes with fantastic animals and birds, and sets that are so imaginative that you want to believe they are real. But as well as this, the actual locations are beautiful.

I would recommend this film to anyone, even those who do not usually enjoy fantasy films. What I would say to them is – go and try it! Like me, you might find that the film lifts you out of your everyday life into a world you will not want to leave. I can watch it again and again, and never get bored.

DO remember to mention important or memorable characters, but don't spend too much time just describing them.

DO remember to link ideas clearly, and to link paragraphs together.

DO support your opinion with clear reasons.

2 Sample answers

The following scripts were written by students. Read the Paper 2 marking guidelines on page 180, and use them to help you assess each answer and decide on its strong and weak points. Then read the comments given and the suggested band score, and compare your ideas.

2.1 Essay
(Part 1)

TASK

In your English class you have been talking about what people do in their free time. Now, your teacher has asked you to write an essay.

Write an essay using **all** the notes and give reasons for your point of view.

Many people in cities go shopping in their free time.
Do you think this has any value as a leisure activity?

Notes

Write about

1 relaxation

2 social activity

3 .... (your own idea)

Write your **essay**. (You should write **140–190** words.)

Sample answer

I believe that shopping can be one of the important things people do, like eating and sleeping, and for some shopping is their chance to do their favourite things like walking and meeting friends.

On the one hand, I think that is true that shopping has no value in some lifestyles. People think of shopping only as a chance to do whatever they want, and then it is an escape from doing things they should do. I mean people go shopping instead of do work.

However, others think of it as a chance to meet some friends who you only see from time to time. In addition, it is useful time to discuss every day problems – for example, if you have got some problems, in that shopping time you might listen to others problems and think that yours are nothing compared to theirs. It can make a break from every day work pressure and so it is valuable for some who have a hard job and lifestyle.

In conclusion, it's true that buying things has little value, but people are different, which means that shopping will be priceless for some.

Comments

This answers the question clearly and uses a wide range of vocabulary and some good expressions (e.g. *think that yours are nothing compared to theirs*). The paragraphs are clearly introduced with linking words (e.g. *On the one hand*). However, there are some grammatical mistakes (e.g. *instead of do work*). The style is appropriate, and the writer has included interesting ideas of their own about discussing problems with friends when shopping. The conclusion clearly returns to the question and gives a nice summary of the writer's opinion. It has a positive effect on the reader. **Band 4**

TASK

In your English class you have been talking about consumerism. Now, your English teacher has asked you to write an essay.

Write an essay using **all** the notes and give reasons for your point of view.

Write your **essay**. (You should write **140–190** words.)

Nowadays people buy products that come from all over the world instead of things that come from their local area. Do you think this is a good idea?

Notes

Write about

1 employment

2 quality of products

3 .... (your own idea)

Sample answers

A

Everything in the world always has advantages and disadvantages. As local products, it doesn't have famous brand, but it can help many people get a good job, and get a high income.

To begin with, it contributes various types of jobs for people. As a country able to educate their citizens to produce their own product, this will bring plenty of careers for these people.

Also the products can be more fresher and more healthier because they are home made without any chemical that harmful people's health.

On the other hand if we live in that area and we use that products too, we can know clearly how they made it, because we can go to the company or places where they were made. For example, bread, if we want to know how it was made and what they put in it, we can go to the place where it made. So we can give the people feedback and help them to improve.

So in my opinion it is better to buy local products rather than bought products from other countries.

B

There are many reasons to support domestic products in our country. Firstly, jobless in own country can be reduced because more people will have employment.

Another point is that having local products is more convenient and more reliable. For example, if you get some products that are not related to our country you may get products that don't have our native language on it. This, how can you read the use or the benefit of it? And this will cause you a great deal of problem.

On the other hand there will still have some disadvantages about this point. Some people want to buy product from all over the world because they want to try new thing, for example food they want to try new tasty, or for mobile phone, they want to try if it's better than local product or not.

The conclusion I strongly disagree about the sentence that it is good thing to buy local products imported from all over the world because most of the people, they want to try new things, get new experience.

Comments

A This has a fairly good range of grammar, and the answer is well organised in paragraphs with appropriate linking words. The introduction is a little confusing but the conclusion works well, and it is possible to understand the writer's viewpoint. The writer has used the idea of working with local producers to give feedback as his/her third point. There are some grammatical mistakes (e.g. *more healthier, harmful people's health*). The style is generally suitable for an essay. It has a satisfactory effect on the reader. **Band 3**

B This has no introduction to the topic, and the ideas are not clearly expressed. The writer mentions the lack of native language and trying new things as his own ideas, and uses this in his conclusion. There are grammatical mistakes with articles and some sentences are not clear (e.g. *for example food they want to try new tasty*). The conclusion does not seem to follow the argument logically. The essay just about has a reasonably satisfactory effect on the reader, and would just reach **Band 3.**

2.2 Informal letter/email
(Part 2)

TASK

You have received this letter from your English-speaking friend Tom.

I'll definitely be able to visit you next July – is that a good time to come? What will we be able to do together then, and what would you recommend I see? Should I bring anything special with me? Any advice for me? How can we travel around?

Write your **letter**. Do not write any postal addresses. (You should write **140–190** words.)

Sample answers

A

Dear Tom,

Hi! How are you? Thank you for your letter! I'm very happy about your plan!

OK! If you let me know your arrival time, I will come to you, at Narita airport. I've thought about our plan in Japan. I know you really like football! So, how about visiting stadiums of the World Cup? You can visit a locker room in Yokohama International Stadium where the final was held, and you can see autographs of Brazilian national team members.

In July, Japan is very hot, but sometimes there is a heavy rain so you have to bring an umbrella. And there are lots of mosquitoes, you must bring a medical cream to protect yourself against them.

Do you have any special requests? If you have any, please let me know. I'll try to do it!

I'm looking forward to your reply and to meeting you in July!

Lots of love,

Yuka

B

Dear Tom,

Nice to hear from you. I'm so surprised that you are on your way to come here this summer. I have to say that you've made a good decision.

First of all, I would like to recommend you some places where you shouldn't miss such as Sentosa island. You can have different activities there. For example, if you would like having sunbathing. I think 'Sun World' is the best choice to relax. Don't forget to bring swimwear. I don't think Bird Park is a good place to visit. It's quite boring I have to be honest to say that. However if you are really interesting in visiting there I could show you around.

Secondly, it's the best time come here if you enjoy the shopping. We have big on sale in July. Therefore, I can arrange the shopping table for you.

I don't think you need to bring any special stuff. That's because you can buy them here. Don't forget to prepare some more empty suitcase for your shopping.

If you have any question just ask me. I'll do my best to solve them.

Best wishes,

Carel

A All parts of the question are dealt with, in an appropriately informal style. There are some grammatical mistakes (e.g. *there is a heavy rain*) and problems in pronoun use (e.g. *I'll try to do it!*) but the student uses tenses accurately and shows a good range of vocabulary, and the paragraphs are clear and well constructed. The letter has a positive effect on the reader. **Band 4**

B This is a full answer to the question, with a fairly good range of grammar, but there are quite a few grammatical problems (e.g. *recommend you some places where you* instead of *recommend some places to you which; interesting in* instead of *interested in*). Vocabulary problems sometimes make the meaning unclear (e.g. *I can arrange the shopping table for you*). Paragraphs and connecting words are well used and the style is generally suitable for a letter from a friend. It has a satisfactory effect on the reader. **Band 3**

2.3 Semi-formal letter
(Part 2)

TASK

You have received this letter from the organisers of a competition you entered.

Write your **letter**. Do not write any postal addresses. (You should write **140–190** words.)

Congratulations! You have won first prize in our competition – a two-week trip to Vancouver OR San Francisco. Your prize includes FREE return flights to the city of your choice, a two-week English course and FREE accommodation with a family.

Which city would you prefer, and when? Would you like us to make any special arrangements for you?

Sample answers

A

Dear Mrs Thompson,

Thank you very much for the letter. I am very pleased that I've won the prize. I would like to go to San Francisco because I have never been to the USA before. However, there are several questions I would like to ask.

First of all, I would like to know whether the return flight is a direct flight or not. I would like to book a direct flight because it is much more comfortable.

Secondly, I would like to know how long we are being teached every day and if there are classes in the morning or the afternoon. Is there a difference between Vancouver and San Francisco concerning this point?

You wrote about a free accommodation with a family. Are the meals included and/or do I have the opportunity to cook by myself? Please let me also know the distance from the school.

Finally, I would like to ask you if it is possible to stay at school for an extra week. If it is possible please let me know the price I have to pay.

I like to thank you in advance for your assistance and I look forward to hearing from you soon.

Yours sincerely,

Anders Moser

B

Dear Sir or Madam

Thank you very much for your letter which I received yesterday. I would like to go to Vancouver, because I have never been there. As I know that the weather in Canada is very nice in summertime, my preferred month is July.

Furthermore, I would like to enquire whether you could let me have some more information about my prize. First of all, I am interested in my course: how many lessons in a week do we have? And only in the morning, or in the afternoon as well? In addition to this. I would like to know if my flight is a direct one or not. My other questions concern my host family. As I am vegetarian, I would prefer to go in a family who cooks not only meat dishes. Is this possible? And how far do students usually have to walk to school?

I would be grateful if you could reply to these questions as soon as possible.

Yours faithfully

Andrea Larssen

Comments

A There is no irrelevant information and the student answers the question with interesting details. There are some grammatical mistakes (e.g. *we are being teached; a free accommodation*), but these don't cause problems in understanding the meaning. He uses quite a wide range of structures, although he tends to repeat *I would like to know*. Ideas are organised in paragraphs with appropriate vocabulary. The style is sometimes too formal (e.g. *concerning this point*) but the letter would have a positive effect on the reader. **Band 5**

B There is a grammatical mistake in word order *'who cooks not only meat dishes'* but she uses a wide range of structures accurately including the present perfect. The vocabulary is appropriate, and there is clear paragraphing although the use of 'furthermore' is not appropriate. All parts of the task are dealt with. The style is semi-formal and appropriate, and the letter would have a positive effect on the reader. **Band 5**

2.4 Report
(Part 2)

TASK

The principal of your school wants to make some changes to the school classrooms and has asked students for ideas about what should be done to make the classrooms better places to study in. Write a report making suggestions for how the classrooms could be improved.

Write your **report**. (You should write **140–190** words.)

Sample answer

Introduction

This report is to suggest what we need to make the classrooms better in our school. I asked students for their ideas.

Background situation

What it's need to be inside a good school classrooms is that they all have all the equipment students might need starting from the essential things like chair, blackboards, finishing with accessories like televisions.

Suggestions

I certainly believe that two things need to start our plan to improve the school classrooms, they are money and good management. My idea of improving the classrooms is to start with what we have and see what needs to be repared and what has to be thrown away and replaced with a new equipment and some computers that the students might need also having a massive liberrary is one of the more important things that students request. Heating and air conditioning are necessary to make the atmosphere in the classrooms cosy.

Personal opinion

In conclusion, the chance of having a good classrooms looks easy from a distance, in fact it isn't, and that we must try to find the balance between having a very good school and not spending too much.

Comments

This report makes some relevant points, but the style is more suitable for an essay than a report. It would be much better in bullet points.

It is not easy to identify the main suggestions because of problems with sentence linking and punctuation. *My idea of … is to start with what we have* is good. The problem is the sentence is too long and needs splitting up, e.g. *My idea of improving the classrooms is to start with what we have. Then we can see …* There are some problems with passive forms (e.g. *what it's need* instead of *what is needed*) but also some good expressions (e.g. *to start with what we have; we must try to find the balance between*). The student has a good range of vocabulary although this is not always appropriately used (e.g. *massive, cosy*) and there are some spelling mistakes (e.g. *repared, liberrary*). It has a satisfactory effect on the reader. **Band 3**

2.5 Article
(Part 2)

TASK

You have seen this advertisement in a magazine for young people.

> ## I'd love to have ...
>
> Write an article about something you would like to have, saying why you would like to have it and what difference it would make to your life.

The writer of the best article will win a laptop computer. Write your **article**.

Sample answers

A

I'd love to have ...

Now, I'm living in England to study English. I came from Japan. Have you been there? It takes 13 hours to get there by airplanes. The most thing which I really need is not airplane tickets, it's a good tablet computer.

Yes, I know. Most people's opinions are same as me. In my case, the situation is slightly different. In my tablet, I could have lots of digital photos. They remind me many memories of my friends in Japan and friends who I make in England. When I get a homesick, they help me. I can feel that I'm not alone. Indeed, I could connect with my parents and friends by emails. The fact that we live in foreign countries is sometimes very stressful, but I could consult to them whenever I want. It's very convenient! And writing to my foreign friends is very good writing practice, isn't it? The problem is that it expensive for students.

If you studied abroad, I would recommend you to have a tablet. Trust me! It will make life so much easier for you.

B

Money would be lovely!

I'd love to have a lot of money although I think money is not a perfect solution. Of course not! However, if I had enough money I could do plenty of things which I want to do.

Above all, I want to study in other countries, because. It is a good chance to develop my abilities. In this case, I don't need worry about the fee of education in my life. I can only concentrate on studying as long as I do my best.

Secondly, I would like to prepare a lovely house for my parents. Although they didn't say to me at all, I think the work of electric services is so hard to continue at their ages within 10 years. Therefore, I hope that I could make them relax and enjoy their life.

On the other hand, I can help the other people who are suffering from lack of food, illness and so on. When I saw a TV programme which announced those people's stories, I thought if I were them I would get really depressed.

Sometimes, money can be used in a bad way, but if I am a rich person I will spend them on not only for me, but I also give an opportunity to others.

Comments

A The language is informal: *Yes, I know,* and *Trust me!* are more like spoken English although the style is also engaging for the reader. There is an attempt to use a range of language but there are grammar mistakes (e.g. *a homesick, recommend you*). The paragraphing is clear, but the introduction is confusing. The answer would have a reasonably satisfactory effect on the reader. **Band 3**

B There is a range of structures and vocabulary but there are mistakes (e.g. *if I am a rich person I will spend them on not only for me*). It is difficult to understand what she says about her parents *Although they didn't say to me at all, I think ….* Paragraphs are well planned but there are mistakes with punctuation and linking words (e.g. *Secondly, On the other hand*). There is informal and formal language (e.g. *Of course not!, Therefore*), and it is a little long. It has a satisfactory effect on the reader. **Band 3**

2.6 Review
(Part 2)

TASK

You see this advertisement in an English language film magazine.

Write your **review**. (You should write **140–190** words.)

Reviews needed!

We want to compile a list of the best-loved films of recent years. Write a review of your favourite film. Include information on the plot, main characters, anything special about the film and why you would recommend this film to other film-goers.

The best review will be published in next month's edition of the magazine.

Sample answers

A

I want to tell you about a movie really discussed in Italy, 'L'Ultimo Bacio' (The Last Kiss) directed by Gabriele Muccino in 2001.

It is set in an Italian city in the same time in which actors play, in fact, the director's purpose is take a plausible picture of people's life. The movie tell us about the crisis of two different generations worried by the difficulty of grow up and take their responsibility.

On the one hand, there are thirty years old people who think wedding like an important change of life but sad and serious, therefore they are very frightened of doing it, preferring an affair with someone else to solving their couple's problems.

On the other hand, fifty years old people are frightened of growing old.

I think the story is really topical and show a widespread situation, the actors' performance is really good, the dialogues are fast and accurate. Although is a great film I must admit that it is a bit too shouted, but this is Muccino's style.

A good story, great actors and good dialogues and editing, 'L'Ultimo Bacio' is really interesting, not boring at all.

B

My favourite film is called 'If only'. It's the best romantic film I have ever seen, and I really love watching it again and again.

It's set in London and about a hard-working businessman and a lovely violinist woman. The man is too busy to take care his love. He thinks work is more important than his girlfriend. On the concert of her graduation he meets a taxi driver and talks with him about their love. He realises something but it's too late because his girlfriend dies by car accident. He regrets everything, but surprisingly there is a great chance of living with her again. Finally he can appreciate her, but sadly he has to die instead of his girlfriend.

I have seen it 5 times. Until I saw it 3-4 times it was just love story with strange situation, but last time, I can feel character's feelings. So it was a really romantic film. The plot and the song of the actress was fantastic. The story could be a bit artificial and far-fetched. But if you focus on character's feelings you can be given a good precept. Don't calculate your love, just appreciate her!

If you fall in love or like romance you'll love this film.

Comments

A This review is a bit long, has some style problems and is not always easy to follow. *On the one hand/ On the other hand* does not link well to *two different generations*. There is a good range of vocabulary (*plausible picture, take responsibility, widespread situation*) but some words are misused, e.g. *too shouted*. There are basic grammatical mistakes, e.g. *-ing* form after prepositions (*difficulty of grow up*). The review only has a satisfactory effect on the reader. **Band 3**

B This is a bit long, but is organised and easy to follow. The style and paragraphing are both generally appropriate, and the writer has given her opinion. There is some interesting vocabulary although some words are misused, e.g. *precept*. The sentences are simple, but there is a range of structures including present perfect and modals. Mistakes do not usually impede communication. The review generally has a satisfactory effect on the reader. **Band 3**

3 Marking guidelines

Both parts of the Writing paper carry equal marks. Here are some guidelines for assessment.

Band	Content	Communicative achievement	Organisation	Language
5	All the content is relevant. The reader has all the information he/she needs.	Communicates both straightforward and complex ideas effectively within the conventions of the task.	The text is well organised and coherent, with a variety of connecting words. The overall effect is good.	Uses a range of vocabulary, including less common words, appropriately. Uses a range of simple and complex grammatical forms with only occasional errors which do not confuse the reader.
4	A mix of bands 3 and 5			
3	Nearly all the content is relevant. In general, the reader has all the information he/she needs.	Communicates straightforward ideas effectively.	The text is generally well organised and coherent, with a variety of connecting words.	Uses a range of everyday vocabulary appropriately. There may be occasional errors with less common lexis. Uses a range of simple and complex grammatical forms. There may be some errors, but these do not cause difficulty for the reader.
2	A mix of bands 1 and 3			
1	Some of the content is irrelevant. Some information needed by the reader is omitted.	Generally communicates straightforward ideas appropriately.	The text is connected and coherent, using basic linking words.	Uses everyday vocabulary generally appropriately, while occasionally using some words too much. Shows good control of simple grammatical forms. Errors are noticeable, but the meaning can still be understood.
0	The content is totally irrelevant. The reader does not have the information he/she needs.	Below band 1		

4 Guide to writing genres

The range of task types in Parts 1 and 2 of the Writing Paper give you the chance to write in different styles and for different purposes. This means you can show a range of language across the paper, and in Part 2 you can choose to write in a style you feel comfortable with.

4.1 Part 1

Essay

An essay is written for a teacher or tutor. The purpose of an essay is to present an argument or point of view that the reader can easily identify and understand. You should answer the question provided in the task by discussing the two content points you are given, and adding a new idea of your own. You should organise your essay into clear paragraphs with a new paragraph for each point. There should be an introduction to the topic in the first paragraph and the essay should finish with an appropriate conclusion that rounds off the argument and sets out your point of view. The style will probably be semi-formal and ideas should be linked with appropriate words and phrases.

4.2 Part 2

Email/Letter

An informal or semi-formal letter or email is written as a response to part of a letter or email provided in the task. There may also be a situation you have to respond to, such as an advertisement for a job or course. The letter or email may be written to an English-speaking friend, a possible employer, a college principal, or an editor of a newspaper or magazine. It is important that you write in a consistent and appropriate style for the reader of your letter or email, and that you include all the information required so that the reader is fully informed.

Article

An article is usually written for an English language magazine, newsletter or website and is on a topic of general interest to both the readers and the writer of the article. In your article you may have to give examples to support an idea or comment on a topic. The purpose of an article is to interest, entertain and engage the reader, and to do this you should try to use techniques such as rhetorical questions, expressing personal opinions or feelings and using a range of interesting language.

Report

A report is usually written for a teacher, principal or a fellow member of a club or similar organisation. In a report you usually have to give factual information about a given situation, and make suggestions or recommendations about that situation. The purpose of a report is to give information to enable the reader to decide on a course of action. This means the information and recommendations in the report should be well organised and expressed clearly. It may be helpful to use headings for the different sections of the report, and bullet points for recommendations. The introduction should include a summary of the purpose of the report, and the conclusion should highlight the recommended course of action.

Review

A review is usually written for an English language magazine, newspaper or website. Reviews may be about a film, a book, a holiday, a product, a website and so on. The purpose of a review is to inform the reader by describing something and giving a personal opinion about it in an interesting and engaging way so that the reader can form his/her own opinion about it. You should give a brief description of the film/book, etc. you are reviewing, and provide clear reasons for whether or not to recommend it to others. It is important for you to describe whatever you are reviewing well, and explain your opinions clearly so that the reader understands whether you are recommending the film/book, etc. or not, and why.

5 Additional tasks with suggested plans

You should always plan your answer before you start to write. In the exam you should allow time for this, and also for checking for mistakes after you have finished. Here are some tasks, and suggested plans. Read them to see how the plan works with the task, then try writing your own plan and answer.

5.1 Essay
(Part 1)

> **TASK**
>
> In your English class you have been talking about students doing part-time jobs. Now, your English teacher has asked you to write an essay.
>
> Write an essay using **all** the notes and give reasons for your point of view.
>
> Many students do part-time jobs. Is this a good idea?
> ---
> **Notes**
> Write about:
> ---
> 1 disadvantages of time
> 2 advantages of experience
> 3 .... (your own idea)
>
> Write your **essay**. (You should write **140–190** words.)

Plan

Introduction
Introduce the topic in a general way, but don't give your own opinion.

Paragraph 1
Describe disadvantages of time, e.g. not being able to do homework/see friends.

Paragraph 2
Describe advantages of experience, e.g. learning about the workplace, being independent.

Paragraph 3
Add an extra point, e.g. improved attitude to life/earning money.

Conclusion
Give your own opinion about whether a part-time job is a good idea or not.

5.2 Letter
(Part 2)

> **TASK**
>
> You receive this letter from a travel company about a recent holiday you booked with them.
>
> We understand that you were dissatisfied with the holiday you have recently taken with our company, and we would like to find out what happened. Write to us explaining what the problems were, what your experiences were and what you would like us to do.
>
> Write your **letter.** (You should write **140–190** words.)

Plan

Introduction
Say when and where you went on holiday.

Paragraph 1
Describe the problems, e.g. location of hotel, extra costs for meals, lack of evening activities.

Paragraph 2
Explain your experiences, e.g. disappointment with holiday, poor organisation, boredom.

Paragraph 3
Say what you want the company to do.

5.3 Informal email
(Part 2)

> **TASK**
>
> You have received this email from your English-speaking friend Tom.
>
> **From:** Tom
> **Subject:** Jo's birthday
> Hi – we're planning a get-together next Saturday in town to celebrate Jo's birthday. I know that you can't come because you're visiting your grandparents, but what do you think the rest of us should do together? What should we get her as a present? What's the best way to contact everyone to tell them where to meet? Let me know your thoughts.
> Cheers
> Tom
>
> Write your email. (You should write **140–190** words.)

Plan

Introduction

Thank Tom for the email, and apologise for not being able to attend the celebration.

Paragraph 1

Suggest things the friends could do together, e.g. go to the cinema, have a meal in a restaurant.

Paragraph 2

Give ideas for a present, with reasons, e.g. a book because she likes reading/a voucher for downloading music because she likes discovering new singers.

Paragraph 3

Suggest ways of contacting the other friends, e.g. a message on Facebook/setting up a group chat but not a letter as it would take too long.

Conclusion

Finish the email appropriately and ask Tom to pass on your best wishes to Jo.

5.4 Article
(Part 2)

TASK

You see this advertisement in a local English language newspaper.

Articles wanted: Life today

Is life better for young people now than it was for our parents? What has improved? What is worse?

Write us an article answering these questions. We will publish the best articles in the newspaper.

Write your **article**. (You should write **140–190** words.)

Plan

Introduction

Introduce the topic generally – maybe with a rhetorical question.

Paragraph 1

Describe something that is better, e.g. technology, entertainment.

Paragraph 2

Describe something that is worse, e.g. pollution, stress and financial pressure.

Conclusion

Give your opinion, with an amusing or interesting ending.

5.5 Report
(Part 2)

TASK

Your college principal wants to improve the area around the college buildings to make it more attractive for students. He has asked students to write a report on the current situation, and make recommendations for using the area.

Write your **report**. (You should write **140–190** words.)

Plan

Introduction

Explain the purpose of the report and who you interviewed.

Current situation

Explain why the area is not nice now.

Suggestions

Make recommendations for the use of the area based on student feedback, e.g. a garden, sports pitches.

Conclusion

Highlight what the results of following your suggestions would be.

5.6 Article
(Part 2)

TASK

You see this announcement in an English language magazine.

Book reviews wanted

Have you read a book in which the main character is particularly interesting? Write us a review of the book, explaining what makes the main character so interesting and why you liked him or her. Tell us whether you would recommend this book to other people or not.

Write your **review**. (You should write **140–190** words.)

Plan

Introduction

Introduce the book and the main character.

Paragraph 1

Explain what makes the main character interesting and why you like him or her. Give examples from the book.

Paragraph 2

Sum up the reasons you recommend the book to others.

Conclusion

Finish with an interesting or amusing concluding sentence.

6 Discourse markers and linking words and phrases

6.1 Time sequencers

Examples include *before, after, after a while, eventually, later, then, finally, as soon as, at first, at last, when, while.*

*I immediately phoned the police. **While** I was waiting for them to arrive, I watched the house.*

***At first**, no one got out of the car, but **after a while** the driver's door opened.*

*And **then** I **finally** found what I was looking for.*

6.2 Listing points

Examples include *first, firstly, first of all, to begin with, secondly, thirdly, finally.*

*Our holiday was spoiled, **firstly** because the hotel was uncomfortable and **secondly** because the weather was bad.*

6.3 Adding information/Emphasising points

Examples include *as well as (that), in addition (to), moreover, furthermore, not only … (but also…), what's more, on top of that, to make matters worse, in fact, as a matter of fact.*

*The hotel was miles from the beach. **On top of that**, the view from our bedroom window was terrible.*

***Not only** was the hotel miles from the beach, **but** the view from our bedroom window was terrible too!*

***In fact**, everyone is different when it comes to personal taste.*

6.4 Giving examples

Examples include *for example, for instance, such as. I like singers **such as** Adele.*

*My town has a lot of things for young people to do. **For example**, there are three cinemas.*

6.5 Reasons, causes and results

Examples include *as a result, because, because of (this), so, therefore.*

*I have visited Britain several times and, **as a result**, my English is quite good.*

*By the end of the day, you haven't managed to find anything that you like. **So**, you go home frustrated.*

6.6 Contrast

but

But links two contrasting ideas. It is not normally used at the beginning of the sentence.

*Many people argue that TV is bad for you, **but** I disagree with this.*

however

However can come at the beginning or end of a sentence. It must be separated off by commas.

*The advert claimed that there were huge discounts for students. **However**, the discount was only five percent.*

*I love travelling. I don't enjoy long flights, **however**.*

although, even though, though

These expressions introduce a subordinate clause of contrast. If the subordinate clause comes first, it is separated from the main clause by a comma.

***Although** he practised every day, he didn't manage to improve.*

*I walked home **even though** it took me two hours.*

NOTE *though* can be used after a comma at the end of a separate sentence that expresses something surprising.

*We lived in the middle of a city. We still had a large garden, **though**.*

whereas, while

- *Whereas* and *while* are used to compare two things and show how they are different.

*She likes football **whereas** I prefer tennis.*

*My sister is very like my father, **while** I take after my mother.*

- *While* is also used in the same way as *although*.

***While** computers are important, we shouldn't let them rule our lives.*

in spite of (the fact that), despite (the fact that)

These expressions must be followed by a noun or *-ing* form.

Despite is slightly more formal than *in spite of*.

***In spite of** the fact that they are expensive, many people want to buy designer clothes.*

***Despite** all the research that has been done, we still haven't found a cure for cancer.*

in fact, the fact of the matter is

This is used when you are saying what the 'real' truth of a situation is.

*According to the brochure, the service is free for students. **In fact**, students are charged at the same rate as everyone else.*

on (the) one hand, … on the other hand, …

These expressions are used to introduce opposite points in a discussion.

*(**On the one hand**,) if I take the job in Milan, I'll be able to go to the opera. **On the other hand**, if I take the job in Barcelona, I'll be able to go to the beach.*

otherwise

This is used to say what will happen if something else does not happen first.

*You have to choose your holiday carefully. **Otherwise** you could be disappointed.*

7 Academic language

For the Writing paper, it is important to use the correct style. If you are writing an essay or report, it may be appropriate to use language that is academic. Here are some examples of sentences using: **1** non-academic English, and **2** academic English.

7.1 Nouns

function

1 I still don't understand what they will use the new building for.
2 The **function** of the new building is still unclear to me.

area

1 This is something that we don't know much about.
2 This is an **area** that we know little about.

role

1 An important way to improve people's eating habits is by educating them.
2 Education **plays an important role** in improving people's eating habits.

source

1 We don't know where this information comes from.
2 The **source** of this information is not known.

factor

1 If people are poor, they may commit crimes as a result.
2 Poverty seems to be **a key factor** in many crimes.

aspect

1 If you are ill, that can affect many different parts of your life.
2 Ill health may affect **many different aspects** of your life.

concept

1 Some people find it hard to understand the idea of climate change.
2 Some people cannot **grasp the concept** of climate change.

feature

1 The new sports stadium is an important building in our city.
2 The new sports stadium is **a major feature** of our city.

7.2 Adjectives

beneficial

1 The effects of the internet are not all good for people who use it.
2 Not all the effects of the internet are **beneficial** to its users.

varied

1 People replied to our question in lots of different ways.
2 Many **varied** responses were given to our question.

significant

1 Technology is very important in people's lives.
2 The effect of technology on people's lives is very **significant**.

financial

1 Often, young people don't have enough money.
2 Young people often suffer from **financial problems**.

specific

1 The speaker talked about the special problems that people around here have.
2 The speaker **discussed the specific problems affecting** people living in this area.

sufficient

1 I hope there will be enough money from the government to finish the project.
2 I hope to have **sufficient government funding** to complete the project.

7.3 Verbs

establish

1 They started the company in 1978.
2 The company **was established** in 1978.

assess

1 They did research to find out how much long-distance runners were affected by diet.
2 **Research was carried out to assess the effects** of diet on long-distance runners.

identify

1 We can see three big problems in the plans.
2 Three **major problems can be identified** in the plans.

occur

1 Some bad flooding happened in places round the town.
2 Serious flooding **occurred** in areas around the town.

assume

1 The students think they can use the school hall.
2 The students **assume** they can use the school hall.

require

1 The main thing a mountain climber needs is a good head for heights.
2 The main thing **required of** a mountain climber is a good head for heights.

Exam focus

Contents

Reading and Use of English Paper

(1 hour 15 minutes)

Part 1 (Multiple-choice cloze)

What is being tested?

Part 1 tests your awareness of vocabulary, including words with similar meanings. It also tests some grammatical features, e.g. phrasal verbs and fixed phrases.

What do you have to do?

- Read a text with eight missing words.
- Choose the correct word or phrase from each set of four options.
- Mark the correct letter A, B, C or D on your answer sheet.

Strategy

1 Read the title and the text quickly to get a general idea of what it is about, without trying to fill any of the gaps.

2 Read the text again. Stop at each gap and try to predict what the missing word or phrase might be.

3 Look at the options for each gap carefully. Try putting each of the options in the gap to see which one fits best.

4 Check the words on either side of the gap to see if the option you have chosen goes with these.

5 Read the whole text again to make sure the options you have chosen make sense. Do not leave a blank; if you are not sure, choose the one which seems most likely.

6 Transfer your answers to the answer sheet.

Part 2 (Open cloze)

What is being tested?

In Part 2, the focus is on grammar and the missing words will be grammatical words like auxiliary verbs, articles, prepositions, pronouns, phrasal verbs, etc.

What do you have to do?

- Read the text with eight missing words.
- Put one word in each of the eight gaps. Contractions (e.g. *won't*) count as two words.
- Write the correct word for each gap clearly on your answer sheet. Check your spelling.

Strategy

1 Read the title and text quickly to get a general idea of what it is about, without trying to fill any of the gaps.

2 Think about what kind of word is missing, e.g. preposition, article, pronoun, etc.

3 Write in the missing words in pencil. Only write one word in each gap.

4 When you have finished, read through the whole text again. Check it makes sense, and check the spelling.

5 Transfer your answers to the answer sheet.

Part 3 (Word formation)

What is being tested?

Part 3 focuses on both vocabulary and grammar and tests your knowledge of how words are formed using prefixes and suffixes, etc. You'll have to understand what kind of word is required in each gap (e.g. noun, adjective, adverb), and be able to form it.

What do you have to do?

- Read a paragraph with eight gaps.
- Use the word in capital letters at the end of each line with a gap to form a word which fits each gap.
- Write your answers on your answer sheet.

Strategy

1 Read the title and the text quickly to get a general idea of what it is about.

2 Read the text again. This time stop at each gap. Think about whether the missing word is positive or negative, plural or singular, a noun, verb, adjective or adverb. Use the words before and after each gap to help you decide.

3 Write the correct form of the word in the gap.

4 Read the text again to make sure your answers make sense and the words are spelt correctly.

5 Transfer your answers to the answer sheet.

Part 4 (Key word transformation)

What is being tested?

Part 4 tests a range of grammatical structures as well as vocabulary, and shows examiners that you can express yourself in different ways.

What do you have to do?

- Complete six sentences using two to five words, including a key word which is provided. You must not change the key word in any way. Your completed sentence must have a similar meaning to the lead-in sentence. You get two marks for each transformation.
- Write your answers on the answer sheet.

Strategy

1 Read the first sentence and the key word. Work out what is being tested, e.g. you may need a passive form in a future tense.
2 Identify what is missing from the second sentence.
3 Think about what kind of words need to be used with the key word.
4 Write down the missing words. Do not change the key word in any way.
5 Make sure you have not written more than five words (contractions, e.g. *don't*, count as two words) and that you have not changed the meaning at all.
6 Check your spelling and that the sentences make sense.
7 Transfer your answers to your answer sheet.

Part 5 (Multiple choice)

What is being tested?

Part 5 focuses on your ability to understand a text in detail. Questions will focus on different things such as the main idea of a text, specific details in a text, the writer's opinion, attitude or purpose, your ability to understand the meaning of words or phrases from the context, and to follow features of text organisation such as examples and references.

What do you have to do?

- Read the text and answer six questions. Each question has four possible answers (A, B, C or D) and the questions follow the order of the text.
- Choose the correct option for each question, based on the information in the text.
- Mark the correct letter A, B, C or D for each answer on your answer sheet.

Strategy

1 Read the instructions, title and sub-heading of the text.
2 Skim the text to get a general idea of what it is about.
3 Read each question and highlight the key words (don't worry about the four options yet).
4 For each question, highlight the part of the text that the question relates to.

5 Read the text again carefully. When you find a part of the text you have highlighted, look at the question and the four options and decide on the answer. The meaning will be the same but the language will be different.
6 Check all the options again carefully, crossing out ones that are obviously wrong.
7 Make your decision. If you are not sure, choose the option that seems most likely.
8 When you have completed all the questions, transfer your answers to the answer sheet.

Part 6 (Gapped text)

What is being tested?

In Part 6, you will be tested on your understanding of how a text is structured.

What do you have to do?

- Read through the text, from which six sentences have been removed.
- Read the seven sentences (there is an extra one which doesn't fit anywhere) and decide which sentence best fits each gap.
- Mark your answers on your answer sheet.

Strategy

1 Read the title and sub-heading to get an idea about the topic of the text.
2 Read the main text carefully to make sure you understand what it is about.
3 Read the section before and after each gap and predict what information is missing from each gap.
4 Underline any nouns, pronouns, linkers, etc. which will help you to find a link.
5 Read the seven sentences and look for clues that will connect them to the gaps. Look for topic words, synonyms and reference words.
6 If you are not sure about what goes in a gap, go on to the next question and return to it later.
7 When you have finished, read through the completed text to check that it makes sense. Make sure you have filled in all the gaps and not used any sentences more than once.
8 Try the extra sentence in each gap again to make sure that it doesn't fit anywhere.
9 Transfer your answers to the answer sheet.

Part 7 (Multiple matching)

What is being tested?

Part 7 focuses on your ability to search through a text (or texts) to find specific information, and on understanding writers' opinions and attitudes.

What do you have to do?

- Read four to six short texts around the same theme, or one longer text divided into four to six paragraphs. To answer the questions, you will have to read quickly to find specific information.

- Match ten questions or statements to the text or paragraph that it relates to. The questions do not follow the same order as the text.
- Write the correct letter for each answer clearly on your answer sheet.

Strategy

1 Read the title and any subheadings.
2 Skim each text quickly to get an idea of what it is about.
3 Read the questions carefully and highlight key words.
4 Scan each section of the text to find the information in the questions. You do not need to read in detail. Look for words or phrases which are similar in meaning to the words or phrases in the questions.
5 Underline or highlight possible answers. Do not mark them on your answer sheet yet: you may find similar – but not exactly the same – information in other sections.
6 Read the information carefully to check which one is an exact answer to the question.
7 Leave any questions that you are not sure about; but always go back and answer them at the end as you will not lose marks for a wrong answer. Choose the most likely answer.
8 When you have finished, transfer your answers to the answer sheet.

Writing Paper (1 hour 20 minutes)

Part 1 (Essay)

What is being tested?

Part 1 tests your ability to write an essay outlining and discussing issues on a particular topic.

What do you have to do?

- Write an essay based on a title and notes to guide your writing.
- Write in an appropriate style (formal or informal).
- Write 140–190 words.

Strategy

See Writing reference page 166.

Part 2 (Choice of task)

What is being tested?

There is a choice of tasks in Part 2, and the testing focus depends on the task. You will have to communicate clearly in a style appropriate to the task. You may also have to advise, compare, describe, explain or recommend.

What do you have to do?

- Choose one task out of the three tasks you are given.
- Write an answer to the task using an appropriate format and style. The three options could be from the following: an article, a review, a report, a letter or email.
- Write 140–190 words.

Strategy

See Writing reference pages 168–172.

Listening Paper
(approx. 40 minutes)

Part 1 (Multiple choice: short extracts)

What is being tested?

Part 1 tests a range of listening skills. You may be asked about the main idea, the attitude or opinion of the speakers, whether they agree or disagree, etc. You will be given eight seconds to read through the questions before the extracts are played.

What do you have to do?

- Listen twice to eight short extracts which last about thirty seconds each on different topics. These may be monologues or dialogues.
- Answer one multiple-choice question about each of the eight extracts.
- Write the correct letter A, B or C on your answer sheet. (You are given five minutes at the end of the test to transfer your answers from the question paper to the answer sheet.)

Strategy

1 Read the questions and options and highlight the key words before you listen.
2 The first time you listen, mark the answer you think is best on your answer sheet.
3 Check your answers the second time you listen and make sure the options you have chosen answer the questions correctly.
4 If you aren't sure, choose the answer you think is most likely – you don't lose marks for wrong answers.

Part 2 (Sentence completion)

What is being tested?

In Part 2, the focus is on listening for detail, specific information and opinion in a longer text. You will be given 45 seconds to read through the questions before the recording is played.

What do you have to do?

- Read the ten sentences with gaps about the recording.
- Listen twice to a monologue which lasts about three minutes on a particular topic.
- Complete the ten sentences with a word or words from the recording.
- Write your answers on your answer sheet.

Strategy

1 Before you listen, read the rubric, title and sentences carefully. Highlight key words and think about the kind of information that is missing. You have some time for this.

2 As you listen, try to complete the sentences. The sentences are in the same order as the information in the recording. Write a word or short phrase to complete each sentence. You should write the words you hear; you do not need to change these words.

3 If you can't complete a sentence the first time you listen, leave it blank.

4 The second time you listen, complete any remaining sentences and check your answers. Don't leave any of the gaps blank – you don't lose marks for a wrong answer.

5 Check that your spelling and grammar (e.g. singular/plural) is correct and that the sentences make sense grammatically.

6 Be careful not to make any mistakes when you copy your answers onto the answer sheet at the end of the test.

Part 3 (Multiple matching)

What is being tested?

In Part 3, the focus is on your ability to understand the main idea. You may also have to listen for specific details, understand a speaker's attitude or opinion, etc. You will be given 30 seconds to read through the questions before the recording is played.

What do you have to do?

- Listen twice to five short monologues which last about thirty seconds each on a related topic.

- Match one of eight options to each monologue. There are three extra options which do not match any of the monologues.

- Write the correct letter A–H for each answer on your answer sheet.

Strategy

1 Read the rubric carefully. This tells you what topic the speakers will talk about.

2 Read each option. Highlight key words/phrases and think of synonyms/paraphrases for these words.

3 The first time you listen, try to identify the main idea of what the speaker is talking about, and mark the option which you think matches most closely.

4 During the second listening, check that the options match exactly what the speaker says. Don't choose an option just because it contains a word from the monologue.

Part 4 (Multiple choice: longer text)

What is being tested?

Part 4 focuses on your ability to follow a longer text and listen for the main idea, for a speaker's attitude or opinion, or for specific information. You will be given one minute to read through the questions before the recording is played.

What do you have to do?

- Listen twice to an interview or a conversation which lasts about three minutes a topic.

- Answer seven multiple-choice questions.

- Write the correct letter A, B or C for each answer on your answer sheet.

Strategy

1 Before you listen, read the introduction to the task to get information about who the speakers are and what they will talk about.

2 Read the questions and options and highlight key words/phrases. Think about the kind of information you need to listen for.

3 Listen for paraphrases of the words and phrases on the recording and choose one of the options A, B or C. If you are not sure of an answer, continue answering the other questions and come back to it in the second listening.

4 During the second listening, check the options you have chosen. If you aren't sure, choose the one that seems most likely.

Speaking Paper
(approx. 14 minutes)

Part 1 (Interview)

What is being tested?

Part 1 focuses on your general interaction and on social language skills.

What do you have to do?

- The examiner will ask you and the other candidate for some personal information.

- You will be asked different questions about things such as where you live, your family, what you do in your spare time, your work/studies, future plans.

- This will take around two minutes.

Strategy

1 Speak clearly. Try to relax and speak confidently.

2 Try to sound interested and interesting. Try not to speak in a monotone.

3 If you don't know a word, say it in another way. Don't leave long pauses.

4 Listen carefully both to the examiner and to your partner.

5 If you don't understand the question, ask for it to be repeated.

6 Give relevant, personal answers. Avoid giving one-word answers, but don't speak for too long.

Part 2 (Individual long turn)

What is being tested?

In Part 2, the focus is on your ability to organise your ideas and express yourself clearly. You will have to compare two photographs, and answer a question about them.

What do you have to do?

- The examiner gives you two photographs on the same topic.
- Listen to the examiner's instructions.
- Compare the photos and answer the question which is also printed on the page with the photographs. You have one minute.
- Then listen to the other candidate speaking, and look at his/her photos.
- When he/she has finished, you will be asked to give a short 30-second answer to a question related to his/her photos.

Strategy

1 Listen carefully to the instructions. It's important that you understand exactly what you need to talk about. Ask the examiner to repeat the instructions if necessary but remember that the question is also written above the photographs.

2 Summarise the main similarity and any differences between the two photos. Talk about general ideas and don't be tempted just to describe the photos or go 'off topic'.

3 You may need to speculate about the photos if you are not sure what they show.

4 Make sure you have enough time to answer the question.

5 Keep talking for the whole minute. Use paraphrases and 'fillers' if necessary. The examiner will say 'thank you' when the minute is finished.

6 Listen carefully while the other candidate is speaking. Look at his/her photos, but don't interrupt. When the examiner asks you a question related to the photos, give a short answer (about 30 seconds).

Part 3 (Collaborative task)

What is being tested?

In Part 3, you'll be tested on your range of language and your ability to interact with another person. You'll be expected to exchange and discuss ideas and opinions, and invite and respond to your partner's contributions.

What do you have to do?

- In this part of the test, you work with a partner to discuss something together.
- The examiner gives you a written question and prompts to look at.
- The task has two parts. The first part will usually involve talking about each of the prompts in turn. The second part will involve making a decision, etc.

- Discuss the question and prompts with a partner for about two minutes. Then the examiner will ask you a question about making a decision. Discuss this for about a minute.

Strategy

1 Read and listen carefully to the instructions. Ask for repetition if you do not understand.

2 In the first part of the task you should discuss the prompts in relation to the question. (Don't spend too long on any one prompt – you only have two minutes to do this. You don't need to talk about all of them.)

3 One of you should start the discussion. Then take turns to give your opinions, agree, disagree, etc. You are tested on the language you use to work together.

4 Turn-taking skills are important. Avoid dominating the discussion or interrupting rudely. It is important to involve and encourage your partner and follow up on what he/she says.

5 Explain things in a different way if you can't think of a word or phrase and don't leave long pauses. Use words such as *right* or *OK* to 'fill the gaps'.

6 Try to use a range of functional language, such as asking for and reacting to opinions, agreeing and disagreeing, suggesting, speculating, opening and summarising the discussion.

7 When you are discussing the question about the decision you don't have to agree.

Part 4 (Discussion)

What is being tested?

Part 4 focuses on your ability to discuss issues in more depth by giving and justifying opinions, agreeing and disagreeing, etc.

What do you have to do?

- In this part, the examiner asks you both questions which develop the topic in Part 3 and may lead to a more general discussion.
- You may add to what your partner has said or agree/disagree with his/her ideas.
- The discussion will last for around four minutes.

Strategy

1 If you don't understand the question, ask the examiner to repeat it.

2 Give opinions and express your feelings about issues. Give reasons or examples.

3 Listen to what your partner says and ask him/her questions or give follow-up comments.

4 Use a wide range of language, but don't dominate the discussion.

Practice test

Reading and Use of English

Part 1

For questions **1–8**, read the text below and decide which answer (**A, B, C** or **D**) best fits each gap. There is an example at the beginning (**0**).

Example:

0   **A**   <u>group</u>   **B**   crowd   **C**   band   **D**   gang

---

Photography Walks with Tina George

Join professional photographer Tina George on a morning photography walk through the stunning woodland of the Redbridge Forest. There will be no more than ten people in each (**0**) ....

As the guided walk gets underway, you will develop a deeper consciousness of the nature (**1**) .... you thanks to some special strategies that you'll be (**2**) .... to that will lead to enhanced powers of perception. You will be able draw (**3**) .... from what you see which will, in turn, boost your creative confidence and help you to significantly (**4**) .... your own photography skills.

Tina will spend the morning taking you through a programme of activities that require you to (**5**) .... use of your entire range of senses to 'notice' – become aware of what's immediately around you. At each step, Tina will also encourage you to personalise your response to what you see by (**6**) .... your feelings through either creative writing or doing rough drawings.

Although you will be with others, you will experience your own personal journey as you walk through Redbridge Forest, seeing the natural (**7**) .... through fresh eyes. As the session draws to a close, you will pause to (**8**) .... on what you have seen, and share your thoughts with the others as to how you might use these insights in your photography in the future.

1	**A** attaching	**B** surrounding	**C** enclosing	**D** connecting
2	**A** announced	**B** taught	**C** introduced	**D** known
3	**A** creation	**B** brilliance	**C** vision	**D** inspiration
4	**A** swell	**B** alter	**C** develop	**D** enlarge
5	**A** do	**B** have	**C** take	**D** make
6	**A** saying	**B** recording	**C** telling	**D** remarking
7	**A** situation	**B** environment	**C** scene	**D** location
8	**A** reflect	**B** consider	**C** wonder	**D** judge

Part 2

For questions **9–16**, read the text below and think of the word which best fits each gap. Use only one word in each gap. There is an example at the beginning (**0**).

Example

0	of

The Treasure Hunter

Have you ever dreamt **(0)** .... finding buried treasure? Having dug up **(9)** .... than 5,000 silver coins in the South of England, an amateur treasure hunter could now receive over a million pounds. The coins, among the largest collections ever found in the UK, are around a thousand years old. These perfectly preserved pieces, each of **(10)** .... features the face of an ancient king, **(11)** .... discovered in a bucket buried almost a metre underground.

The person **(12)** .... made this discovery was digging with members of his archaeology club when he found the coins. Club leader, Paul Walsh, described the find as an exciting one. He said that they aren't sure if all the coins are the same or if **(13)** .... is any variation. He also added that once they have checked the coins, they will know just **(14)** .... significant the discovery actually is.

The coins will be taken to the British Museum in London for identification. Then a court will come to a decision as to **(15)** .... they are legally treasure. If so, the money from their sale will be split equally **(16)** .... the landowner and the treasure hunter.

Part 3

For questions **17–24**, read the text below. Use the word given in capitals at the end of some of the lines to form a word that fits in the gap **in the same line**. There is an example at the beginning (**0**).

Example:

0	charitable

Oxfam

Oxfam is an international association of **(0)** *charitable* organisations, which was founded in Oxford in 1942. It is still based in Oxford today. — **CHARITY**

In its early days, Oxfam was mainly involved with providing food in areas which had been struck by famine. However, with the passing of time, the organisation has also adopted methods to address the underlying causes of famine. Oxfam **(17)** .... supplies medicine as well as food to people — **CURRENT**
who need it. Additionally, it offers a variety of equipment that **(18)** .... people to provide — **ABLE**
for themselves. It makes people more self-sufficient by facilitating **(19)** .... trade and — **GLOBE**
ensuring that any crafts or produce made by local **(20)** .... are sold profitably. — **PRODUCE**

Oxfam mainly works through local associations with the aim of improving their **(21)** .... — **EFFECTIVE**
Its programmes explore the reasons behind **(22)** .... The organisation declares that its — **POOR**
goal is to offer assistance in the **(23)** .... of policies that benefit disadvantaged people — **DEVELOP**
internationally, and also to help people **(24)** .... when it is either beyond the capabilities — **DIRECT**
of local associations or is inappropriate for them to do so.

Part 4

For questions **25–30**, complete the second sentence so that it has a similar meaning to the first sentence, using the word given. **Do not change the word given.** You must use between two and five words, including the word given. Here is an example (**0**).

Example

0   A very friendly taxi driver drove us into town.

   DRIVEN

   We .... a very friendly taxi driver.

The gap can be filled by the words 'were driven into town by', so you write:

Example: | 0 | | WERE DRIVEN INTO TOWN BY |

---

25   Dimitris asked the manager to find out what had gone wrong.

   INTO

   Dimitris wanted .... what had gone wrong.

26   There wasn't any fresh bread left in the bakery.

   RUN

   The bakery .... fresh bread.

27   Aliya wouldn't object to you going early today.

   OBJECTION

   Aliya would not .... your going early today.

28   Michel started learning Japanese two years ago.

   FOR

   Michel .... two years.

29   The journey wasn't as easy as she had expected.

   MORE

   The journey .... she had expected.

30   I demanded to see the manager to make a complaint.

   SEEING

   I .... the manager to make a complaint.

Part 5

You are going to read part of an article about an awards ceremony for scientists and other experts. For questions **31–36**, choose the answer (**A**, **B**, **C** or **D**) which you think fits best according to the text.

The Rolex Awards for Enterprise

Tom Rowley meets British scientist Joseph Cook who is unlocking the secrets of why and how fast Arctic ice is melting, and whose work has taken him from Sheffield to Greenland.

At the home of the Oscars on Hollywood Boulevard, 500 sets of golden cutlery had been laid out. The well-groomed guests and an uncommonly smart group of reporters had flown into Los Angeles. Passing the metal stars on the pavement of the world-famous Walk of Fame, they hung around the café enjoying snacks, and now they were taking their seats in the theatre. On the stage, the orchestra warmed up and in the wings, the Hollywood stars who were acting as presenters for the evening awaited their cue. And there in the front row, nervously awaiting his moment of glory, sat a little-known man who spends much of his time staring into puddles.

Not just puddles, actually. Some of the pools he likes to examine, far away in the Arctic, more closely resemble drill holes, just a centimetre across. Some days he flies drones (aircraft with no pilot) over them. Other times, he bends over them himself, gathering their contents into test tubes.

On this November evening, the man, Joseph Cook, arrived at the theatre with his family. In the moments before the ceremony began, his father stepped up to the stage to take a picture of Cook and the two women sitting beside him: his wife, Kylie, and his mother, Angela. Cook had never known them to fuss so much about their outfits. They were not the only ones. Searching for their seats in the rows behind the Cooks were mathematicians in tuxedos and biologists in cocktail dresses. One elderly man wore a hearing aid and a bow tie, but the dress code was apt for they were here to witness the science world's closest approximation of the Academy Awards.

Every two years, the Rolex Awards for Enterprise honour scientists, explorers and assorted other geniuses who have ambitious plans to chart unknown corners of our planet or develop life-enhancing technology. Launched 40 years ago, this latest ceremony would welcome five new 'laureates' – who would each receive 100,000 Swiss francs (£79,000) towards their projects – and another five young laureates, who would be given 50,000 Swiss francs (£39,000). This being a Rolex affair, just before the ceremony the engraved watches the laureates also received were put on, and they were entertained to a luxury dinner of lobster salad and filet mignon, served on the same stage from which Hollywood A-listers deliver their Oscar acceptance speeches. Hence the golden cutlery.

'It's another world,' Cook told me. 'So extravagant. It's not what you expect when you're sat at your desk in Sheffield just quietly getting on with stuff.'

Why, then, had Cook been singled out as one of this year's winners, when 2,312 applicants had been rejected? The answer lay 3,700 miles away on the vast expanse of the Greenland ice sheet. Try to picture this 650,000 square miles of frozen water and you will probably imagine a vast piece of ice, all of the brilliant white of a snowstorm in a Hollywood movie. In fact, the ice is awash with colour. 'There are colours there that I've seen nowhere else,' says Cook. 'You see these wonderful neon blues, deep purples and pastel shades everywhere.' Risking encounters with polar bears and being eaten alive by mosquitoes, Cook loves the view and confides that 'it's totally got under my skin', but he knows these colours are important for more than their beauty. They also hold long-kept, scientific secrets, and Cook, as one of only around 200 glacial microbiologists in the world, is trying to discover them. Put simply, his *line 39* research focuses on how, as the ice darkens, it melts more quickly and the effect this has on the harm already caused by global warming.

31 According to the first paragraph, why were Hollywood stars there on the evening?

    A They had been invited to join the audience to watch a ceremony.

    B They had been asked to carry out a specific role.

    C They had been asked to attend a special dinner.

    D They had been invited to receive some awards.

32 How did Cook's wife and mother feel on the evening?

    A confused about the seating arrangements

    B thrilled by the photo opportunities that arose

    C concerned about the impression they would make

    D overcome with emotion due to their relative's achievements

33 In the fourth paragraph, what does the writer tell us about the Rolex Awards?

    A A single winner is awarded a gift of cash.

    B The ceremony was initially held over half a century ago.

    C Winners are presented with more than one type of prize.

    D Attendees are treated to a simple meal before the ceremony.

34 When Cook talks about being at the Awards, we learn that

    A he is making the most of being spoiled.

    B he is unaccustomed to this level of luxury.

    C he had expected to be treated like a celebrity.

    D he would much rather be getting on with his work.

35 What does Cook say about the landscape in Greenland?

    A It is hazardous.

    B It is primarily one colour – white.

    C It is extremely delicate.

    D It is unique in nature.

36 What does 'them' refer to in line 39?

    A the secrets

    B the colours

    C the mosquitoes

    D the microbiologists

Part 6

You are going to read a newspaper article about the health benefits of coffee. Six sentences have been removed from the article. Choose from the sentences **A–G** the one which fits each gap (**37–42**). There is one extra sentence which you do not need to use.

Why caffeine is cool

Scientists have discovered that there are many advantages to drinking coffee.

The number of coffee bars in the UK has increased dramatically in recent times. Britons are now estimated to drink 2.1 billion cups of coffee outside their homes, and the good news is that our heavy caffeine intake comes with some health benefits. Of course, as with any foodstuff, moderation is key, but as various scientific studies show, the outlook for coffee lovers is certainly not as depressing as was once believed.

Austrian research shows that caffeine gives people a mental boost for 45 minutes. Research from Johns Hopkins University in the UK also found that caffeine can improve memories. **37** Those who had had coffee were better able to distinguish between the visuals than those who were caffeine-free.

Researchers at Harvard University found that even after a burst of mental stimulation, people should probably keep on drinking coffee. Studies carried out in 2015 showed that drinking several cups of coffee a day may cut the risk of Parkinson's disease in half. **38** Earlier findings suggested that caffeine can help with common symptoms of the disease, such as mobility problems.

Science also backs up the belief that caffeine also makes people more logical and speeds up their reaction time. When scientists at the Walter Reed Army Institute of Research were trying to discover the best ways to overcome tiredness in soldiers, they found that a daily dose of 800 mg of caffeine (about eight cups) over successive nights is an 'effective strategy to maintain cognitive function when optimal sleep periods during the day are not available'. **39** But it's good to know that a cappuccino helps if you've had a sleepless night.

German researchers have found that, under laboratory conditions, caffeine stimulated human hair growth. **40** And their beliefs shaped the development of caffeinated shampoos.

People who drink more than four cups of caffeinated coffee daily have a 49 percent lower risk of developing throat and mouth cancers than those who drink it only occasionally. This was the finding of American research that was ongoing for more than a quarter of a century. They studied almost one million men and women over a period of 26 years to find the relationship between the two. **41** There was no such similar link for people who drink decaffeinated coffee and none at all for tea.

The study's lead author said: 'We are not recommending people drink four cups of coffee a day. This is just a little bit of good news for those of us who enjoy coffee.' **42** The main thing is that we now know much more than we used to about the effects of caffeine.

A They concluded that it 'may have an important clinical impact' on the management of baldness.

B Caffeine may also be good for people who already suffer from the condition.

C A new global study into the effects of caffeine on our skin will be carried out early next year.

D And a little bit of that is better than none, surely.

E Participants in the study were given two different sets of images to learn over two days.

F However, it was a different story when it came to drinks which do not have a high caffeine content.

G However, it's clearly not recommended that people should replace a good night's rest with a visit to a local coffee shop.

Part 7

You are going to read part of an article about young people choosing careers in engineering. For questions **43–52**, choose from the sections (**A–D**). The sections may be chosen more than once.

In which section does the writer

give examples of common objects that have involved engineering? | 43 |

say that people think engineering is a wise choice of profession? | 44 |

mention the importance of receiving advice from experts? | 45 |

say that having too few engineers is a problem for a country's wealth? | 46 |

highlight the similarities in ways of thinking among certain groups of people? | 47 |

point out that engineering has long been considered a safe career? | 48 |

recommend how understanding of engineers' work can be increased? | 49 |

explain how different groups are encouraging students to become engineers? | 50 |

mention the difference between how men and women choose their careers? | 51 |

mention that students are unfamiliar with the type of work that engineers do? | 52 |

Young people in engineering

A recent report focused on encouraging more young people to choose careers in engineering has shown a division between the sexes.

A Although the shortage of young engineers is no longer news, the potential consequences of this news are still a concern with regard to the future of the UK economy. A study by the Royal Academy of Engineering estimates that there will be a need for 800,000 new science, engineering and technology professionals in the next few years. Industry leaders, educators, the government and other agencies are trying to overcome the challenge and tempt young people at career fairs and with graduate training schemes. But all of the different agencies involved need good data as well as specialist advice on how to use the information. A new report, *Engineering Skills for the Future*, produced by a charity organisation for Science, Engineering and Manufacturing Technologies (Semta) hopes to address the gender divide and getting new people into an engineering career.

B The shocking division in gender was the main subject of the report. Only six per cent of registered engineers and technicians are women and, even more worrying, females make up just four percent of participants in engineering training programmes. The report analyses data from men and women in engineering. 'This latest report suggests that males are more interested in financial reward and females are more interested in the prospect of interesting work,' explains Stephen Howse, from Semta. According to Howse, gender is a more significant divide than age with people aged 14–15, 17–18 and 21–22 years old, the reasons for young people choosing a career are similar. One of the most useful – if shocking – pieces of information provided by the report is that the engineering industry as a whole doesn't think the imbalance between the genders stops people going into engineering. Only three percent of female engineers see the gender divide as a problem.

C That, argues Howse, just doesn't make sense. The *Engineering Skills for the Future* report comes up with some suggestions for positive action. 'The best thing engineers can do is describe to non-engineers their day-to-day job,' says Howse. 'There's still a lot of incorrect information out there around what an engineering job actually involves, including amongst young people. Having evidence from an engineer that says: "Actually, my job isn't dirty and it isn't boring" is so much more powerful. We need to show young people, especially females, that modern engineering offers them the chance to be creative and inventive, and can also offer them the chance to shape the world around them. Everything they touch has been engineered – their phones, their games consoles and their bikes – we need to get that message across.'

D There are, however, some positive points shown in the report, for example more women than men think about encouraging other women to join them in an engineering profession. Also, in general there is still a belief that engineering is a good career choice and can offer a secure job for life. 'That's a really strong selling point now just as it was 40–50 years ago,' explains Howse. 'Technological change is going to create lots of exciting new job roles. Getting into engineering now gives people – whatever their gender, whatever their nationality – the perfect route into to a strong career. We're always going to need engineering after all.'

Writing

Part 1

You must answer this question. Write your answer in **140–190** words in an appropriate style.

In your English class you have been talking about the internet. Now, your English teacher has asked you to write an essay.

Write an essay using all the notes and give reasons for your point of view.

The internet has more advantages than disadvantages. Do you agree?

Notes

Write about:

1 immediate access to information

2 people spend too much time online

3 .... (your own idea)

Part 2

Write an answer to one of the questions **2–4** in this part. Write your answer in **140–190** words in an appropriate style.

---

2   You see this announcement in your college English-language magazine.

Book reviews wanted

Have you read a book in which there was a character who did something funny?

Write us a review of the book, explaining what the character did and why he/she was funny. Tell us whether or not you would recommend this book to other people.

The best reviews will be published in the magazine.

Write your **review**.

3   You see this announcement on an English-language website.

Articles wanted

How much television do you watch?

How often do you watch television? What types of programmes do you watch at weekends? What do you think of the quality?

Write us an article answering these questions.

The best articles will be posted on our website.

Write your **article**.

4   You have received this email from your English-speaking friend Oliver.

From: Oliver

Subject: City visit

Some friends of mine would like to visit your city for a weekend. They would like to see some of the places of interest there.

Can you tell me about some of the places they should visit? When's the best time of year to come and why?

Thanks,

Oliver

Write your **email**.

Listening

Part 1 ▶ 39

You will hear people talking in eight different situations. For questions **1–8**, choose the best answer (**A**, **B** or **C**).

1 You hear a man talking to a friend about a DIY job he has recently done. What does he say?

   A He wishes he had had some help with it.
   B He got better results than he had expected.
   C The job took longer than he thought it would.

2 You hear a woman leaving a voicemail message. Why is the speaker calling?

   A to respond to a complaint a customer has made
   B to apologise to a customer about a delivery
   C to provide a customer with an update on an order

3 You hear a mother talking to her son about doing some shopping. She believes that her son should

   A buy better-quality products.
   B do his own shopping in future.
   C reconsider how to buy a particular product.

4 You hear a man leaving a message for a colleague. What does he say about his staff?

   A Some staff will soon be promoted.
   B Some staff will be made redundant.
   C Some staff will be taken on at a later date.

5 You hear a man talking to his manager about a training session. It has been cancelled due to

   A lack of availability among the players.
   B the weather conditions.
   C another important event.

6 You hear a woman making an announcement at a train station. What does she say?

   A Passengers should wait for additional information.
   B Passengers need to move to a different platform.
   C Passengers must use another form of transport.

7 You hear two people talking about a coffee shop. What do they both think about it?

   A The drinks are too expensive.
   B The atmosphere is depressing.
   C The choice of baked goods is limited.

8 You hear a woman leaving a message for her friend. What is she talking about?

   A a website
   B a course
   C a magazine

Part 2 ▶ 40

You will hear a talk by a man called Harry Carter, who is a pilot. For questions **9–18**, complete the sentences with a word or short phrase.

Pilot with Emperor Airlines

Harry explains that the airline's **(9)** .... are to be found in Texas in the USA.

Harry says that his experience at a local **(10)** .... greatly influenced his career choice.

Harry was persuaded to apply to the airline by his **(11)** ....

Harry explains that he could only start his training because of the airline's **(12)** ....

The airline operates a **(13)** .... scheme which Harry feels provides new pilots with invaluable help.

Opportunities for promotion depend on how many **(14)** .... there are within the company as well as the pilot's acquired experience.

Harry says that as part of the paperwork, the flight paths are prepared so that the necessary quantity of **(15)** .... can be established.

Harry explains that one pilot performs a/n **(16)** .... outside the plane which plays a central part in safety control.

Harry says that some people may find the **(17)** .... he has to work a negative aspect of the job.

Harry says that knowing he can count on his **(18)** .... gives him a boost.

Part 3 ▶ 41

You will hear five short extracts in which professional sportspeople are talking about what motivates them most. For questions **19–23**, choose from the list (**A–H**) what each speaker says. There are three extra letters which you do not need to use.

A	being admired by fellow athletes	Speaker 1	19
B	improving his/her timings	Speaker 2	20
C	providing inspiration for the youth	Speaker 3	21
D	being remembered in the future	Speaker 4	22
E	getting a gold medal	Speaker 5	23
F	making family members proud		
G	improving his/her level of fitness		
H	participating in an international competition		

Part 4 ▶ 42

You will hear an interview with a health and lifestyle expert called Sam, who is talking about ways people can make themselves happy. For questions **24–30**, choose the best answer (**A**, **B** or **C**).

24 Sam says that our decisions can be affected by
  A our own negative thoughts.
  B other people's negative opinions.
  C our previous negative experiences.

25 According to Sam, when it comes to sleep, the most important thing is
  A where people get their sleep.
  B the quality of sleep people get.
  C the amount of sleep people get.

26 What does Sam recommend that anyone having a bad day should do?
  A try to take things less seriously
  B spend time with their kids
  C visit one of their friends

27 Which example of getting back to basics does Sam give?
  A meeting new people
  B painting a picture
  C taking the dog for a walk

28 When Sam talks about love, he says that it is
  A an essential element in establishing relationships.
  B a feeling that people sometimes fail to show.
  C a quality that all people naturally show.

29 How does Sam suggest that people can improve their self-confidence?
  A helping others with their problems
  B doing more physical exercise
  C extending their knowledge

30 Sam says the phrase 'I need you to' is an example of language that
  A shows the speaker has already got an opinion on something.
  B states clearly what the speaker wants from someone.
  C expresses the speaker's dissatisfaction with someone.

Speaking

Part 1

2 minutes (3 minutes for groups of three)

▶ 43 Listen to the recording and answer the questions. Pause the recording after each bleep and give your answer.

Part 2

4 minutes (6 minutes for groups of three)

Candidate A: Here are your photographs.
They show people listening to music in different places. Compare the photographs, and say why you think the people have chosen to listen to music in these places.

Candidate B: Do you enjoy going to concerts? Why/Why not?

Candidate B: Here are your photographs.
They show people who are attending different celebrations. Compare the photographs and say how you think the people are feeling at these celebrations.

Candidate A: Which of these celebrations would you prefer to go to? Why?

Part 3

4 minutes (5 minutes for groups of three)

Here are some things people often do when they are learning a new language. Discuss the question.

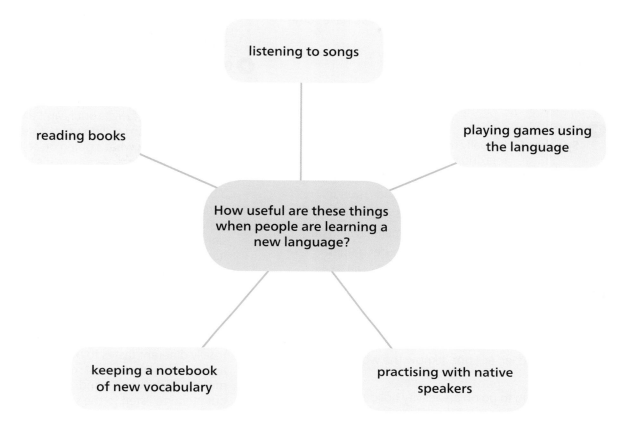

Now decide which two things are most useful when learning a new language.

Part 4

4 minutes (6 minutes for groups of three)

▶ **44** The Interlocutor will ask you and the other candidate questions related to the topic of Part 3.

Listen to the questions and when you hear the bleep, pause the recording and discuss the question with the other candidate.*[pages 198-199]*

Audio scripts

▶ 01

1 How do you usually relax when you have some free time?

2 What do you do when you stay in? Where do you go when you go out?

3 Do you like being in a large group or would you rather be with a few close friends?

▶ 02

Speaker 1: I usually find watching TV quite relaxing but it depends on my mood.

Speaker 2: I tend to stay in on weekdays though I sometimes have friends round.

Speaker 3: Playing the guitar is good fun.

Speaker 1: Doing yoga helps me to switch off.

Speaker 2: I'm really into computer games.

Speaker 3: I go out for a pizza now and again.

▶ 03

Julia 1

The subject I enjoyed most was maths but I don't know why. Maybe it was because it is easy for me and I got good, er, er, I don't know the word for this …

Julia 2

I'm hoping to go on an activity holiday in this country and learn water-skiing and other things, but my parents want me to go to the beach with them in Italy.

Stefan 3

His name is Thomas and I've known him all my life. He's the person I'd phone if I had any problems because he's always there for me and he gives me good advice. I'm really fond of him and I think we'll always stay in touch.

Stefan 4

I'm sorry. Would you repeat the question, please? OK, thanks. Well, some people think it's a bit boring, because there isn't a lot to do in the evenings, but I love it. It's near the mountains, but also not too far from the beach.

▶ 04

1

I suppose I've always been mad about music. I used to listen to my dad's favourite rock bands from the sixties but now I'm just into the same stuff as everyone else – hip hop mainly. Some people I know always want to be different so they'll only listen to new bands that haven't become popular yet. My friends and I will spend hours playing different tracks to each other and making up new playlists. It's fun. I don't really bother with following my favourite bands on Instagram or anything like that – it's the music I'm interested in, not celebrities.

▶ 05

2

A lot of people I know only use online streaming to create their playlists but I can't always find the albums I want so I still download some stuff. I like to keep up with what's going on so I will check Instagram or Twitter regularly. It's the best way of finding out about gigs and release dates for new albums. I listen to music on my phone all day – I hate it when I can't find my earphones! I used to watch a lot of videos on YouTube before going to sleep but not so much anymore. I mainly like upbeat happy songs – I don't like slow depressing ballads.

3

I think you can be friends with people you have musical differences with. You can have other things in common with people besides music. Having said that, I could never go out with someone who had totally different tastes to me. And I do have a lot of arguments with some of my friends who love heavy metal, which I can't stand. I enjoy making playlists but I tend to listen to the same tracks again and again until I'm bored of them. I use a free online streaming service – I don't see the point in paying for whole albums when you don't have to.

4

Whatever I'm doing there's always music on in the background and when I'm out I'm always wearing earphones. I used to be obsessed with music videos too but now I find they're all the same. Before I go out I like playing music really loud – it puts me in the mood. Luckily my parents don't mind. They're really into music too and have influenced me a lot. When I was growing up, my mum would often play seventies disco music and dance around the kitchen. I think that's what's made me so open to all kinds of music.

5

I like being one of the first to discover a new band. I think artists are at their most creative when they're just starting out, so you probably won't be familiar with what's on my latest playlist. Once a band's become really famous and everyone's following them on social media, I start to lose interest. I try to see as much live music as I can because it's a completely different experience to watching a video. Often I'll download an album after I've seen a band play live.

Unit 2

▶ 06

sociable, comfortable, lovable, predictable, reliable, adventurous, cautious, generous, realistic, dramatic, pessimistic, sympathetic, practical, emotional, thoughtful, careful, harmful, helpful, hopeful, meaningful, useful

▶ 07

P = Presenter   M = Max

P: As the youngest of four children, I know my older brothers and sisters always thought I had a much easier time. I didn't use to do as many jobs around the house and my parents were more relaxed about letting me do things as I got older. But has this affected my personality in any way? Our reporter, Max Berry, has been listening to psychologists at Southfield University who are doing some research into what's known as 'the birth order effect' – how your position in a family can affect your life. They've been asking people whether they believe there's any truth in this. Max, what can you tell us?

M: Well, Esther, it seems that the vast majority of people believe that the oldest child's always the most successful in later life. But apparently, there's a lot of evidence to show that it's actually middle children who have the best chance of leading happy, as well as successful, lives. People also believe that the youngest child always has a problem learning to be responsible and independent, which again isn't supported by any real facts.

▶ 08

P = Presenter   M = Max

P: So, is it true, for example, that oldest children perform best in intelligence tests?

M: Well, yes. There are lots of studies which prove this to be the case. One explanation for this might be that parents often encourage the oldest child to help their younger brothers and sisters to learn new skills, especially learning to read, and this actually helps the older child become more confident and independent.

P: Interesting. So what other characteristics do oldest children have?

M: Some psychologists believe that first-borns like me often take life too seriously and worry too much. They may feel under pressure to be the best all the time, though I must say that isn't something that's ever been a problem for me. But as a young child, I do remember hating my younger brother and thinking that he was my parents' favourite, and this is something that's quite common in oldest children.

P: What about youngest children, like me?

M: Well, in families where there are three or more children, the baby of the family's often treated as just that – a baby. They're allowed to grow up more slowly. But their good points are that they're likely to question everything and to be imaginative and artistic. Just like you, Esther.

P: Are there any factors which increase the 'birth order effect' in some families?

M: According to some psychologists, it seems that in families where there are either two boys, or two girls, the birth order effect is stronger. But it can have hardly any impact on large families, or where siblings aren't close in age. Although some people believe the birth order effect is so important that it should influence really important decisions such as our choice of marriage partner.

P: So, if you're the oldest, should you marry someone who's also the oldest in their family?

M: Well, it's been suggested that two first-born children will have to work very hard to make a marriage a success, but that it'd be much easier for two third-born children because they're likely to be more relaxed. And two middle children will probably want to compete with each other, so it could be difficult for them to get on well.

P: That does make things complicated! But surely birth order isn't the most important thing which affects people's personalities?

M: Absolutely not. Before you start to examine every aspect of your life in relation to whether you were born first, middle or last, a word of caution. The influence this can have when we are children doesn't necessarily last as we become adults.
Our relationships outside our family can have just as much influence on the development of our personalities.

P: Right. So it might be wise to resist blaming your brothers and sisters for everything that's gone wrong in your life! Thanks very much …

▶ 09

1

I've always found my nephew really cute, but it took me ages to have the confidence to be on my own with him without feeling nervous. I hadn't been around babies before so I found it a bit scary, but it's fine now.

2

I get on well with most of the family but one of my cousins is a bit weird. He's so argumentative. It's not worth talking to him really because he just disagrees with whatever anybody says. It's a good thing he doesn't live that near.

3

My mum got married again a few years ago and my stepfather has a daughter. Luckily, she's about the same age as me and we both love riding, so it's great to have something in common.

4

I don't see my granddad that much as he lives hundreds of miles away. We'd like him to come and live nearer. He's quite old now but when I was younger we used to support the same football team so we always had loads to talk about on the phone.

5

I was quite surprised when my sister married Charlie, because he's very different from her other boyfriends. But actually he's a really nice guy to have as a brother-in-law and I've promised to give him tennis lessons.

▶ 10

A = Alana   F = Federico

A: I think the relationship with a twin sister would be very important because you would probably be very close and tell her stuff you wouldn't tell other people.

F: Yes, that's very true. Even if I argue with my brother, we're still very close. But don't you think grandparents have a big influence on your life, too, because …

A: I suppose so, but it depends how often you see them. I didn't see mine very often but I did learn a lot from them and they were very patient and kind to me.

F: So were mine, even if there was a generation gap. What's your view on the father/son relationship?

A: I'm not sure, but I imagine perhaps they would share hobbies together, like, er, well, learning to drive or playing football together.

F: I suppose so. My father was much older than most fathers but I suppose it depends on your personality, too, and if you have things in common.

A: I see what you mean. If you get an inspirational teacher, they have a huge effect on your life too. I know somebody who took up, er, drama and became an actor because of the encouragement a teacher gave them.

F: Then there's …

Unit 3

▶ 11

My name's David Burton and I'm here today to tell you about the work I do for charity and why I've decided to give all my money away – well most of it anyway!

By the time I was thirty, I was already a multimillionaire. That was something I'd never really dreamt of as a kid. Like all small boys my ambition was to become a footballer. But I soon realised that wasn't realistic and then I thought about becoming a policeman. My uncle was one and he always looked really cool in his uniform and he told me stories about exciting car chases. But my dad wasn't so keen on this plan – he wanted me to be a doctor or a lawyer – but his hopes were crushed when I dropped out of university to set myself up as an entrepreneur selling shoes on a market stall.

Without a degree or any money behind me I faced an uncertain future. And I think this experience has been very useful. I learnt that taking risks is something that you have to do to achieve anything in business. But I worked hard and I was lucky and within a few years I had 250 shops and employed 7,000 people.

I had far more money than I knew what to do with. I spent a lot on fast cars and even a helicopter but being able to afford this actually brought me little satisfaction – in fact I was emptier and lonelier than before. I realised I wanted to do something that would help transform people's lives, especially young people from disadvantaged backgrounds. So I began funding a charity which provided training in basic business skills.

I then decided to start running charity projects full time. While travelling in India, I heard about a charity that offered support to people who wanted to start a small business. I thought that was the most effective way of escaping poverty and I liked the idea of helping people to help themselves. The idea was to lend small amounts of money to individuals, which they would then pay back. The amount can be as little as £100 but the average is more like £450. The great thing is that in 99 percent of cases, the loan has been paid back on time.

So far we've made 1,450 loans worth over £1 million and helped change the future prospects of hundreds of families.

More recently I've been working on projects to improve facilities and opportunities for villagers in Malawi. The charity has been able to help build new schools and provided investment for farm machinery. One of the things I'm proudest of is being involved in a construction project for a new hospital in a small town in Malawi. Seeing that finally up and running was a truly great feeling, far better than any business deal. What I learnt from this experience in particular was that being part of a community makes people far more content than becoming a millionaire.

I would advise anyone to give up dreaming of making loads of money because it doesn't make you as happy as you think. Of course having too much money isn't nearly as difficult as not having enough money – but it does make a lot of people miserable. Having said that, there are some advantages – not greater security as I imagined when I was younger – but greater freedom. I feel very privileged to be able to do something that I think is important and that makes the world a better place.

▶ 12

In both pictures there are people doing something which is very important to them. In the first picture the people look very happy because they are celebrating success. It looks like a graduation ceremony. In the second picture the man looks as if he's very proud of his car because he's taking very good care of it. It looks like hard work. He probably spent a lot of money on it and it looks like it's very valuable.

I'd say that both pictures show an achievement but the first picture is celebrating an experience whereas the second picture shows someone who values an expensive thing. The graduation photo is more special because it's something you can remember for your whole life. The car can be sold or it could be damaged in an accident – it's not something that lasts in the same way. While the man might really love his car, his passion is something he does on his own. The girl in the graduation photo seems happier because she's sharing her success with her family and friends. She looks like she's having more fun than the man.

UNIT 4

▶ 13

P = Presenter L = Leo

P: Today on *The Travel Programme*, we're interviewing the explorer, Leo Stone. He's talking about his recent expedition to the South Pole in the steps of his hero Ernest Shackleton, who, as we know, famously failed to reach the South Pole in 1908. Welcome to the programme, Leo.

L: Thank you.

P: First of all, can you tell us something about your team?

L: Sure. The really unusual thing about them is that we all have some kind of connection to members of Shackleton's team, whether directly or indirectly. I myself am a relative of a member of that 1908 expedition, who is, of course, no longer alive today.

P: So you had some unfinished family business.

L: Exactly. Shackleton had had to turn back before reaching the South Pole so some of us felt we had a special motivation to try to do what he so sadly didn't manage to accomplish. For me, it was my lifetime's ambition to give it a go.

P: Amazing. Did the trip take a long time to organise?

L: Yes. It took us five years to prepare for it. First and foremost, we had to find the money, which was no easy task. As you can imagine, the costs involved were enormous. Then there was the physical training. You'd think this would be the hardest part, but a couple of us have been in the army so we were used to this kind of thing. And one of the team members had run a few marathons – I think we were all relatively fit. It was actually the mental challenge that we struggled with the most; having to get our heads around a nine-hundred-mile journey.

P: So was the trip any easier for your 21st-century team than the original one?

L: In some ways, yes. But we still had to walk for ten hours a day with all our equipment. And then we had to put up our tent and cook a meal in what can only be described as a 'frozen hell'. But Shackleton was travelling into the unknown with only a compass to guide him, while our team had a map and modern navigation equipment.

P: And did you experience any of the same problems?

L: We did. For example, we had to spend two days in our tent because high winds made it impossible to continue, which Shackleton also endured. But it was worse for Shackleton because they were also very low on food at that point. And one of Shackleton's men fell seriously ill, which luckily our team was spared.

P: So what were your feelings when you were crossing the Antarctic plateau?

L: Well, I knew it was going to be very tough going, but I still wasn't prepared for the harsh reality. Apparently, it was when Shackleton came face to face with the brutal conditions there, that he began to doubt that he'd ever reach the Pole. I never got to that stage but it was really hard. Like Shackleton, we went up the Beardmore Glacier, which was incredibly dangerous with huge crevasses everywhere.

And when we finally arrived at the Antarctic plateau it was even worse – it being the coldest, driest place on earth. As with Shackleton's team, we experienced symptoms of altitude sickness but none of us lost confidence in what we were aiming to do.

P: Looking back, which part of the trip did you enjoy the most?

L: The highlight was definitely arriving at the place where Shackleton decided to turn back. The excitement and sense of joy was really inspiring and memorable – better even than getting to the Pole itself or the huge sense of relief at making it back to our families.

P: Do you think Shackleton deserves his reputation as a great hero?

L: Yes, I do. I've always really admired Shackleton, and anyone who doesn't know anything about him should definitely read one of the many books about him. His decision to turn back to save his men took great courage. That's why I respect him so much. He never did reach his goal and it was Roald Amundsen who finally made it to the South Pole in 1911. There are so many lessons we …

▶ 14

A: So which two skills do you think would be the most useful?

B: Top of the list for me would be finding water and making a shelter because without these things you can't survive.

A: I'd put making a fire above making a shelter. I think learning to make a fire would be the highest priority for me because a fire can keep you warm and you can also use it to boil water so that it's safe to drink and for cooking.

B: That's true. So out of these five skills, making a fire and finding water would be the most useful.

Unit 5

▶ 15

N = Narrator   S = Sarah

N: You are going to listen to an extract from a radio programme in which a food writer called Sarah Willis is talking about the history of cooking.

S: My name is Sarah Willis and I'm a food historian. Have you ever wondered what our lives would be like without cooking and how easy it would be to survive in the wild eating only raw food? Well, the answer is that humans are not very good at eating food

that hasn't been cooked and would find it almost impossible to survive on the diet of a chimpanzee, for example. Chimpanzees do eat a lot of fruit, which would be OK for us, not just bananas but all sorts of berries too, and this accounts for 60 percent of their diet. But the remaining 40 percent is made up of other plant food, which wouldn't really be suitable for human consumption. These plants don't contain sugar so they taste very bitter. The other problem with the chimpanzee diet is that human teeth aren't strong enough to chew the huge quantities of plants and we'd also need a bigger stomach to digest it all.

But long ago, before people discovered cooking, our human ancestors must have had a diet that was quite similar to a chimpanzee's. They would have spent an awful lot of time chewing in order to digest the raw food properly. They might spend eight hours a day finding food to eat and then about six hours actually eating it. Which didn't leave them much time for any leisure activities. So when people started cooking, life began to get a lot better. They had more time for other things and the food also tasted much better. But as well as that, cooking made it possible to preserve meat for longer, which meant they could save some for the next day – in case they didn't manage to find any.

No one knows exactly when people started cooking. But a lot of scientists believe the discovery of cooking was a really important development. They think that because of cooking, our mouths gradually became smaller and the brain became much bigger. These changes happened over thousands of years, of course. And as well as bringing about physical changes, some scientists believe the activity of cooking also introduced significant social change. They say that cooking food meant that everyone in the family ate at the same time, so it's where the tradition of sitting down together and having a family meal may have begun. But there were new risks involved too. For the first time, people couldn't eat their food immediately because it had to be cooked first. The long wait between catching or finding the food and then eating it meant there was always the possibility someone might take it. So the female cooks had to be protected against any thieves by the men who were also responsible for the hunting and gathering of food.

Until a few years ago, it was thought that cooking was a relatively recent development but now tests indicate that our ancestors started cooking in Africa a very long time ago. Scientists have discovered that fire may have been used for this purpose over one million years ago, which is far earlier than was previously thought.

Scientists do know that people began cooking routinely during the last ice age around twelve thousand years ago. Cooking food was a good idea in the extreme cold because it gives more energy than raw food so cooking helped people survive this harsh environment.

▶ 16

OK, well obviously both photos show restaurants but the similarity ends there, I think. The one on the right is a much more special kind of place. It's probably really expensive and the food will be more adventurous and interesting than in the other photo. The photo on the left shows a self-service restaurant so the atmosphere will be more casual and the food is probably more basic, such as burgers or pizza.

I'd imagine the young people at the expensive restaurant are there because they are celebrating a special occasion and they wanted to do something different. But actually, they would probably prefer to be eating in a less formal situation, like in the other photo. The people in the fast-food restaurant probably go there because it's cheaper, they can eat quickly, and they don't have to dress up.

Unit 6

▶ 17

E = Examiner   R = Roberto   B = Beata

E: Roberto, which do you think you need more of to succeed in the arts: luck or talent?

R: I think a lot depends on luck. You need the opportunity to succeed and not everyone gets the right opportunity even if they're really talented. Then there are lots of examples of people who are really famous and successful but not very talented. I think these people need to have a lot of ambition and determination as well as luck. Would you agree with that, Beata?

B: I'm not sure. Basically, you're saying you don't really need talent to succeed. But you can't become successful without any talent at all.

R: Yes, I suppose you are right. You don't need a lot of talent to succeed but you do need a lot of luck.

▶ 18

1

It's one of my favourite plays so I was really excited about seeing it again. But I have to warn you – it's

probably quite different from any other production you may have seen by this company. On the whole, I think it works. The futuristic set is stunning, very cleverly contrasted with the present-day jeans and hoodies the cast have on. The specially composed music is a welcome addition and really helps to create a threatening atmosphere. But for some reason most of the action takes place in semi-darkness, so I just wish I'd been able to see everything a bit more clearly.

▶ 19

2

A: OK. So shall we meet in the theatre café at 6.30? That should give us time to have a coffee first.

B: But the play starts at 6.45, which means it probably won't finish until ten. I'll be so starving by then I won't be able to concentrate on the last act!

A: Well, why don't we meet a bit earlier and grab something quick at a pizza place nearby?

B: Yeah. I can't get there earlier than six though. I'm not sure that'll give us enough time, will it?

A: We should be OK. We've already got our tickets, remember.

B: Have we? OK then. Anyway, it's irritating that it starts so early. I don't know why they've done that.

3

Next up, information about another popular actor – for all you Josh Willard fans, we have some exciting news. Josh's new film, set in nineteenth-century Scotland, has its premiere next week and Josh will be here in London to attend. This is the first time he's appeared on the silver screen for quite a while, and the action-packed movie might well be a contender for all the awards going, if the critics are to be believed. Josh, who famously doesn't do many interviews, will appear on Channel 3's *Live Tonight*, so make sure you don't miss him talking to Ned Bryan. Then it's back to New York where he'll be starring alongside Natasha Reynolds in *The Holly Tree* at the District Theatre from the end of April ...

4

Once again the comedy festival will be held in Lenbury, but with a few changes to the usual programme. The organisers have decided that this year it'll be held in the third weekend in July rather than the first. The main stage is also moving from the Lenbury Theatre to a tent in the park, where there will be much more seating availability, although most of the smaller gigs will continue to take place in the theatre. The implication of the move of course is that more tickets'll be available for the main events, which will be a very popular decision, especially with local students, who usually make up the large and enthusiastic majority of the audience.

5

A: So, Maria, is it true you're going to retire soon?

B: Yes. I'm shortly going to be thirty-five and I'm finding it's getting harder and harder for me physically. In fact, I still haven't totally got over that last back injury which kept me away from the stage for three months. But I could cope with that – the main issue is that all the overseas visits keep me away from my little boy for weeks at a time. He's only two and he's growing up so fast.

A: So you don't enjoy being on tour anymore?

B: Actually, if I could find a practical solution, I'd definitely carry on. It'll actually break my heart to give up dancing.

6

A: So, as usual, The View will be the biggest contemporary art event of the summer in terms of the number of artworks on display.

B: That's true, there'll be a huge collection. However, for me it's more the *range* of work which makes it stand out. Everything from landscape to abstract, and mostly by young artists who must surely be on the point of making a name for themselves in the art world.

A: That's right. Although it'll be the one or two big names which'll attract most art lovers.

B: Absolutely. It's a shame, though, that a permanent venue can't be found for the show. The museum's a bit old-fashioned and I don't think the displays are that imaginative really.

7

I'm really excited about the play. It's the first time I've worked with this particular director and that's always quite a challenge to begin with until you get used to each other's ways of working. Actually, I'm not sure how successful the show will be in this country because of course it tackles rather a depressing subject and people might prefer not to spend an evening at the theatre watching something that they may well find upsetting. But personally I think the play addresses an important issue and I believe strongly that the theatre is an excellent way to do it. That's why I agreed to produce the play and I do hope people will support it.

8

A: So who do you think will get the main part in the next musical?

B: I expect it'll be Zoe. She's probably the best singer and dancer, although my mum thinks it could be Molly. I agree she did an excellent audition. Mr Paignton says he's going to tell us in our next drama class.

A: When do you start rehearsals?

B: On Friday. It's going to be really hard work because the show opens in three weeks' time. In fact, I think I'll go now and read the script.

A: I'll help you learn your lines, if that's any help.

B: That'd be great, actually. My sister said she'd do it but she's very busy with her new job.

▶ **20**

1

A: What're you doing this weekend?

B: I'm going to the dance festival in the park. It's on all weekend.

A: Oh, I'd really like to go but my brother's moving house and I have to help him.

B: Oh, that's a shame!

A: Never mind. I'm sure you'll enjoy it.

B: Yes. It should be fun, especially as I think the weather's going to be good.

2

A: Hi, Ben! Are you going to the film festival at the weekend?

B: Yes, on Saturday. I'm going to buy the tickets online this afternoon.

A: How much are they?

B: Only £15. I'll get you one if you like.

A: That would be great. What time does it start?

B: At 7.30. But I'm going to leave home early, at six o'clock because of the traffic. I'll pick you up on my way if you want.

Unit 7

▶ **21**

Well, I'm not absolutely certain what the place on the right is but it could be an underwater hotel. The other one seems to have been built in the trees and is a hotel too. The underwater hotel looks quite luxurious, whereas the treehouse appears to be more basic; but it's eco-friendly and it would definitely be less expensive to stay at.

It must be an interesting experience to stay at both of them, although I'd imagine the treehouse might not be such fun in bad weather. The hotel under the sea must feel a bit weird and scary at first, I think. Having said that, it would be wonderful to watch the fish without having to get wet.

Of the two, I think the treehouse would be more enjoyable to stay in because, although the underwater one would be the experience of a lifetime, guests would probably always be wondering what would happen if something went wrong.

▶ 22

1   Well, I'm not absolutely certain what the place on the right is.
2   It could be an underwater hotel.
3   The other one seems to have been built in the trees.
4   The underwater hotel looks quite luxurious.
5   The treehouse appears to be more basic.
6   It would definitely be less expensive to stay at.
7   It must be an interesting experience to stay at both of them.
8   I'd imagine the treehouse might not be such fun in bad weather.

▶ 23

bustling, cosy, inspiring, magnificent, mysterious, peaceful, polluted, remote, run-down

▶ 24

N = Narrator   P = Presenter   O = Olivia

N: You will hear a journalist interviewing a travel writer called Olivia Rees about a place called Shangri-La.

P: Today we turn to Shangri-La, a synonym for an earthly paradise, used all over the world as a name for hotels, restaurants and holiday homes. But the name actually comes from a famous novel called *Lost Horizon* by James Hilton, which was published in the 1930s. Why do you think this book became so popular, Olivia?

O: It's surprising really, because when it was published in 1933, Tibet, where the book was set, was a remote and insular place. It was also a very beautiful place, as people saw when the film based on it came out some years later. In my view, because the 1930s were a hard time, people were keen to forget their troubles and only too happy to read a fantasy about somewhere that was both peaceful and spiritual.

P: But why do people these days still relate to the novel?

O: Mmm, good question. It's a good story, of course – you know, a plane crashes into mountains in an isolated area and the survivors are taken to a tranquil and idyllic place. I suspect though that what makes it a classic novel is its timeless theme of how you deal with potential alternative paths in life – are you tempted to

stay in paradise or do you go back to the life you know? The people rescued from the plane all came to different decisions about this, as you know, which caused conflict amongst the two brothers.

P: In what way were the people who lived in Shangri-La unusual?

O: The author describes how there was little interest in material wealth in Shangri-La – the emphasis being on simplicity and a slow pace of living. Perhaps this accounts for why the inhabitants there, amazingly, lived for centuries, only showing any physical signs of age when they got to around a hundred. The monastery in Shangri-La also had a magnificent library containing the world's greatest works of literature – a place which contained all the wisdom of humanity – although it is unclear how many people made use of this facility.

P: You were obviously very interested in the author, James Hilton?

O: Yes, I read a lot about him and found his life very interesting. He'd been inspired by articles published in *National Geographic* magazine during the 1920s by early travellers to Tibet, and this provided fascinating, detailed descriptions of the scenery and the Buddhist way of life there. Hilton himself actually travelled no further than the British Library in London to research the location of *Lost Horizon*. But many, many people have since travelled to the region to try and find Shangri-La and to discover more about Buddhism.

P: Aren't there similarities between the story of Shangri-La and the Tibetan legend of Shambhala?

O: Indeed. Shambhala was also a kingdom, cut off from the outside world, where the people also lived in peace and harmony and which was also dominated by a magnificent white mountain. But I don't think these parallels are accidental or show that Hilton couldn't come up with anything new. It simply illustrates the strength of the appeal that the culture had for him and his desire to show how a perfect society should be run.

P: Why is the county of Zhongdian now known as Shangri-La?

O: It changed its name in 2002 for marketing reasons, even though Shangri-La was not actually based on one single place. Investment in the tourist industry provides a better living for the inhabitants of Zhongdian and means they're no longer so reliant on the tea trade for survival. Thousands of tourists visit every year to see the monastery which they believe – rightly or wrongly – could've been the inspiration for Hilton's monastery in Shangri-La.

P: How do visitors react when they visit the modern-day Shangri-La?

O: Inevitably, visitors to modern-day Shangri-La often find it doesn't live up to their expectations. After all, although it's a fictional place, people have an idea in their mind of what it will be like and if it isn't exactly as the writer described it, they often find it a bit of a letdown. For one thing, there's no white mountain although nobody could deny the countryside is absolutely breathtaking. Finally, I'm afraid, you're more likely to meet a group of tourists than anyone over the age of one hundred.

Unit 8

 25

Speaker 1

In my work as a counsellor, I'm already seeing a huge increase in the number of victims of cyber-bullying on social networking sites and this is a trend that can only get worse. To deal with bullying or other problems that can occur online, social networking counsellors will support people in their cyber-relationships using the same counselling skills we use today. The only difference is that, because we'll be online, it'll be easier for people to contact us when they need us – in the evenings, for example. This may mean that we'll have to change our working patterns and work out-of-office hours when required.

Speaker 2

I work as a robotics engineer for a company that makes robots to perform operations in hospitals. Robots are increasingly being used in this field, and it's a trend that'll continue to grow. We'll eventually get to a point where all operations are performed by robots, as they're perfect for doing highly skilled work. Building robots is slowly becoming more affordable. This means that routine operations like bypass surgery will be cheaper in the future because highly paid surgeons won't be needed as much. This'll be good news for patients who are waiting for operations.

Speaker 3

The company I work for is currently developing spaceships for leisure space travel. We aim to have six spaceships taking people on trips into space, each able to carry six passengers. I'm working as a test pilot at the moment, but eventually my role will be to recruit airline pilots and train them in the skills they'll need to become spaceship pilots. We're expecting there to be a lot of public interest

in our service, even though it'll only be something very wealthy individuals can afford. But it'll be the experience of a lifetime and something a lot of people will be willing to pay for.

Speaker 4

My company has been operating virtually for a few years now and this is a trend that's likely to continue across the globe. I work as a part of a team of virtual lawyers, all specialising in employment law. It means I don't have to live close to the city, which saves me a lot of money in rent and train fares as well as not having a long commute into work. Being accessible on the internet has encouraged people to contact us who, before, wouldn't have considered hiring a lawyer. So I can see that, instead of spending most of my time with clients from big firms in the city, I'll be dealing with people from all sorts of companies.

Speaker 5

I work for a large vertical farm, where vegetables are grown on shelves in giant glasshouses. I think it's the answer to feeding an increasing population, especially in towns and cities where space is so limited. Vertical farmers will be able to get food from the farm to the supermarket in under two hours. I think most of our vegetables will be produced in this way in the future because there are so many advantages. We don't use pesticides, all the water we use is recycled, and soon all of our electricity will be run on wind and solar energy and we don't have to worry about the weather.

26

1 Actually, I'm not sure about that.
2 I agree up to a point but …
3 I suppose so.
4 That's just what I was going to say!
5 That's a good point.
6 Really? That's not how I see it.

27
1

Boss: So how are you getting on with the report, Amy?

Amy: I've done most of it but I still need to get some information from the sales team in Brazil before I can finish it.

Boss: OK. Good. Remember to keep it brief. Don't write loads of detail, and summarise the data in graphs if you can. No one has time to read very long reports.

Amy: Don't worry, it won't be more than four pages long.

2

OK, so, it's your dream job and you know they're interviewing at least ten other people. Who wouldn't be nervous? But remember, experienced interviewers want you to do your best and aren't there to catch you out, so try to forget about being nervous. One thing that can really help with the nerves is being sure of your facts. So memorise key information about where you worked and for how long. Also, find out as much as you can about your prospective employer. And ask one or two questions to show you've done your homework.

3

A = Angela   M = Mike

A: I've just had JPS on the phone and they say they've left three messages for me but that I haven't phoned them back. Why wasn't I given the messages?

M: Oh dear. Well, I haven't taken any calls from JPS. They must've rung yesterday when I was out of the office on my training course.

A: OK, Mike. Sorry. But I really must find out who took those calls. We can't afford to upset such an important customer.

M: No problem, Angela. I'll look into why the messages weren't passed on if you like.

▶ **28**

I = Interviewer   L = Lauren

I: Lauren, how did you hear about this job?

L: Well, I spotted the advert while I was on the internet. I think it's something I'd be good at.

I: Being an entertainment coordinator will involve looking after very young children. Have you had much experience of doing this?

L: Well, I look after my niece and nephew every month and I'm taking them on a cycling holiday tomorrow.

I: Well, you might be unlucky, I'm afraid, because I've heard that it's going to rain.

L: Oh, I'm sure we'll still have a lot of fun.

I: Well, you sound very positive, and this is one of the qualities we're looking for. Anyway, enjoy your weekend!

L: Thanks.

I: Lauren, thanks for coming. We'll write soon, but don't worry if you don't hear anything for a few days.

Unit 9

▶ **29**

Well, most top sportspeople would claim that their success is not so much down to natural ability but rather to effort, dedication and long hours of practice. Luck is rarely mentioned, unless they happen to lose, and that's sometimes blamed on something they couldn't control, like the weather.

▶ **30**

N = Narrator   P = Presenter   M = Max

N: You will hear an interview with a journalist called Max Wilson about success in sport.

P: With me in the studio today is sports writer Max Wilson. Max, in your experience, how do successful sportspeople account for their success?

M: Hi. Well, most top sportspeople would claim that their success is not so much down to natural ability but rather to effort, dedication and long hours of practice. Luck is rarely mentioned, unless they happen to lose, and that's sometimes blamed on something they couldn't control, like the weather.

P: And do you have an explanation as to why records keep on being broken? Why do sportspeople seem to be continually improving their performance?

M: Well, this improvement in sport can't be because athletes are much bigger and stronger than they were fifty, or even a hundred years ago because experts say physical changes develop over a much longer time span. So it must be that people are getting better all the time because they're practising longer and harder. Sure, improvements in running shoes, tennis rackets and other technological advances play their part, but they can't account on their own for the differences in standards.

P: Could it also be that there are more talented young children around?

M: It is certainly true that successful tennis clubs like Spartak, in Moscow, recognise talent at a very young age and nurture it, with huge success. But a seemingly exceptional natural talent in a young child is often only the product of hours and hours of expert tuition and practice, and the child is unlikely to continue to make progress at such a fast rate.

P: So, I know you have read Matthew Syed's book *Bounce*, which is about how he became a successful table tennis player. In his book, what explanation does Matthew Syed give for his success?

M: Well, as you know, Matthew Syed used to be a British number one and top international table tennis player and he examines the relationship between talent, success and luck. He lists several factors which he believes contributed to his success and which had very little to do with his own talent. Matthew says his first piece of good fortune was that when he was eight, his parents decided to buy a full-size, professional table-tennis table, which they kept in the garage, as a way of keeping their boys occupied and out of trouble. Matthew says he was also lucky that his older brother was happy to fight out endless battles in the garage.

P: But Matthew must also have had a huge advantage by being able to join a very good table tennis club for young people near his home. This was called the Omega Club, wasn't it?

M: That's right. And it was while he was playing table tennis at the Omega Club that he was lucky enough to be spotted by the man who not only ran the club but was also one of the leading table tennis coaches in the country, Peter Charters. Charters also happened to be a teacher at Matthew's primary school. In those days, the Omega Club hadn't yet become a well-known club but the tiny group of members could play whenever they liked, day or night, even though there was only one table.

P: I see. And how does Matthew explain the success of the Omega Club members?

M: It's extraordinary how the members of the Omega Club – not just Matthew – soon started to attract a lot of attention. The street where Matthew lived, Silverdale Road, contained an astonishing number of the country's top players. Was this inevitable, given the quality of the coach, the talent of the players and the location of the Omega Club, or was it, as Matthew argues in the book, just a combination of lucky events? If he hadn't lived in Silverdale Road, he would have gone to a different school and he wouldn't have met Peter Charters, nor become a member of the Omega Club.

P: What do we know about the importance of luck?

M: Interestingly, a ten-year investigation into what makes people lucky or unlucky has concluded that people do make their own luck. Obviously, Matthew couldn't have succeeded without some raw talent, but he also took full advantage of the opportunities given to him, and this is what ultimately made him so successful. Lucky people are better at taking chances and finding ways to improve their situation. Unlucky people are less likely to take risks and don't like change. If there are lessons to be learnt …

▶ 31

E = Examiner   C = Clara   R = Ralf

E: What do you think makes some people more successful at sport than other people?

C: I'm sorry, did you say successful?

E: Yes, that's right.

C: Thanks. Well, it's difficult to say, of course, but I suppose a lot depends on your personality: whether you are self … erm … I mean sure of your ability.

R: Yes, and also really, really want to win. You have to be… erm … hungry. What I'm trying to say is, you need to be very determined.

C: But it's not enough if you … you need the ability in the first place otherwise it doesn't matter how you are … or rather, how ambitious you are.

R: Maybe, but some people say if you practise a lot …

C: Yes but it isn't enough. There is also … right, a … you need a good body, for example, good health and you also need …

Unit 10

▶ 32

1 Dylan

We grew up together, went to the same school, spent holidays together when we were kids. He's got to know my parents, and brothers and sisters, and grandparents over the years – so he's almost part of the family. Like having another brother. And we fight like brothers, too, about all sorts of things; politics, music and sport, mainly. Watching sport on TV with him is a nightmare. Sometimes he makes me change my mind about something, so it's good in a way, because he helps me to see things from a different point of view. And he makes me laugh a lot too, which is really important.

2 Martha

Even if we haven't seen each other for a few months, we can catch up really easily. We've got such a strong connection. Our relationship's built on trust – she knows she can call me up about anything and I'd help her in whatever way I can and she'd do the same for me. She's the best listener I know. She understands what I'm talking about even though her life is so different. I'm single and she's married. I work in a huge office and she works in her family's business. But we're not always serious; we do have a laugh together too.

3 Alex

We met about ten years ago at a party at college when we were both studying law. We have the same taste in music and films so he's the one I call if there's a gig on or a film I want to see. Or he calls me. Sometimes we go out to eat as a foursome with our girlfriends, other times it's just a boys' night out. He loves football as much as I do but he supports a different team, so we never go to football matches together. Otherwise we end up arguing. We usually get to see each other about once a week but we message each other all the time too.

4 Amy

We keep in touch by phone or online. That's OK – we're still very close but I'd like us to spend more time together. We can have conversations about anything from politics to music to family problems. We both feel strongly about politics but generally we see eye-to-eye on everything and rarely disagree. I suppose that's why we get on so well. When we first met, we used to go out together all the time but now I travel a lot for my job and she just got promoted so, unless we're very organised, it can be hard to arrange to go out. As long as we plan ahead, it's fine.

5 Ed

I suppose people sometimes wonder why we're such good friends. For example, he loves being the centre of attention whereas I'm quite shy. But apart from that, I think we've got a lot in common. I mean, we have a lot of shared experiences. We do the same job. We're both married with a young child and we've both lived in the same town for a few years. I'd really miss him if he moved away. We don't meet up or even text that often but I like just being able to call him up at short notice to see if he wants to go out.

▶ 33

A: OK, shall we begin?

B: Yes. We could start with childhood. What's really important to young kids is their friends, don't you think?

A: I suppose so, although maybe not so much if they have brothers and siblings to play with.

B: That's true, and they're still quite close to their parents at this age. Maybe friends are more important when you're teenagers, then.

A: Definitely, especially if you're quite shy. That's why they message each other a lot and go on Snapchat and so on. But what you need to have at that age as well is friends to go out with.

B: Yes, and as well as that to give you confidence because at that age it can be difficult. When you're older – between nineteen and twenty maybe – they're not so …

A: Actually, … oh sorry …

B: No, that's OK. Go on.

A: I was just going to say that at college, friends are very important too. Otherwise you'd be very lonely.

B: It must also be lonely for adults if they're living on their own. So it's really important to have friends at work if you don't have a family, don't you think?

A: Yes, like you said, it must be lonely when you leave college and get a job in a new city or maybe in another country. I've got no experience of this yet but I'd imagine that friends are essential or you'd have no one to talk to! Would you say men and women have a different kind of friendship?

B: I think they're probably very similar. Although I think men like doing sport together or even just watching matches together, whereas women generally just like talking.

A: Yeah and as you say men like doing things together so … er … when you retire from your job it must be good to have someone to go out with and do things.

Unit 11
▶ 34
1

Some people are 'risk-takers' and enjoy taking unnecessary and sometimes stupid risks, while others are 'risk-averse' and avoid taking the smallest risk at all costs. As someone who gets a thrill out of extreme mountain biking, I'm definitely a risk-taker. A lot of people find that quite hard to understand and wonder how I can enjoy something that they think's frightening and dangerous. But so long as people take safety seriously, I think everyone needs to be more adventurous. I feel quite strongly that using all your skill and strength to push yourself to the limit gives you the greatest sense of being alive. There's nothing quite like it.

2

A: Emma, what are you doing outside by yourself? Aren't you enjoying the party?

B: Not really. Parties aren't my thing. And it's so hot and crowded in there.

A: I know what you mean. But it's nice to meet new people.

B: Mmm, I never know what to say and also it's almost impossible to have a conversation when the music's so loud. And if you're not into dancing, there's not much point. So I think I'll make my excuses and head home soon.

A: I don't think I'll stay much longer either. I've got an early start in the morning.

3

A: Have you enjoyed this Mandarin course so far, Becky?

B: Yes, it's been really good. I was never any good at languages at school so I surprised myself. The biggest challenge has been learning the sounds – and the intonation is so different from English – but I knew that already.

A: Definitely. Other stuff I thought would be really hard has actually been quite straightforward. I mean, the verbs are simpler than English and there aren't any articles to worry about.

B: Right. I think it's good that we focused on speaking and haven't bothered with writing yet.

A: Yeah. That might not be as bad as we think either!

4

Now you said last time you liked the idea of doing a journalism course after you graduate. But you weren't sure whether you should get some experience first. I'd say that even with a degree in zoology it's not that easy to get a job with a conservation magazine. So what about getting a job volunteering for a conservation charity? There are some really interesting and worthwhile things you could do – like working with endangered species in Borneo. I've got a list of organisations I could put you in touch with. You could start writing a blog while you're there. Then you'd have some evidence that you're serious about a career in journalism.

5

A: It annoys me that a lot of people are so negative about rugby. I don't think there are any more injuries than in lots of other sports – skiing for example.

B: Or horse riding. I think that's probably the most dangerous.

A: I wonder. It might be interesting to find out.

B: But it's a great game. I prefer watching it to any other sport. And I'm so glad I had the opportunity to play at school. Not many girls did at that time.

A: To me it just seemed an organised form of fighting! It's funny I used to dread playing it at school but I'm completely hooked now. I never miss a game on TV.

6

A: So how are you getting on with your new boss?

B: Fine. She's actually given me a lot of responsibility already, which is good. But the scary thing is she just expects me to get on with things – like I should already know what to do. And I don't like to keep bothering her with questions because she's so busy. Her management style is quite laid back – she doesn't try and motivate you all the time or tell you what to do. So it's challenging but better that than the other way round. In my last job I always felt my boss didn't trust me enough to let me do anything without constant supervision. I felt she was always looking over my shoulder.

7

A: How do you feel about travelling alone? I'm not sure I'd like it.

B: Oh, it's fine most of the time. I like the fact that you don't have to make compromises about where to go or what to eat. You've got a lot more freedom. The only thing is that when you get home, you haven't got anyone to talk to about the trip. And it's nice to have someone to remember things with.

A: What about if you're feeling ill or when things go wrong?

B: Well, you meet people while you're travelling and someone's always there to help you sort things out. People are generally very kind.

8

Listen, I'm really sorry but I won't be able to get home to pick you up. I've been held up in a meeting. But don't worry because everything's been arranged. I've just booked a taxi to take you to the station at two o'clock. Oh, there's some money on the kitchen shelf to pay the fare. So you will be ready in time, won't you? And don't forget to clean your shoes. I'm hoping to get out of here in about half an hour and then I'll pick you up after the interview. So good luck. Just do your best and try to relax.

▶ 35

I was pretty good at skateboarding and I used to love going to the park with my two sons. The problem was that, as my sons got older, they didn't want me hanging out with them. I always wished I'd had a skater friend my own age. I was lonely and self-conscious. I wasn't worried about having an accident because I was always careful and wore protective clothing and a helmet, but everyone kept saying 'It's time you stopped. You're too old for this.' So I gave in and stopped. And then last year they opened a brand new skate park, and I said to myself, 'If only I hadn't given up. If only I could start again!' But I've lost confidence. I wish I was twenty years younger, and I wish my wife wouldn't tell me I need a new hobby all the time.

▶ 36

E = Examiner   L = Layla

E: Layla, here are your photographs. They show people taking risks in different situations. I'd like you to compare the two photographs and say which person you think is taking the most risks, and why.

L: OK. Well, both photos show sportspeople who have to take risks while doing their chosen sport. The boxer faces risks of injury every time he has a fight. There's also the risk of permanent, long-term brain damage. The yachtswoman is in a similar situation because she has to rely on her skill to avoid getting into danger or being injured. Both the boxer and the yachtswoman have to be extremely fit and well trained. They're probably both aware of the risks they're taking. In a way, it's harder for the yachtswoman because she's completely alone, whereas the boxer has a team of people to help and support him. I think you'd have to be quite fearless and determined but also a little bit crazy to want to do dangerous sports like these.

But although the possible dangers to the yachtswoman are serious, she has all kinds of technology available to her to help her avoid dangerous situations, so I'd say that she's taking less of a risk than the boxer. I'd imagine the chances of her getting injured out at sea are quite small compared to the boxer, who probably gets injured every time he has a fight.

▶ 37

E = Examiner   L = Leo

E: Which of these activities would you prefer to do, Leo?

L: To be honest, I've never thought about doing either of them. But I'd choose sailing because it's out in the open air, you're surrounded by sea and sky and it must be a wonderful feeling.

Unit 12

▶ 38

N = Narrator   J = Journalist

N: You will hear a journalist talking about a new type of hotel for paying guests.

J: You'd think a prison would be the last place anyone would willingly spend money to stay in, but you'd be wrong. Former prisons all over the world've been opening their gates to paying guests. Some have been converted into luxury hotels, but others, like the Karosta Prison in Latvia, are left almost unchanged, with none of the usual comforts, thanks to the rise in popularity of what's become known as 'reality tourism'. Unlike luxury tourism, people are given the chance to have an authentic and challenging experience.

Constructed in 1905 as a jail for sailors who didn't obey orders, Karosta Prison was taken over in the 1970s by the USSR's secret service, the KGB. Today, it's a hotel with a difference.

The extreme package offers the opportunity to experience life as a prisoner for a few hours and hundreds of people actually choose to stay here every year. Admittedly, most are on trips organised by their school, but there are growing numbers of businesspeople who come here on team-building exercises. Not too many on their honeymoon, I suspect.

I recently spent one night as a guest in Karosta prison. The extreme package started at 9p.m. when the prison guards lined everyone up in the courtyard and shouted out orders. Before we were taken to our cells, we had to put on a prison uniform and then one of the guards took a photo of each of us to include with the papers they kept on each 'prisoner'. I half-expected them to take our fingerprints too, but that didn't happen. After that it was 'dinner' – which consisted of a hunk of dry bread and black tea. If you wanted coffee or a cold drink, too bad. We were then shut in our cells for the night. There were four people in every cell, so we weren't alone, but we were given strict instructions to keep silent, until we were told we were allowed to speak.

After a very uncomfortable few hours, we were finally allowed to leave, which all of my cell mates did, along with almost everyone else, without waiting for breakfast. As it says in its publicity, the service is 'unfriendly and unwelcoming', which sums it up nicely. For me it was memorable, but not something I'd wish to repeat in a hurry, even though they only charge around ten euros. If this appeals to you, Tarceny Travel offer a three-day journey around Latvia during the summer, which includes staying at Karosta Prison for one night.

The Alcatraz prison hotel, near Frankfurt in Germany, is also located in a former prison and is named after the famous Alcatraz prison near San Francisco. Guests have the option of choosing one of the basic cell rooms, which are very small, or one of the rather better 'comfort' rooms, which have private showers. Although the cells are clean and cheerful, there's still some discomfort; the beds, which are original and made by prisoners, are very narrow and there are still bars on the windows.

But if it's an authentic prison experience you're looking for, then the Alcatraz probably isn't for you. For a start, the staff couldn't be more friendly and welcoming, a huge contrast with what a convict would've experienced in the past.

The cost of staying at the Alcatraz is comparable to other budget hotels in the area, although I would've expected to pay a bit more. Prices range from forty-nine euros for a single to sixty-nine euros for a double in the less spacious cell rooms, while the larger rooms cost about twenty euros per night more.

If you've experienced a night in a prison hotel, we'd love to hear from you. Contact us at www dot …

Practice Test

Part I

 39

N = Narrator

N: You will hear people talking in eight different situations. For questions, 1-8, choose the best answer (A, B or C).

Question 1. You hear a man talking to a friend about a DIY job he has recently done.

A: So, was tiling the kitchen floor straightforward?

B: Yeah, not too bad. This wasn't the first floor I'd tiled though. I did our bathroom floor last year and that turned out all right. The secret's in the planning and preparation, and if you get that right, it should be easy enough.

A: Hmm … and your kitchen's quite big too.

B: It is, so I thought it'd have taken me days to tile the floor but I actually surprised myself! I tell you what though … my knees were aching by the time I'd done. My mate offered to give me a hand, but I told him I could manage by myself. I really should have accepted his offer!

N: Question 2. You hear a woman leaving a voicemail message.

A: Good morning. It's Zara from Atlantic Fish Supplies here. Sorry to take so long to get back to you. I've received your order, but unfortunately I can't get hold of that particular fish at the moment. But there's no need to be disappointed because I've found a very close substitute for it at a similar price. I'm sure it'll be great at the event you're catering for. It'll really impress your client as it's not the sort of thing their guests would typically have at home. So, if you want to go with this, let me know and I'll make sure I get it delivered to you in good time.

N: Question 3. You hear a mother talking to her son about doing some shopping.

A: Leo, I had a good look around for that computer game you wanted, but it seems to be out of stock everywhere at the moment.

B: Thanks, Mom. I'll check again when I'm in the shopping mall next week.

A: And as for the laptop battery you need … well, the guy in the store says it'll apparently only be half the price if you order it online. So why don't you try that then? I know that I certainly wouldn't waste perfectly good money in a store downtown when I can go elsewhere. There's no point.

B: OK. Actually, that's a really good idea so that's what I'll do!

N: Question 4. You hear a man leaving a message for a colleague.

A: Helen, it's Jack here in Human Resources getting back to you regarding your proposal to hire software developers for the new project. The thing is that due to all the company-wide cuts, it was agreed at last month's senior management meeting that there'll be a freeze on hiring until the new financial year, so we'll have to make do with current resources. Bad news for some team members I'm sure, but those in certain key roles will have the opportunity to boost their income by doing extra hours. And who knows … that may even lead to some people working their way up the career ladder, which would be a good thing obviously.

N: Question 5. You hear a man talking to his manager about a training session.

A: Well, it looks unlikely that training'll go ahead tonight.

B: Oh! Why?

A: Well, several team members, especially those living in remote areas, won't be able to get into town as visibility's practically zero now. And after what we've had all morning, the pitch is in no state to have us running over it.

B: We'll just have to make up for this before the big day by putting in some extra practice. We can review the situation again tomorrow I guess, but yeah … for now there's not much we can do.

A: Exactly! It's just a case of waiting. I just hope that some of our men don't come down with that nasty virus that's going around.

N: Question 6. You hear a woman making an announcement at a train station.

A: We are sorry to have to announce that the 16.20 express service to Windsor Central from Platform 10 has been delayed due to a mechanical fault further down the line at Oxford. Could all passengers who have been waiting to board this service please make their way to the waiting room at the end of the platform. We hope to be able to provide further travel updates in due course and in the event that a replacement bus service will operate, all previously purchased train tickets will be valid for travel. A selection of hot drinks and snacks is available from the coffee shop on Platform 11.

N: Question 7. You hear two people talking about a coffee shop.

A: I must say they've done a good job with that new coffee shop in the high street. It's got a bit of a buzz to it and it's always packed, so obviously plenty of people think the same as me.

B: Yeah, and you get a really decent cup of coffee for your money too, unlike some of those other coffee chains where they hand you half a cupful! And the lemon cake's incredible too …

A: … which is great if you like lemon cake, of course. To be honest though they could do with adding a few more cakes to the menu!

B: I think you're right. I'd thought that too, actually.

N: Question 8. You hear a woman leaving a message for her friend.

A: Hi Lisa, sorry to take so long to get back to you. You were asking about courses. Well, I definitely recommend the digital photography one at Oakwood College. There's one for all levels really, so don't worry if you think you don't know enough to join a class. I wouldn't leave it too long to sign up though, as classes usually fill up almost as soon as the new brochure's published. If you do decide to go ahead, I've got some material you can use as well … I signed up for a monthly publication to help me with what I'd learnt. And there's loads of stuff online too. Let me know, OK?

N: That is the end of Part One. Now turn to Part Two.

Part 2

 40

N = Narrator   H = Harry

N: You will hear a talk by a man called Harry Carter, who is a pilot. For questions 9–18, complete the sentences with a word or short phrase. You now have 45 seconds to look at Part 2.

H: Hello everyone. I'm Harry Carter and I'm here to talk to you about my work as a commercial pilot for Emperor Airlines, which, as you may know, has offices in many cities in the United States. Its headquarters are in Texas, though, and I moved there from California to take up the role.

My love of flying started in childhood. My dad was a pilot, and from an early age, I travelled on planes where I was often lucky enough to sit in the flight deck. Later, I studied Aeronautical Engineering and regularly visited a flying club not far from where I lived to get a feel of what it would be like flying a plane. It was learning the ropes like that, more so than my university degree, that confirmed this was the career for me.

After qualifying, I came across a sponsorship opportunity with Emperor Airlines in a magazine, and funnily enough it was my instructor, rather than my father, who pushed me to apply. It was a lengthy process with many tests and interviews. All things considered, I was fortunate to be offered a place. I didn't have much in the way of savings, but fortunately the airline provided funding, and though it wasn't enough to cover the whole period, it at least meant that I could get on with my training.

At Emperor Airlines, I was immediately allocated to a Senior First Officer and we had weekly email catch-ups. In addition, he visited me and other trainees. It's a hugely successful support system that they run for trainee pilots, where they can discuss the whole process, ask questions and so on – and get lots of encouragement! And without all that I think the whole thing would have been far harder.

So, how do you move up the ranks? Well, initially you start at the bottom as a First Officer on a particular type of aircraft. You then need to do a certain number of flying hours on that aircraft, as well as have the relevant training and industry experience. Clearly the airline also needs to have vacancies.

Now, what's my typical day like? Well, before departure, as First Officer I'm obliged to run through the day's paperwork, which covers flight paths and weather. Then, to work out how much fuel is required and the approximate flight times, the other pilot who'll be flying the plane with me, and I go through the details together. We brief the crew so everyone knows what to expect for the flight.

Then, it's down to one pilot to set up the flight deck – the routes, charts and so on – while the other carries out an external check to ensure all's in order in terms of safety. And obviously this is pretty crucial. Once everyone's on board and we're happy that everything's in order, the doors are closed and we take off.

My favourite part of the job's the view – my office window changes every day! And with the sheer variety of passengers and crew I get to meet, there's never a dull moment. Hearing my friends moan about their nine-to-five jobs makes me laugh – I mean, I could very well feel sorry for myself because the shifts I work are often long and can be a bit antisocial. But I really don't mind getting up at the crack of dawn or getting home at four in the morning when I have to.

Although I don't come into as much contact with passengers as the cabin crew obviously, I do enjoy getting out of the cockpit when I can to go and say a quick hello to people. Most passengers are actually pleasantly surprised to see the pilot. And knowing that my colleagues would do anything to help me out gives me a real boost! Pilots have a lot of responsibility and there's nothing like being part of a strong team – and that's what we really are.

N: Now you will hear Part Two again.

That is the end of Part Two. Now turn to Part Three.

Part 3

 41

N = Narrator

N: You will hear five short extracts in which professional sportspeople are talking about what motivates them most. For questions 19–23, choose from the list (A–H) what each speaker says. There are three extra letters which you do not need to use.

You now have thirty seconds to look at Part 3.

Speaker 1

For me sport's not so much about pushing myself so that I get to be one of the top athletes in the world … winning gold medals all over the place, and so on. Or even beating my own personal best by getting faster each time I go out there on the track, though that's great when it happens. Sport's actually more about keeping my body in tip-top condition and making it better if I can. Health is wealth, as they say, and unfortunately people often only realise that when it's way too late, so I want to stay ahead of the game.

Speaker 2

I care about lots of aspects of being involved in sport actually, and in the case of my sport … boxing … I really want to show people what's achievable. And especially females who might not be traditionally drawn to this sport. I guess when I'm old and grey I'd like to be seen as a person who pushed the boundaries a little. I know that my dad, who was a boxer himself, is already so proud of what I've done and though that's not what pushes me forward, it's a lovely bonus, as is knowing that other boxers respect me because they see me as being at the top of my game.

Speaker 3

Well, there's no doubt about it that it's nice being looked up to by lots of other athletes, but that admiration can only take you so far. I train hard and I know that lots of young people out there feel inspired by my success to date, but what drives me forward now is that really strong desire I've got to become world class … you know, being right up there with the best there are. I suppose the ultimate aim's getting through to the European championships. I know what I have to do and I'm up for the challenge! I just hope that all my hard work will be worth it.

Speaker 4

I enjoy the competitive element of being a professional sportsperson, I really do. It's always great to win and to know that you're the best there is in your sport. That's short-lived though … you come down from that high that you get after a win fairly soon. What has a much longer-lasting effect is knowing how I can influence people everywhere … you know … instil in the next generation the will to go out and have a go at playing football. That's very rewarding indeed. It's always great to hear reports of the admiration people have for me and my team, and what that's led to. That's what really keeps me going!

Speaker 5

I took part in the long jump in the last Olympics and that's definitely going to go down as one of the most unforgettable experiences of my entire life. What made it all the more special was having my kids there with me. They're still very young, but actually old enough now to understand what it is I do and how strict my training schedule needs to be. They encourage me to do better in each jump I do, and it's knowing that they feel so much pride regarding my achievements that really makes me want to do better and better each time. It's a hard feeling to describe really.

N: Now you will hear Part Three again.

That is the end of Part Three.

Now turn to Part Four.

Part 4

 42

N = Narrator   I = Interviewer   S = Sam

N: You will hear an interview with a health and lifestyle expert called Sam, who is talking about ways people can make themselves happy. For questions 24–30, choose the best answer (A, B or C).

You now have one minute to look at Part 4.

I: Today, our health and lifestyle expert, Sam, is going to tell us some simple tricks for making ourselves feel better when we're a bit down. So, Sam, my first question is 'What's the link between our mood and making decisions?'

S: Mood's really important when it comes to making decisions. Many people have problems with internal dialogue … you know, that little voice inside your head that says, 'Oh, you'll never be able to do that' or 'You'll fail'. That's very damaging … we mustn't allow it to affect our judgement. It's all about being more positive. And luckily this is something that everyone can do, regardless of age or gender.

I: Yes, that makes sense. And I imagine sleep's important too, isn't it?

S: Definitely. It's actually more about how well we sleep rather than how much. We should make sure that we're ready for sleep when we settle down for the night. That means spending time winding down beforehand … you know, just relaxing, and giving our brain a chance to slow down. People who have trouble getting to sleep should try sleeping in different rooms in the house.

I: Right. Now we all get bad days. What advice would you give for when that happens?

S: Hmm … er, I'd say laughter's important. You've heard the old saying 'laughter's the best medicine' … well, there's a lot of truth in it! Laughing improves your mood so if you're having a bad day, just try being silly now and again. If you haven't got time to go and see a friend, look up some jokes online or watch something that'll make you laugh. Basically it's about learning to lighten your mood and seeing the funny side of life. Be a child again!

I: Uh-uh … good tips. So, is there anything else?

S: Yes, there's what I call getting back to basics … we're all so busy these days and we don't have time, or rather we don't make time for doing the simple stuff … you know, like meeting up with friends you haven't seen for ages, walking your dog or going to a gallery and seeing some interesting art work. It's actually these little things that often make us happiest.

I: I'm with you on that. And how would you say love features in our personal happiness?

S: Well, it may seem obvious, but don't be afraid to let love into your life. After all, the ability to give and receive love is quite a desirable human quality. It seems to me that, as a society, we're either not as close to each other as we might be, or we often forget to show how much we value our loved ones. And that can cause negative feelings like anger or loneliness, for example. So, if you really want to work on making your attitude more positive, find a way to reconnect with people, especially those close to you.

I: That seems reasonable. Would you say that self-confidence plays a part in being happy?

S: Certainly. Participating in new mental activities improves confidence levels and the way we cope with problems in life. Building confidence could be as easy as discovering the meaning of new words or learning about new topics. Or, if you're right-handed, try using your left hand more frequently. This is because the left hand connects with the right side of the brain, which is more creative.

I: I see. We're nearly out of time unfortunately. Any final points to add, about, say, the language we use when we're communicating?

S: Yes, I'd say that people use too much negative language. Focus on positive things instead, and learn to communicate your needs more effectively. For example, instead of telling people 'you shouldn't have done that', express your requirements by using phrases like 'I need you to'. The difference is that this peaceful language expresses <u>needs</u> and doesn't judge, so that can change the way the speaker's viewed and make them seem so much more positive.

I: Well Sam, it's been very interesting talking to you, but unfortunately we'll have to end it there. Thanks for joining us today.

S: And thank you!

N: Now you will hear Part Four again.
That is the end of Part Four.

Speaking Part 1

 43

Where are you from?

Tell me about a dish that's popular in your country.

Do you cook every day?

What kinds of things do you like doing with your family at weekends?

Do you prefer hobbies that you do alone or hobbies that you do with other people?

Is there a new hobby that you would like to start?

Speaking Part 1

▶ 44

What are the advantages of learning another language? Why do you think this is?

Is it easier to learn a language when you're young?

What do you think is difficult about learning English?

Some people say the best way to learn a language is to go and live in the country where the language is spoken. Do you agree?

Do you think that speaking another language helps people to understand the culture of that country?

Some people say it would be better if there was just one language that was spoken in all countries. What do you think?

Thank you.

That is the end of the Speaking test.

Pearson Education Limited
KAO Two, KAO Park, Harlow,
Essex, CM17 9NA, England
and Associated Companies throughout the world

www.pearsonELT.com/gold

© Pearson Education Limited 2018

Main Coursebook: Jan Bell and Amanda Thomas
Writing reference and Grammar reference: Jacky Newbrook
and Judith Wilson
Practice Test: Imelda Maguire-Karayel

The right of Jan Bell, Amanda Thomas, Jacky Newbrook, Judith Wilson
and Imelda Maguire-Karayel to be identified as authors of this Work has
been asserted by them in accordance with the Copyright, Designs and
Patents Act, 1988.

New Edition first published 2018
Fifth impression 2019

ISBN: 978-1-292-20226-6   (Gold First New Edition Coursebook
                         for MyEnglishLab pack)

ISBN: 978-1-292-20227-3   (Gold First New Edition Coursebook)

Set in Frutiger Neue LT Pro Thin
Printed in Italy by L.E.G.O. S.p.A. Lavis (TN)

Acknowledgements
The publishers would like to thank the following people for their
feedback and comments during the development of the materials:
Iñigo Casis (Spain), Victoria Clifford (Italy), Louise Manicolo (Mexico),
Maria Giulia Pettigiani (Italy), Maria Stanny Winzcura (Poland), Cindy
Steiger (Switzerland), Kate Taylor (Italy), Christopher Thirlaway (Brazil),
Jacky Newbrook, Judith Wilson (UK).

The authors would like to thank the exam consultants for their advice, the
team at Pearson for their hard work and their families for their support.

We are grateful to the following for permission to reproduce
copyright material:

Text
Extract on page 8 adapted from "Coachella 2016: Bonfire of the Vanities
- how a music festival turned into a money-making monster", *The
Telegraph*, 25/04/2016 (Jonathan Bernstein), copyright © Telegraph
Media Group Limited 2016; Extract on page 31 adapted from "All you
need is love (and a scarf)", *The Times*, 25/05/2005 (Alyson Rudd),
copyright © The Times / News Syndication; Extract on page 39 adapted
from "X-men: meet the real mutants", *The Telegraph*, 22/05/2017 (Jake
Wallis Simons), copyright © Telegraph Media Group Limited 2014; Extract
on page 53 adapted from "Lunch with Rob Rhinehart", *The Financial
Times*, 21/07/2016 (Tom Braithwaite), copyright © The Financial Times
Limited. All Rights Reserved; Extract on page 63 adapted from "Sharing
the (self) love: the rise of the selfie and digital narcissism", *The Guardian*,
13/03/2014 (Tomas Chamarro-Premuzic), copyright © Guardian News
& Media Ltd 2017; Extract on page 68 adapted from "Yakutsk: Journey to
the coldest city on earth", *The Independent*, 21/01/2008 (Shaun Walker)
and extract on page 69 adapted from "Dining on insects: Anyone for
crickets...?", *The Independent*, 21/10/2010 (Jerome Taylor), copyright ©
The Independent, www.independent.co.uk; Extract on page 71 adapted
from "'I'd love to get my own place': young Europeans on the struggle to
fly the nest", *The Guardian*, 25/03/2014 (Lizzy Davies, Carmen Fishwick
and Richard Orange), copyright © Guardian News & Media Ltd 2017;
Extract on page 91 adapted from "Big decision ahead? Just roll the dice",
The Financial Times, 28/09/2016 (Tim Harford) and extract on page 100
adapted from "France: Claudie Haigneré", *Financial Times Weekend*,
02/04/2011 (Simon Kuper), copyright © The Financial Times Limited.
All Rights Reserved; Extract on page 105 adapted from "Would you

rent a friend?", *The Guardian*, 21/07/2010 (Tim Dowling), copyright ©
Guardian News & Media Ltd 2017; Extract on page 106 adapted from
"Do soulmates really exist?", *The Telegraph*, 09/07/2014 (Marianne
Kavanagh) and extract on page 115 adapted from "Stage fright: Classical
music's dark secret", *The Telegraph*, 26/06/2014 (Ivan Hewett), copyright
© Telegraph Media Group Limited 2014; Extract on page 132 adapted
from "Watch your (body) language", *The Guardian*, 07/03/2009 (Sarah
Wilson), copyright © Guardian News & Media Ltd 2017; Extract on
pages 126-127 from *One Good Turn*, Black Swan (Kate Atkinson 2010)
Published by Doubleday, copyright © Kate Atkinson, 2006. Reproduced
by permission of the author c/o Rogers, Coleridge & White Ltd., 20
Powis Mews, London W11 1JN, The Random House Group Limited and
Anchor Canada/Doubleday Canada, a division of Penguin Random House
Canada Limited; Extract on page 194 adapted from "How fast is the
Arctic ice melting? Meet the British scientist who risked polar bear attacks
and plagues of mosquitoes to find out", *The Telegraph*, 14/01/2017
(Tom Rowley), extract on page 196 adapted from "The surprising health
benefits of caffeine", *The Telegraph*, 18/01/2017 (Henry Wong) and
extract on page 199 adapted from "How to get young people to choose
a career in engineering", *The Telegraph*, 14/03/2017 (Chris Moss),
copyright © Telegraph Media Group Limited 2017.

Photos
The publisher would like to thank the following for their kind permission
to reproduce their photographs:

(Key: b-bottom; c-centre; l-left; r-right; t-top)

123RF.com: 109l, 109r, andresr 20r, Antonio Balaguer Soler 41, Peter
Bernik 62, Elizabeth Engle 97t, goodluz 136bl, Halfpoint 8, Eric Isselee
93, kadettmann 64b, Dmitry Kalinovsky 56, rido 20l, Slavko Slavi 26cl,
Wavebreak Media 12; **Alamy Stock Photo:** Ian Allenden 70, Asiaselects
29t, Robin Beckham 28, Julian Castle 137tr, CFimages 134bl, Cronos 99,
Chris A Crumley 135br, Danita Delimont 114, 137br, Design Pics Inc 44,
dpa picture alliance archive 96, Jürgen Fälchle 124, Christin Gasner 13,
Joan Hall 106, Kiko Jimenez 136tr, Wim Lanclus 58b, Paul Maguire 33,
Mint Images Limited 103, Keith Morris 61, B O'Kane 60, Trajano Paiva 48l,
Roger Parkes 67, Stefano Paterna 73bl, PhotoAlto 18, PhotoAlto sas 102,
robertharding 137bl, SiliconValleyStock 135tl, Silver Image Photographics
122t, Thomas Söllner 81r, Jochen Tack 73br, E.D. Torial 31, Travelscape
Images 108c, Lisa Werner 81l, Tim Woodcock 117l; **Keith Ducatel:** 47;
Getty Images: AFP 53, Axiom 122b, Neil Beckerman 29b, Bloomberg
64t, Brand X Pictures 40, Ian Cumming 27, E+ 35, Raphael Gaillarde
135tr, Jamie Garbutt 118, Soren Hald 136tl, Dimitrios Kambouris 21,
Toshifumi Kitamura 48t, Emma MacIntyre 9, Anastassios Mentis 137tl,
ONOKY 134tr, Pascal Pavani 95, Persefoni Photo Images 38r, Shelby Ross
119l, Henryk Sadura 42, Paul A. Souders 119r, The Washington Post 79,
Steve Welsh 24; **Pearson Education Ltd:** Jon Barlow 15, MindStudio
97b; **Shutterstock.com:** 20th Century Fox / Kobal / Rex 38b, 2happy
112, 74, 129, Africa Studio 204br, arek_malang 96t, bbernard 204bl,
Mihai Blanaru 59, Blend Images 55l, Konstantin Christian 16, cunaplus
75, Danila 26t, Elena Dijour 58t, Elena Elisseeva 10, elwynn 136br,
FreeProd33 51, Giedriusok 26bl, goodluz 23l, Kaspars Grinvalds 125,
Hartswood Films / REX 128, Stefan Holm 94, Alex Hubenov 49, Hurst
Photo 90, IdeaStepConceptStock. 130, ittipon 116r, Ammit Jack 117,
Aleksandar Kamasi 6, Patryk Kosmider 204tr, koya979 92t, London Films
/ United Artists / Kobal / REX 65, Jacob Lund 87, Kamil Macniak 134tl,
Eoin Moore 32, Eldar Nurkovic 85, Odua Images 110, Penson / Rex 89,
pikselstock 7, ProStockStudio 105, Bhushan Raj Timla 76, Alexander
Raths 86, Rawpixel 26r, RFarrarons 135bl, S_Photo 57, Kyle Santee 45,
Sipa Press / Rex 80, Solis Images 82, StockLite 204tl, Syda Productions
55r, 134br, Turtix 50, Popova Valeriya 115, Chuck Wagner 26tl, Evgeniy
Zhukov 23r; **The Random House Group Ltd.:** from One Good Turn:
A Jolly Murder Mystery by Kate Atkinson, published by Black Swan.
Reprinted by permission of The Random House Group Ltd 127

All other images © Pearson Education

Illustrated by Oxford Designers & Illustrators Ltd.